Editors' Introduction

IN HIS famous *Speech on Conciliation with the Colonies* Edmund Burke reminded his listeners that "the people of the colonies are descendants of Englishmen," and then added: "England, Sir, is a nation which still, I hope, respects, and formerly adored, her freedom." The Americans, Burke pointed out, "were not only devoted to liberty, but to liberty according to English ideas and on English principles." In truth, the concepts of constitutional government and civil liberties which the colonists took with them from the mother country distinguished the English colonies in North America from the colonies of any of the other great powers of that era.

This influence of the mother country was by no means confined to public law. In the realm of colonial private law, English customs, court decisions, legislation, and law books had an enormous impact. New Englanders found in the manorial system a plan of organization for their farming communities; Southerners adopted the parish as an administrative unit and found the office of the justice of the peace a model for their local officials. Many colonial towns soon bore the look of English provincial towns as the architecture of old England was imported and adapted. Labor controls after English models were quickly introduced in the colonies, and English religious influences, notably Puritanism, were far reaching. Although few of the gentry actually came to America, the standards of the English country gentleman came to be the accepted standards of the colonial ruling class.

These and many other aspects of the transit of civilization from England to America are considered by Dr. Wallace Notestein. He has brought to life for us the position of the Crown, the courts, and Parliament, the church and the university, town and country, the student, the merchant, the aristocracy, and the peasantry. He has illuminated this picture by fascinating illustrations from contemporary poetry and drama. Drawing upon his mastery of the source material of the seventeenth century, he has captured the inner character of the English people at a time when many Englishmen were building a new life in the New World.

This volume is one of *The New American Nation Series,* a comprehensive co-operative survey of the history of the area now known as the United States, from the days of discovery to the mid-twentieth century. Since the publication a half century ago by the House of Harper of the *American Nation* series under the editorship of the distinguished historian, Albert Bushnell Hart, the scope of history has been broadened and a new approach has been developed to deal with the problems of historical interpretation and presentation. The time has now come for a judicious appraisal of the new history, a cautious application of the new techniques of investigation and presentation, and a large-scale effort to achieve a synthesis of the new findings with the traditional facts, and to present the whole in attractive literary form.

To this task the New American Nation Series is dedicated. Each volume is part of a carefully planned whole, and co-ordinated with other volumes in the series; at the same time each volume is designed to be complete in itself. Some overlapping is doubtless inevitable, but it has seemed to the editors that overlapping is less regrettable than omissions, and from time to time the same series of events and the same actors will be seen from different points of view. While for the most part the series follows a chronological organization, separate volumes or groups of volumes will be devoted to cultural history, constitutional history, and foreign affairs.

Another volume in this series will deal with the important influence of continental Europe on the American colonies; it will describe how the development and exploitation of the resources of the New World affected economic life across the Atlantic. Together, the volumes on the English and the continental European backgrounds of American colonization will serve as a guide to the evolving Atlantic community of the seventeenth century.

HENRY STEELE COMMAGER
RICHARD BRANDON MORRIS

THE ENGLISH

1603-1630 # PEOPLE

ON THE EVE OF

COLONIZATION

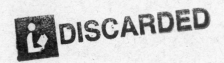
the text of this book is printed
on 100% recycled paper

The New American Nation Series

Edited by Henry Steele Commager and Richard B. Morris

A comprehensive survey of United States history since the days of discovery, in forty-odd volumes written by leading historians for both the general reader and the scholar. Each volume, complete in itself, is coordinated with others in the series, which is largely chronological. However, some volumes are devoted to cultural history, constitutional history, and foreign affairs. All take into account new evidence about the American past and include the role of science, technology, religion, culture, and government.

Now available:

THE ENGLISH
1603-1630 PEOPLE
ON THE EVE OF
COLONIZATION

BY WALLACE NOTESTEIN

HARPER TORCHBOOKS
Harper & Row, Publishers
New York, Hagerstown, San Francisco, London

TO

A. L. C.

κἀριπρεπὴϛ μὲν ἐν γυναιξὶ γίγνεται
πάσησι, θείη δ' ἀμφιδέδρομεν χάριϛ.
τοίαϛ γυναῖκαϛ ἀνδράσιν χαρίζεται
Ζεὺϛ τὰϛ ἀρίσταϛ καὶ πολυφραδεστάταϛ.

THE ENGLISH PEOPLE ON THE EVE OF COLONIZATION

Copyright 1954, by Harper & Row, Publishers, Incorporated
Printed in the United States of America

This book was originally published by Harper & Brothers
in 1954, in The New American Nation Series edited by
Henry Steele Commager and Richard B. Morris.

First HARPER TORCHBOOK edition published 1962

Harper & Row, Publishers, Incorporated
10 East 53rd Street, New York, N.Y. 10022

Library of Congress catalog card number: 54-8978

ISBN: 0-06-133006-X

78 79 80   20 19 18 17 16 15 14 13

Contents

Illustrations and Maps

These illustrations, grouped in a separate section,
will be found following page 142.

1. JAMES I

2. SIR EDWIN SANDYS

3. LADY OGLANDER

4. Nottingham and the Trent

5. A Farmyard with Figures

6. PHINEAS PETT

7. INIGO JONES

8. A reading country gentleman

9. Prospect of Oxford

10. A Small Landscape

11. An Old Ruin

MAPS

Preface and Acknowledgments

TO MEET the space limitations of this little book and at the same time cover the ground meant economy of words. I have had to leave out the proofs for many statements, to give few examples, and to omit the stories I would like to tell. Moreover, while I have mentioned London incidentally again and again, I have written no chapters on London because the subject should either be treated at length or not at all, and because the English who came to the New World were mostly from the country and brought with them country modes and country outlooks. Those I have tried to set forth in the brief chapters on classes and occupations. The schools and universities were so important in explaining English life that they could not be omitted, nor could Puritanism, which affected America in ways beyond estimate. Some account was also needed of the political institutions which affected the colonists. The Kingship, the Privy Council, and Parliament were powers that could not be forgotten even in farthest Virginia. About local institutions I have set down less than I wrote originally, but enough, I hope. The reader will find as much about English country life in the descriptions of county and hundred and village government as in the purely social history chapters. A survey of the activities of the officials of local government should prepare us for the colonial scene.

The English are described as they were in the reign of James I and in the early years of Charles I, say up to 1630, when the great migration to Massachusetts was taking place. Occasionally I have gone back into the last years of Elizabeth's reign and forward into the years just before the Civil Wars, but never, I think, without saying so. It will be said that a large part of the emigration from England to the New World came in the late seventeenth century and in the eighteenth. The English of that later time cannot be taken into account in this brief treatment. It is more than enough to describe the people of something over a generation. That generation was not static and therefore not easy to picture; it was one rather in which medieval ideas and practices were by no means forgotten and in which new conceptions and new ways of doing things were coming in. The American tradition, or that part derived from England, was at least in some degree established by the early colonists. The English who came over later must have found the English Americans somewhat settled in their ways.

The help I have received from others is evident in the footnotes. I have reread the monographs of former students, those of John Raach, George Dodds, Thomas Murphy, Alice Kimball Smith, William Sachse, and Francis Squire. T. Hallinan of Balliol College kindly sent me his long paper on the sheriffs in the Midlands and Miss M. Barratt allowed me to use her Oxford thesis on the clergy in three counties and was kind enough to go over my chapter on the clergymen. The comments, statistics, and conclusions of these several scholars I have used in quotations or with references. Their bibliographies have facilitated my work. Many monographs and learned introductions to collections of materials are mentioned in the Bibliography and have been of great use. But the sources themselves have furnished most of the examples used and have been the basis of many conclusions drawn, though I have now and then modified those conclusions, perhaps not enough, in the light of monographic opinion.

Many varieties of topics I have had to deal with, some of them never in my particular province, and I have consulted experts, submitting chapters or putting questions to them. Among my colleagues at New Haven who have given me of their time and knowledge are Irving Rouse, Roland Bainton, Leonard Labaree, Hartley Simpson, Franklin Baumer, S. F. Bemis, Samuel Thorne, and Norman Pearson. Mildred Campbell of Vassar and David Harris Willson of the

University of Minnesota have read chapters. So have other friends: William Haller of Barnard and the Folger Library, Perry Miller of Harvard, L. J. Trinterud of the McCormick Theological Seminary, and Mark Curtis of the University of California at Los Angeles. In addition I am indebted to Dr. Sidney Burrell of Barnard College for editorial assistance.

Among English friends who have assisted me are Christopher Hill of Balliol, Hugh Trevor-Roper of Christ Church, and J. E. Neale of London. The Reverend J. Howard Brown of Whitfield Vicarage, Dover, gave me advice about grammar schools. F. N. L. Poynter and W. J. Bishop of the Wellcome Historical and Medical Library gave me much help about the matter of physicians. For painstaking criticism of my chapters on local government I am under obligations to F. G. Emmison, F. W. Steer, and J. H. Holmes of the Essex Record Society and to H. C. Johnson of the Public Record Office. For general criticism of various chapters I wish to thank John Cooper of Trinity College, Oxford, and Philip Styles of Warwick and Birmingham University. None of those who have read chapters have seen the last drafts. They cannot be held in any way responsible, except in so far as I have quoted them with their permission.

Many have helped me with the problem of finding suitable pictures. Above everything else I wished to show the look of English landscape, but paintings of landscape at that time are practically nonexistent. I have had to content myself with later paintings of landscapes which were perhaps not too unlike those of the early seventeenth century, and with a few prints which are more nearly contemporary.

I am under obligations to the Print Department of the British Museum for much help and especially for five Hollar prints, two of which give actual prospects from hilltops of field systems. Lord Middleton graciously allowed me to use the unusual painting by Siebrechts of Nottingham and the River Trent. The famous art dealers, Leggatt Brothers, interested themselves in my problem and allowed me to use a Woolton landscape they had just bought at the Ashburnham sale. That painting is no doubt based upon an actual scene in the late seventeenth century, even if slightly romantic in character.

The haymaking scene in the Cotswolds, painted perhaps in the early eighteenth century, has details of various festivities, some of which might have been Elizabethan. For permission to use this curious and amusing picture I am grateful to the president of St. John's College, Oxford, and to *Country Life*.

The Print Department in the British Museum brought out for me a wash drawing by De Jongh, who visited England in 1628–30. The drawing shows a ruin (perhaps in Kent) and, on the left side, part of an English village. A contemporary presentment of even a bit of an English village is worth a place in this book. One of Hollar's prints reproduced, that of Windsor Castle, shows in the foreground part of the town of Windsor along the river.

Two pictures show scenes near London, both of them Elizabethan. The *Wedding Fête at Bermondsey* the Marquis of Salisbury has been good enough to allow me to use. Mr. Robert Drage of Hatfield House has given me help in connection with this picture. The painting of Richmond Palace by Vinckenboons I owe to the kindness of the Fitzwilliam Museum at Cambridge.

For a copy of a water-color drawing by John White of an Indian village in what was then called Virginia, made in the 1580's, I wish to express my gratitude to the British Museum.

The National Portrait Gallery has allowed me to use the portraits of Sir John Glanville and Inigo Jones. The Victoria and Albert Museum has furnished me with a photograph of a fancy drawing by Francis Barlow, *A Farmyard with Figures*. For the portrait of James I, I wish to thank its owner, a fellow worker in the seventeenth century, Sir Michael Oppenheimer. Philip Styles called my attention to the monument in Charlecote Church over the grave of Sir Thomas Lucy 2nd, who was obviously a reading country gentleman. Sir Leigh Ashton of the Victoria and Albert Museum has given me wise advice and Miss Rhoda Welsford of the Courtauld Institute of Art has been of great assistance to me.

I am grateful to General Aspinall-Oglander and to the firm of

Constable for permission to use a copy of the painting of Lady Oglander. I am grateful to them also for permission to quote from *A Royalist Notebook* and to the Hogarth Press for permission to quote from *A Nunwell Symphony*. For permission to use the extract from Stephen Benét's *Western Star* at the close of the book I am glad to thank Mrs. Benét and Farrar and Rinehart, Ltd.

I wish to acknowledge the kindness of University College, London, which in the summers of 1951 and 1953 gave me the use of an office in the History Buildings on Gordon Square. During one winter and two summers Balliol College, Oxford, has put an office at my disposal. There I was within a few steps of the Balliol Library, where Mr. Quinn was always eager to speed my work. Much of this book was planned and written in Balliol College.

WALLACE NOTESTEIN

CHAPTER 1

A Retrospect, England up to 1603

JUST outside Dorchester in Dorset rises a rectangular hill with five concentric rings around the edge of the summit, enclosing a space of nearly a hundred acres. It is a lonesome place except for a few sheep and two or three archaeologists in one corner directing the diggers. Maiden Castle, as it is called, is one of the most impressive spots in England. The diggers find evidence of the activities of various types of men from the third millennium B.C. up to the coming of the Romans. On the summit is a "long barrow," an elongated mound that covers a neolithic burial ground of possibly 2500 to 2300 B.C. Such barrows can be observed from afar denting the horizon on many lines of hills in south England. The downland is a manuscript written over by early man, sometimes in forms we can all read, and sometimes in ciphers understood only by anthropologists. Nowadays, thanks to the airplane, we can even make out on the tops of the downs the outlines of early settlements which had never been recognized from the ground.

To see the work of prehistoric man after he had developed some degree of civilization, an American may well visit Wiltshire three counties west and southwest of London and at its nearest border about sixty miles from the capital. There he may view Avebury and Stonehenge, two temples or centers of some form of religious observance. Those circles and arrangements of great stones—there are smaller stone circles all over Britain—were erected by early bronze

1

men, better known by archaeologists today as "beaker men" (from the type of their pottery). Other visible monuments they left on the tops of many hills, the "round barrows," mounds in the shape of inverted bowls, where they buried their dead. Evidences of their settlements are to be found in Wiltshire, Dorset, Hampshire, Berkshire, the Thames valley and Sussex, and also in East Anglia. The beaker men lived on the hills and in the valleys where the clay was light and easily permeable. The great Midland plain of heavy clay and thick oak woods shows little indication of their settlements. But a good many of the beaker men lived also in the northeast of England near the seacoast, and they were widely scattered over Scotland. A pastoral people, they herded cows and sheep, and were probably sometimes nomadic, but did such light farming as men could carry on before they had plows. They had considerable commerce with Ireland and some dealings with the Continent.

The beaker men, who flourished about 1800 to 1600 B.C., like the battle-ax men of about the same period, were invaders from the Continent. They came up the inlets on the east side of England, following up the Thames, and they entered rivers and estuaries on the southwest, coming across from Brittany and Spain. Probably they did not wholly displace the neolithic men already on the ground, of whom, however, there had never been a great number. European peoples were on the move westward, pushed from behind, and some of those in front made their way to Britain. The beaker men and the battle-ax men were followed by many types, distinguished from one another by the kinds of tools and pottery they used. The middle bronze men and the late bronze men were followed by men of the iron age at some time around 800 B.C.[1] About the language of these various invaders we know nothing until a few centuries before Christ, and then we learn of men coming to Britain who spoke a Celtic language, two forms of it. How far back the early Britons used Celtic we do not know, possibly as early as 1000 B.C., and there are those who suspect that the beaker men spoke a kind of

---

[1] These terms have not been discarded, but anthropologists are now making many subdivisions and using many special terms.

Celtic. Just before Julius Caesar and the Roman legions arrived in 55 B.C., new waves of Celtic people were coming into the country, among them the Belgae, familiar to those who have read Caesar's accounts of his wars. Some of these recent arrivals are believed to have made the great ringed fortifications at Maiden Castle and on many other hilltops.

The Romans stayed just over 400 years, but left little mark on the character of the population. They built many roads and possibly drained some swamps, and no doubt they accustomed the natives to orderly government. With their departure the invasions from the Continent continued almost as before, but now we know much more of the newcomers because of written records. When the Romans went away the Celtic peoples were easily overcome by tribes from northwest Germany, the Anglo-Saxons, who spread out over the country of heavy clay and oak woods. No sooner had they managed to build up a central kingdom than they had to resist invaders from Scandinavia, who finally settled down in the northeast segment of England in a kind of wedge, narrow at the south and broad on the north. Northmen (Scandinavians) continued to enter on the northern and western coasts of Britain in small detachments. In 1066 William of Normandy and his warriors, who were a fusion of Northmen and French, landed on the southeast coast and soon made themselves a ruling class. The Normans were the last invaders, but small groups of skilled workers at one time and another were welcomed into the country. In the time of Elizabeth there was a considerable migration of French Huguenots and Dutch Protestants into the counties northeast of London, from which many Puritans were later to come to Massachusetts. Thus the English, like the Americans, are a very composite stock. In England, however, the waves of immigration followed in such slow sequence that the population became thoroughly mixed.[2] In America the mixture has

[2] Yet one can still find in England little enclaves of people who look like descendants of a single stock. In isolated villages under the downs one can come upon redheaded people that might be almost pure Saxons. In the Yorkshire dales one can talk with farmers who look and speak like Minnesota Swedes and are probably of almost undiluted Scandinavian stock.

been taking place over a comparatively short time and is not yet wholly accomplished.

The Norman Kings justified their conquest, if conquest be ever justifiable, by the strong government they established, thus giving England an advantage over the weak and feudalized nations across the Channel. William the Conqueror, Henry I, and Henry II were able with great effort to hold the restive and ambitious Norman nobles in check. Those Kings developed central institutions and devised writs by which cases could be carried out of baronial courts into the King's courts. They sent out itinerant judges over the country who brought the King's power and his devices for facilitating justice to the people in the shires. Out of inquest juries were developed juries for trying criminals. In local communities the small man was drawn into serving on inquest juries that gave verdicts about taxes and amercements and damages, thus affording him in a modest way political experience. It was the good fortune of the English that out of such practice in government even the lesser folk learned to seek out solutions of differences, solutions that would not please all, but would be accepted by all. Slowly they learned to practice the art of compromise.

The Norman Kings of England had gathered their great barons around them as a council. In the time of Edward I and his successors the King called in representatives of the shires and the boroughs mainly in order to get money from them, and those representatives supplemented the great council. Representation had been tried elsewhere, but it was in England that it became important and continued. Presently there were two divisions of Parliament, the Lords and the Commons. Sometimes they bargained with the King and held up grants of money until he would assent to the petitions in the very words they used. Those petitions came to be enrolled as statutes; thus Parliament made laws as well as voted money. Most of the laws it made were, it is true, suggested by the councilors and the judges. Once in a while the members of Parliament refused to pass such proposed legislation or modified it by amendments. While their powers over money and legislation were increasing by slow stages, they were becoming a considerable reinforcement of the government. The King seemed to his people a stronger and more august sovereign because he was "the King in Parliament," because the Lords and the Commons joined with him in policy. Sometimes the King encountered sharp opposition from baronial factions, which, if they could use the Lords and the Commons as a front, might prevail and force the King to give way. The name of Parliament was becoming a part of English tradition and political theorists were beginning to glory in it as something English. By the last half of the sixteenth century it was commanding some of the best talent in the realm, the country gentlemen accustomed to rule as justices of the peace in their own communities. They had ideas as to what ought to be done at Westminster. By the end of the century, when Elizabeth was letting go, Parliament was ready to claim a greater share in government and to limit the power of the sovereign.

The King's power was limited in another way. When criminals were prosecuted, the case read *Rex* v. *B,* and the juries and the judge gave decisions for the King or for B. In civil actions too it might be the King, a great landowner, against B. There too the juries and the judge decided between King and subject. Slowly the common law, the great body of decisions made by judges, came to have an influence on all later decisions and became the protection of the subject against the royal government.

The strong central government, supported at the top by Parliament and at the base by local government, with many firm crosspieces in between, gave the subject confidence and rendered obedience natural. The English became on the whole a politically disciplined people. That did not mean that all of them always obeyed the law. There might be, as late as in the early seventeenth century, lawless districts in the north and west, there might be enclosure riots in Northamptonshire and restlessness in the Forest of Dean, there might be petty incursions upon land in many shires; but they did not affect the essential peace of the country, nor threaten the government. In the great depression of the 1620's, when thousands of clothing men were out of work, a weaver came to a Gloucestershire justice of the peace to inform him that at least five hundred men were coming to interview him, "with their staves ready at their doors." "I asked him," wrote the justice, "what they intended. He answered to do me no harm, but to make their wants known." [3] Englishmen might make a fuss—they have long known the uses of militancy—but they meant no harm. The Civil Wars of the mid-seventeenth century were another matter, but even then the disciplined Englishman, accustomed to obey what he believed to be his government, was in evidence.

At the same time that the government was slowly gaining general support, a fundamental change was taking place in society. By the middle of the sixteenth century the institution of villeinage, by which the serfs were tied to the land and had to perform "works" so many days a week for their lords, had broken down. As a result of various factors, and in particular as a result of the substitution of money payments for labor, serfdom or villeinage became uneconomic. The significance of that change can hardly be overestimated. Freedom must have given a lift of spirit to thousands of families of hardy country stock who wanted only two or three generations of opportunity. A few of the wise and useful in the days of the Stuarts were great-great-grandsons of bondmen.

A strongly based central government, a representative body, that in some degree expressed public opinion, a common law that protected the subject against the state, a free citizenry, such developments meant that England was politically far ahead of the Continent and well on her way toward becoming a modern liberal state. But a nation needs also to have a consciousness of itself; to cherish heroes, to recall its past, and to gather to itself the loyalty that goes with heroes and memory.

The English were not without their heroes. They recalled King Alfred, the Black Prince, and Henry V; they remembered the brave Talbot of the wars in France, and they were beginning to recognize

[3] R. H. Clutterbuck, "A Dismall Depression in 1622," *Wiltshire Archeological Magazine*, XXII, 80. A similar case of militancy but of touching loyalty as well occurred in Suffolk in 1525. See Edward Hall, *Chronicle* (London, 1769), p. 700.

Sir Thomas More as one of their great and good. They were perhaps more familiar with Dick Whittington, thrice mayor of London, and his cat, and with Robin Hood. Famous men and famous deeds were less in their minds than one would expect.[4] No Robert the Bruce, no Barbarossa, was in the English Valhalla. When the predecessors of Shakespeare, when the great dramatist himself, and his fellows, began turning out historical plays, the English became more conscious of their heroic figures. Shakespeare's historical plays furnished them indeed with something like a Nibelungenlied. It was, however, the reign of Elizabeth that provided them with contemporary heroes to talk and write about, Sir John Hawkins, Sir John Norris, Sir Humphrey Gilbert, and, not least, Sir Philip Sidney. Elizabeth herself was hardly laid in the Abbey when her subjects began to recall stories of her versatility, of her courage, and of her fighting speeches.[5]

Heroes and hero worship fortify the wills of leaders, but the underlying substance of history serves to give character to a nation. The memories of its past afford a stimulus, but it takes reflection upon those memories and interpretation of them to enable a nation to understand itself and thus to move forward consistently and wisely. To the people of the last part of the sixteenth century and of the early part of the seventeenth, familiar with Hall, Holinshed, and other historical works, which were beginning at the turn of the century to appear in increasing numbers, the story of their country was still one of kings and favorites and factions, of battles on Severnside and in Normandy, and of murders in the Tower. It was a story full of moral lessons. Wicked men received their judgments at the hands of God. To our eyes the historians of that day seem occupied with the mere surface of the past,[6] and the public discussions of

[4] Some of my wise friends question this statement. I cannot myself read the history and literature of the time without surprise that there had been so little hero worship up nearly to the end of Elizabeth's reign.

[5] For such a speech see J. E. Neale, *Queen Elizabeth* (London, 1934), pp. 297–298.

[6] The leaders of the opposition to the King would have done their work better had they understood the long struggle between King and Parliament and the zigzag course of English constitutional history. They might have proceeded with more caution and better-considered methods. Conceivably they might have

politics and policy reveal a similar immaturity. If antiquarians such as Sir Robert Cotton and lawyers such as Selden and Coke had some inkling of the underlying meaning of English history, there was, as yet, no philosophic interpretation grounded upon an intimate understanding of constitutional processes. The traditions of the English were concerned with the incidentals of history, and traditions are almost as important to a state as its laws and precedents. It might be argued that a nation is as great as its capacity to interpret its annals and give them significance, and that capacity was still limited. Some time had yet to elapse before the English were to comprehend the slow but orderly and symmetrical evolution of parliamentary powers [7] and of the common law, and make it parcel of their natural saga and their pride.[8] No less important are the loyalties of a nation. The loyalty to the sovereign and the loyalty to the body politic, called patriotism, were features of English life which deserve consideration.

The loyalty to the King was so fundamental that even rebels at the block would express quite honestly, I think, their regret for their misdeeds.[9] Yet although the English had over the centuries been gaining discipline, they had in the last half of the fifteenth century relapsed into the civil dissensions known as the Wars of the Roses. Those wars had not indeed been fought against the sovereign but on behalf of different claimants to the throne. They had nearly de-

---

avoided the Civil Wars. Such political wisdom as they displayed was derived from their reading of Greek and Roman history. There was one man in the early Stuart period who glimpsed the possibilities of historical interpretation, Francis Bacon, and it is worth noting that he gave the House of Commons wise advice. He was the author of *The Historie of the Reign of King Henry the Seventh* (London, 1641).

[7] Tennyson's lines about freedom broadening down from precedent to precedent have become a commonplace because they expressed exactly what was in the minds of intelligent Englishmen at the time that Tennyson wrote.

[8] The fathers of the American constitution were deeply versed in English history. They had read Coke and other seventeenth-century lawyers, or the works based upon them. Moreover some of them had been trained at one of the Inns of Court. It was the lawyers at the end of the eighteenth century who were most aware of the development of the English constitution.

[9] Many examples could be cited, among them that of Robert Devereux, Earl of Essex, who was executed in 1601. See W. B. Devereux, *Lives . . . of the Devereux* (London, 1853), II, 187–188.

moralized the country; the public wished no more of them. Loyalty to the possessor of the throne was a first necessity. Henry VIII had done much to alienate the public; he had been hard and cruel, but he was to be served. The young Elizabeth pleased neither Catholic nor Reformer, but Queen she was, and as such to be supported.

Devotion to the nation had never been wanting. Nationalism, which included not only that devotion but also feeling against other nations, had shown itself as early as in the reign of Henry III and again in that of Edward I. It had not been lessened by the victories of Crécy, Poitiers, and Agincourt in the Hundred Years War against France. In the last decades of Elizabeth's reign Spain had become the most feared foreign power and the enemy. The captures of her silver fleets, the exploits of the great and glorious pirates, quickened the spirit of every Englishman. The Queen was

> The mistress of the ocean, her navies
> Putting a girdle round about the world.

The overthrow of the Spanish Armada did not lessen nationalism. The English had gained a good opinion of themselves. Was not England a little body with a mighty heart? The English were all composed of spirit and fire; they were designed to be warriors and to break through their ring, the sea.[10] Had not Jove chosen them for himself and made them famous over all the earth? Such boasting was utterly Elizabethan and more engaging than the self-complacency of maturer nations.

Patriotism became more than pride; it slipped easily into affection. Members of Parliament could hardly conceal their love of their country, nor could pamphleteers, nor playwrights. Shakespeare

[10] Massinger, *The Maid of Honour*, Act I, Scene I, in *Dramatic Works of Philip Massinger* (London, 1805), III, 15. Massinger goes on:

> "And we by force must fetch in what is wanting
> Or precious to us. Add to this, we are
> A populous nation, and increase so fast,
> That if we by our providence are not sent
> Abroad in colonies . . .
>   we must starve
> Or eat up one another."

makes John of Gaunt speak of "This land of such dear souls, this dear dear land." [11]

England was more than dear. She offered a kind of shield and buckler to the individual, a sense of not going it alone, but of being part of a whole. One can detect that sense in Shakespeare and in Milton, and here and there among the speeches in the Commons. The assurance of the Englishman was fortified by a realization of his country's reputation throughout the world and of her mission. Was she not the supporter of Protestantism, the bulwark of Europe against Rome? In that he had his part. He was God's Englishman. [12]

---

[11] In the reign of Charles I, Sir Kenelm Digby, who flitted from one part of Europe to another, wrote of "little England where time slideth more gently away than in any part of the world." Marjorie H. Nicolson, *Conway Letters* (New Haven, 1930), p. 27.

[12] *Areopagitica,* in *Works of John Milton* (London, 1728), I, 156.

CHAPTER 2

The English Character

I. THE VILLAGES AND THE COUNTRY

In one of Dekker's plays Ludovico says:

In England . . . I ever laugh when I think on't, to see a whole nation should be mark't i'th'forehead, as a man may say, with one iron.[1]

The English people were indeed marked off from other peoples and not only in the forehead. In stock they were more mixed than the Germans or the French or the Dutch. They spoke a language which was a fusion of Germanic and Latin elements, and thus their thinking was different, for forms of language modify thinking as thinking modifies language. Their traditions had roots in the British, the Anglo-Saxon, and the Norman past. Their culture and literature owed not a little to the Anglo-Saxons and their forms of government had Norman organization written all over them. Differentiating factors were also their climate and their separation from the Continent.

However English the Englishman was at the beginning of the seventeenth century, he was as yet not as different from a Frenchman or Dutchman or German as he is today. Time has steadily increased the differentiation. Some of the reasons for that progressive differentiation will appear in the chapters that follow.

[1] *The Honest Whore,* Part II, Act I, Scene I, in J. P. Collier (ed.), R. Dodsley, *A Select Collection of Old Plays* (London, 1825), 3rd ed., III, 330.

11

But we must examine the English more closely as they were in the early seventeenth century. In doing so we have to rid ourselves of some of our fixed ideas about them. In that time they spoke a language more like that to be heard in the southern mountains of our country than like that of the cultivated Englishman of today. Some of the dialects we could not have understood, but we might hear echoes of them today in Massachusetts and Maine villages. Their songs and ballads can still be heard in slightly altered form on the hillsides of Tennessee and the Carolinas.

They were a more oncoming and friendly people than the English of a generation or two ago. Of class distinctions they were much aware—feudalism was not far in their past—but they accepted them so naturally that they were not afraid to pass the time of day with those of a different social status.

They did not live in a finished landscape, like that of two or three generations ago; there were no long set vistas between lanes of trees toward a Norman tower, no spacious, smoothed lawns. Formal gardens there were at the greater country places, and covered walks around them with pollarded trees and pleached branches and vines, and here and there terraces and perhaps a pond. But the rough pasture grounds might come up close to the house. It was not yet a landscape designed by gentlemen and their planners, with each tree set out for the total effect. Hedgerows were small trees planted at intervals and often overgrown. In general one would have looked on wide, open fields and a good deal of waste land and unkept woods. Samuel Daniel thought of the French as having ". . . sweeter fields for beauty to the eye."

The people fitted in some degree into such a scene. In the main they were still a rural folk. The social life of the country was dominated by the gentry and part of that class was interested in little else than their fields, their corn, their cattle, and their sheep. Often miles away from neighbors of their own quality, they consorted with graziers, drovers, and their tenant farmers and were scarcely able to rise above the outlook of such men. Other gentlemen, hardly less rustic, played bowls and went hunting and fishing, and often with the yeomen of the community.

These rustical figures [2] were by no means all the squirearchy, but were enough of them to set the tone in many districts. It was the judgment of George Herbert, who was a younger son and must have known many of the country families in the neighborhood of Wilton, that most of the gentry "Are gone to grass and in the pasture lost," and he ventured to compare them to their own sheep.

If many of the gentry could be thus characterized, what must have been the state of the humbler people? Robert Herrick, who knew good company and missed it in his dull Devonshire, wrote of a village there:

> A people currish, churlish as the seas
> And rude (almost) as the crudest Savages.

Francis Bacon declared: "The rural parts are turned into a den of savage men." In a play a lady complains of the men

> So near the primitive making, they retain
> A sense of nothing but the earth.

One could support such opinions by many kinds of evidence.

Such people were not always nature's noblemen. Quarrelsomeness, which is to be found in all places and at all times, but which is not characteristic of the modern Englishman, was common in the early seventeenth century. The churchwardens and the parishioners would get into a fuss about the allocation of pews in the church; the authorities of a borough would wrangle over the choice of a schoolmaster; the parson would carry on a long war with his flock over tithe hens and pigs; two country gentlemen would continue a vendetta started by their great-grandfathers over a ditch or hunting rights.

Quarrels led to fighting. Violence on a large scale was out of the

[2] The English of the early seventeenth century were never far from the country. The portraits show us mainly men and women who had a country look to them. The similes and metaphors they employed were those of folk familiar with woods and fields. Even city-born men would draw their illustrations from the country.

question, but petty violence was not far under the surface of life in some places. In the Yorkshire dales an old Norse fury would break forth and groups of more-or-less armed men would march across the moors to attack a house or to occupy fields of which they claimed ownership; occasionally they were able to terrorize justices and to frighten sheriffs. With such episodes the Privy Council and the Star Chamber were often occupied, restoring to the weak what the strong had taken from them. In the more tamed parts of the country men still moved with servants and friends on fields where they asserted rights. Was not possession nine tenths of the law? On such trespasses the justices of the peace spent much of their time.

A lack of compassion was characteristic of many. People gathered by hundreds to watch executions. The congregation in the parish church listened to the poor girl, barefoot and in penitential white, confessing her frailty, and were as little sorry for her as the Salem characters in *The Scarlet Letter* were for Hester. When a good workman fell from a ladder and was permanently disabled, his misfortune stirred less sympathy [3]—so far as we can tell—than fear that he might become a public charge.

The want of compassion came at times close to cruelty. Massinger makes a character say:

> The people apt to mark calamity
> And tread on the oppressed.

The rejoicing of the crowd over the downfall of the great might be attributed to their interest in the dramatic, but seems to us almost sadistic. Certainly the interest of common men and women in the whipping of vagrants and in the ducking of miserable women was unwholesome.

Of some villages, indeed, little good can be said. Smyth of

[3] It is true that pity for misfortune, one of the tests of a civilization, is to be seen among the nobler characters in the plays of Shakespeare and other dramatists, and also in occasional letters and diaries. Reginald Scot, who dared in 1584 to attack the persecution of witches, took up his mission because "the mighty help themselves together, and the poor widow's cry, though it reach to heaven, is seldom heard here upon earth," and his whole *Discoverie* is full of pity. There were others like him, and their pity for the oppressed and poor is occasionally recorded in epitaphs against church walls.

Nibley [4] tells us about the squatters and riffraff along the Severn estuary and on the western slopes of the Cotswolds. Many hamlets in Gloucestershire and Worcestershire, in the moorlands of the north, and even in the counties near the capital abounded in rude people who lived miserably and were up to little good. Unfeeling as children, they enjoyed pelting the wretch caged in the stocks; they followed with shouts the drunk man led away by the constable. They were ungrateful for kindness and many of them seemed wanting even in natural family affections. They made trouble: they listened of nights to catch bedroom secrets at windows not high above the pavement; they lifted articles from clotheslines and out of rooms; they started quarrels at the alehouse and fell to blows. The constable found them a problem and the good parson seldom saw them in church.[5]

Many of them were no doubt unfortunate in the location and circumstances of their dwelling place. The villages they inhabited were often remote from larger centers or from regions of business activity. In some cases a change in the use of the highways or the silting up of a stream or a shift of industry had caused them to fall off from their former estate, and the ensuing poverty had led to a gradual relaxation of standards. Other villages had been swamped by the incursions of squatters, and still others had been settled originally by a ne'er-do-well population which received little impact from more civilized districts. Such stock can vitiate the character of a village for generations.

These remote villagers must not be judged by modern standards. Serfdom and numbing poverty had been the lot of their ancestors, and they themselves were seldom better off. They had little to think about except their beasts, their fields, and the common; the neighbor and the wrong he had done. Their minds had been too much occupied with small matters to look at things from another's point of view.

The picture was not all dark. The country gentleman and the

---

[4] Sir John Maclean (ed.), *The Berkeley Manuscripts . . . a Description of the Hundred of Berkeley* (3 vols., Gloucester, 1883–85), III.

[5] See the chapters on local government (Chapters 17, 18, 19, and 20).

parson were sometimes men who set an example of civility and good manners, which the villagers imitated. Certainly those parts of the country where manor houses and vicarages abounded were more decent and law-abiding than those districts where they were far apart.[6]

But there were many worthy people in villages in any case. In their somewhat restricted lives the better sort, perhaps not so hard-driven to keep going, exhibited virtues learned from the parson and from God-fearing parents. Their kindness to their neighbors and their compassion for the poor were enjoined upon them. But they had also virtues that arose out of their work. The men who wrought in iron and stone, on wood and wool and leather, the skilled workers, many more of them to be found then in villages than later, had been taught by their fathers and grandfathers in the same calling to be thorough, to be worthy of their "mystery," to have pride in careful craftsmanship. It is true that in Tudor and Stuart England all workmen were not as careful as once, and complaints were common about poor cloth turned out. But the tradition of fine workmanship was strong and the country was full of good men who were utterly honest in their work. They were likely to be honest in speech, given often to few words and downright.[7] Such men were seldom called upon by the constable;[8] they had a good name in the parish. In emergencies some of them could show great character. It was the good fortune of the Massachusetts Bay Company that it was able to command many such artisans.

We know more about the workers on the land,[9] and shall in later chapters deal with them in detail. Here one can only mention a characteristic quality of the best of them, a certain serious-mindedness and a toughness of fiber. Of a small gentleman in Tudor Devon-

[6] Yet sometimes in districts where manor houses were few and well-to-do yeomen were many, the people were lively and spirited, if not always tamed to the law.

[7] A type still to be met with in the deep country, and not uncommon in New England.

[8] But in an industrial district such as Staffordshire, where skilled workers were many and close together, they could make trouble for constables and justices.

[9] Many artisans of course worked also on the land.

shire, whose forbears had been yeomen and whose own outlook was yeoman, it was written: "He was a man earnest in his talk, a very wise, sad [sober], and grave man." He had reason to be so. Under gray skies and cold drizzles [10] his fathers and he and his sons had cleaned their ditches, repaired their boundary walls, and inserted new stones in their houses and barns.[11] By denial and hard work over the generations the family had added field to field. Such families had won a position among their neighbors, but their struggle had not been easy. The chilly houses of the time afforded men and women few comforts. Many a farmer watched one wife after another die in childbirth, or of a consumption, and saw child after child yield up its soul in convulsions or fever. A son that survived the perils of childhood had perhaps gone to sea and never been heard of again. The sorrows of our ancestors we fail to realize, because they recorded their losses with little comment. Some solace they received no doubt from what the parson promised, but it was a kind of stolid endurance that carried them through. They did not pity themselves. They were not philosophic and they did not rationalize their experiences; they went on doing the next things as well as they knew how. People of that kind could even face perilous seas and settle on a stern and rockbound coast. Their daily lives had given them a hardness that was not soon bred out of the English stock in Devon or Massachusetts.

That hardness and serious-mindedness showed itself time and time again in the character of the island people and enabled them to stand up to the shocks of war. It is possible that it had something to do with their susceptibility to Puritanism. Could a sophisticated Englishman of our day, however, one with a quietly quizzical outlook, find himself transported, as in a play, back into that time, he might feel the atmosphere oppressive.

For the English, or at least those who wrote diaries and letters,

[10] The English are pitifully appreciative of the little sunshine they get. The influence of climate upon national character is not for the mere historian to estimate but cannot be overlooked.

[11] That repair work over the centuries can often be traced in old houses, barns, and walls.

were sober and serious-minded even in their good-fellowship. Their merriment seems to us a little arranged and forced. Sir John Oglander describes a festive gathering in the Isle of Wight, with tables set out under the trees. The youths put on a play, and the young yeomen danced the morris, and there was laughter about the misadventure of a lad who fell asleep in a tree. The people of that time had possibly some French gift of making the most of an episode. But the lightheartedness and carefree gayety were not such as to make the reader envious. Nor is one impressed when Smyth of Nibley tells us how he would walk in summertime after evensong with his wife to Hodley's Green to behold his neighbor's children and his own run at barleybreak and dance in the ring. Sir John and Smyth took their pleasures soberly, as became gentlemen of gravity, and so did the yeomen.

Yet Sir John was constantly implying that there had been more merriment in the days of his youth. He could remember when Mistress Worsley and Mistress Milles, two handsome, tall, proper women, would dance after a poor tabor and pipe from Heasley House to the foot of the hill. Richard Corbet, who graced two bishoprics and had once been the merriest and maddest of young fellows, wrote memorable verses in which he lamented that the fairies no longer danced on any heath, and blamed the Puritans. No doubt England had become a soberer place, for many reasons.

There was more humor than one would suppose from a reading of diaries and letters.[12] Some of it was an intellectual type. From the middle of Elizabeth's reign through the reign of James I, Nicholas Breton was writing prose touched here and there with a quiet and subtle humor like the best English humor of our day.[13] Two cen-

[12] If those who wrote letters in the time of Elizabeth had a sense of fun, of the disproportionateness of things and the incongruity of human behavior, they did not often betray it. It is only when we come well down into the next century that we find amusing letter writers. I can think of one gentleman in the reign of James I and two or three in the reign of Charles I (as the second Lord Conway) who wrote letters with humor. Many will remember Dorothy Osborne, an adorable nineteenth-century woman who by an odd chance happened to be on this earth in the time of Cromwell.

[13] Francis Meres suggested that Breton talked Shakespeare's "very way," an

turies earlier Chaucer had used sly understatement, as the English in our time. Whether it amused his readers in the early seventeenth century is hard to discover. But we do come upon humor of a related kind. When Shakespeare makes a carrier say of Robin, "Poor fellow, never joyed since the price of oats rose; it was the death of him," he understood the fun that comes from a want of proportion between cause and effect, and a few in the audience must have smiled.

Exaggeration, misused words, incongruous figures of speech, and sex allusions made citizens laugh.[14] But the embarrassments of Sir John hidden in the basket of dirty clothes and thrown into the river would have made the groundlings roar. Horseplay with an edge of cruelty suited them.

Would that we knew more of the lusty fun of drovers and their kind. In the reign of Charles II, Roger Lowe, a shopkeeping Lancashire lad, could tell stories against himself, of his struggle with a stubborn ram on a rope and of his swallowing hot porridge at the servants' table.[15] His yarns have the ring of an old peasant humor such as might have been found in a Shakespeare scene, or conceivably among Saxon yokels. From bits of evidence one suspects that in the early seventeenth century Jack the carter and Tom the plowman could, when sowing was over or harvest in, be merry fellows at the Crosskeys, as their great-grandfathers before them.[16]

Quiet fun at home over a new-bought pamphlet or boisterous fun at the theater or in the alehouse was all very well for those who liked it, but the worthy lord of the manor, the hard-working yeoman, and

---

overstatement, but Breton did write in a very Elizabethan way and with more humor than most of his contemporaries. He has been too much forgotten.

[14] Some of the satire of the time had a kind of rough and heavy-handed humor.

[15] W. L. Sachse (ed.), *The Diary of Roger Lowe* (New Haven, 1938), pp. 38–40.

[16] Much here set down as characteristic of the English of that time may have been true of other peoples of the same time. Just how much was typically English and no other it is hard to say. Only one who knew intimately the social history not only of the various European peoples but of their subdivisions could answer that question. That the country people of England had more freedom and fewer burdens than those in most parts of France and Germany would hardly be disputed. If so, they had a better chance to take on a certain civility of manners.

the substantial townsman were in general little inclined to light-mindedness. They were men of gravity.

II. ECONOMIC FACTORS

Economic factors and developments were affecting the character of the English. Within the memory of their fathers or grandfathers they had become an adventurous people, seeking out customers and selling goods in far ports. Fortune, it was said, was friendly to folk adventurous. Many a lad who found things slow at home could watch boats from the headland and feel the wind:

> Such wind as scatters young men through the world
> To seek their fortunes.

Not only young men but those established had a "humor to be tampering with contingencies and a longing mind and a liquorish palate after novel projects, if made luscious with probabilities of profits." For the possibility of profit older men had laid plans and young men had sailed into the Arctic White Sea and had ridden camels over deserts toward China. The English were by no means unique in their commercial enterprises, but they believed themselves almost so. Were they not more ready than those of other nations to take chances and even to undergo heavy losses in the hope of great returns? In one of Heywood's plays the merchant Gresham was presented as offering £60,000 for the trade into Barbary during the ruler's lifetime, a gamble continental merchants had refused. Gambling in new business in Russia, Persia, and India was paying off and "eternizing English fame and honor." From a weak and feeble state England was becoming, boasted a member of Parliament, the most opulent and mighty empire of Christendom.[17] His boasting was such as merchants used; they really knew their worth. They would not be afraid to risk money on Virginia and Massachusetts.

They were doing well in enterprises at home as well as abroad. J. U. Nef,[18] who has written the classic work on the coal trade, thinks

---

[17] *Commons Journals,* I, 206, February 10, 1606.
[18] J. U. Nef, *The United States and Civilization* (Chicago, 1942), pp. 18–21.

of two industrial revolutions in England and says that the first took place between 1575 and 1620. Between the Reformation and the Civil Wars the output of coal increased, he estimates, tenfold, and such products as salt, iron and steel, lead, ships, and glass from five-fold to tenfold. Many new or virtually new industries, he tells us, were established, such as the manufacture of copper and brass, paper, soap, sugar, alum for dyeing, tobacco, and the pipes in which it was smoked. No such rapid development took place on the Continent.

The old forms of business were flourishing too. Wool and clothing men, grain buyers, butter-and-eggs dealers, were doing well, as were goldsmiths and scriveners, the bankers of the time. Country lawyers who looked after the legal affairs of gentlemen and well-to-do businessmen were prospering. The circle of the financially successful was widening, thanks in part no doubt to the emancipation of the serfs in the centuries just preceding. We have already seen what a lift that gave to England. The new free were climbing up, finding their way into the old and the new forms of business. Getting on was in the air. The Heralds' College was hunting up or inventing gentle ancestors for the newly arrived. The English were becoming the go-getters of the age, fit rivals of the Dutch and the Venetians.

The results were not always pleasing. The pretentiousness of the business classes gave occasion for satire. Aldermen's wives dressed like ladies of the Court and aped their carriage; they apologized to courtiers for the manners of their husbands; they aspired to be "ladified." Their husbands affected to forget their warehouses and developed a portentous dignity.

The new gentry sprung from the business world were little better. Farmers who had won to gentility over the generations were likely to understand its obligations and to retain a kind of genuine country quality, but the newly rich and the newly emblazoned were too fond of display and lavish hospitality; they overplayed their devotion to their new acres. The general ostentation of the time may be read between the lines on brasses in country churches.

The go-getting in the business world affected the professional classes. It was frankly said that the way to get on was to gain the favor of some great man and through his influence receive at length an appointment. In London were jobs aplenty, political, legal, and ecclesiastical, which carried honor with them and sizable fees, and in which the drudgery could be done by underlings. In the country were petty billets and stewardships in connection with crown lands and commissions, and in various courts and bailiwicks. Not least desirable were church livings, several thousand of them, that promised ease, respectability, and fixity of tenure. The health of every incumbent of a living was watched, and news of an approaching demise sent men scurrying to call on consequential friends.

As often in an age of expansion, the highest honesty was not always maintained. The heads of companies and their subordinates filled their pockets at the expense of their organizations and their factors in foreign ports imitated them. The little dealers over the shires did well for themselves. They were not more scrupulous than those descendants of theirs in the new world, the "Yankee traders," of whom the English have long since made a byword. A contemporary observer wrote: "Conscience is a pretty thing to carry to church but he that useth it in a fair market or shop may die a beggar." The temptations to overstep the line were great. "Let us prosper and purchase," said Bilioso in a play, "our lordships shall live and our knavery be forgotten." [19] By enough sharp practice a man might found a family and give his wife and children leisure and status. Had it not been ever thus that men attained to gentility?

One would like to say that the official classes at the top were better, something like the disinterested civil servants of today. Then one recalls the great houses built by statesmen and scans the letters of their secretaries.[20] Such men were expected to take a rake-off for themselves as part of their wage, but did it on too large a scale. Lesser civil servants awaited gifts from those who wished their suits

[19] *The Malcontent,* Act V, Scene II, in J. P. Collier (ed.), R. Dodsley, *A Select Collection of Old Plays* (London, 1825), 3rd ed., IV, 85.
[20] See J. E. Neale, *The Elizabethan Political Scene* (Raleigh Lecture), *Proc. British Academy,* XXXIV (1949).

furthered. The old English honesty, wistfully alluded to in Parliament, seemed to be on the wane.[21]

The go-getting age from the last decades of Elizabeth's rule to nearly the end of the reign of James I might well be compared to the era of expansion in America when strong men grew rich on railways, steel, or oil. Then some of them, or their sons or grandsons, proceeded to distribute their accumulations for beneficent purposes. Out of the strong came forth sweetness. So it was in England in a different way. The merchant who had come from a small town and made his money in London, or perhaps in Bristol or Norwich, may have used methods that would be frowned upon today, but he was usually a man of initiative and of some vision and intelligence. He was likely to leave part of his accumulations to endow an almshouse in his native village or town. The traveler over England will see many almshouses built in good red brick in the reign of James I, usually to support a fixed number of poor men and women. On the wall will be the carved letters in which the donor set forth his scheme for the charity. Occasionally he was a nobleman, but in most cases a merchant. On the tomb of Robert Gray in St. Mary Magdalene, Taunton, is the epitaph:

> Taunton bore him, London bred him . . .
> Earth enrich'd him; Heav'n carest him;
> Taunton blest him, London blest him;
> This thankful town, that mindful City
> Share his piety and his pity.
> What he gave, and how he gave it,
> Ask the Poor, and you shall have it.

For humanitarianism was and is an English and American habit. It goes back to the early Stuart period and can be found a little earlier. It was not the planned humanitarianism of the late eight-

[21] The men round James I were using the royal favor for financial advantage so brazenly and successfully that they must have affected the moral standards of the whole country. But in the chapters following we shall meet townsmen and country gentlemen of disinterestedness and integrity, most of whom did not frequent the Court and did not get into the records of litigation, as the less honest did.

eenth and nineteenth centuries, directed to helping the unfortunate by doing away with abuses. Few of the English in the early seventeenth century looked that far ahead. But already there was a humaneness of outlook and pity for the poor. As early as in the reign of Elizabeth a country town, shall we say in Devonshire, would vote money for its "poor brethren" in a Yorkshire village who had been burned out or decimated by the plague. The people were offering aid to those they had never seen and never would see.

The go-getters were the kindly givers. It is still true in England. The businessman, especially in the north, will in his office drive hard bargains and in other surroundings prove an openhanded bene-factor.

CHAPTER 3

The English Character, Intellectual and Cultural Influences

HAD AN Italian visited England in the year 1603 and been able to talk freely with an English friend, comparing things Italian and English, he might have raised questions: where are your Donatellos and Michelangelos; where are your palaces and town halls with lines in due proportion and fair façades? Your London buildings are a sprawling jumble of half-timbered houses and the few good structures to be seen are imitations of Italian. You can show some good Gothic cathedrals and some impressive churches and a few memorable monuments and carvings in them. But you seem to have no artistic tradition, no dynasties of painters and architects and sculptors. As for your writings,[1] are not your plays made-over versions of our Italian stories; are not many of your sonnets free translations of ours?

The Englishman might well have admitted that in painting, sculpture, and architecture his nation made a poor showing in comparison with the Italians. He could have pointed, however, to

[1] Samuel Daniel, not a bad poet, thought there was something to be said for English writing against Italian:

"When all that ever hotter spirits exprest
Comes bettred by the patience of the North."

Musophilus, in A. B. Grosart (ed.), *Works of Samuel Daniel* (London, 1885), I, 255.

the English theater, to the companies of players swarming over the realm and beyond, to the dramatists beginning then to be of the first importance. Among poets he could have mentioned Chaucer, Langland, and Spenser.[2] He might have boasted of English music, the most significant in Europe at the time. In view of the location of England at the northwest corner of Christendom, away from the main currents of cultural life, she had not done so badly. Her time was to come.[3]

She was indeed far from the Mediterranean centers of culture. Any modern student of the sixteenth century, as he recalls the flowering of Florence and Venice and other Italian cities, as he considers the works of the Italian humanists, as he gazes at the portraits of the great Italian figures, realizes at once that the southern civilization, if less wholesome, was more highly developed than that of the northern island. Cities breed civilizations and the English were, as we have seen, a somewhat rustic folk.

The intellectual world in which the reading and thinking Englishman lived was, however, not far behind that of Italy and was almost abreast of that in Germany and France. Books and the ideas in them circulate more quickly than artistic traditions. That world in Elizabeth's reign and even up into the early Stuart period was still medieval in its fundamental concepts. Those concepts were derived largely from Plato and his interpreters over the centuries, but in a singular combination with the Old Testament. They have been best

[2] In another poem ("To the Countess of Pembroke," in *Works,* III, 26–27) Daniel wrote:

> "Whereby great Sydney and our Spencer might
> With those Po-singers being equalled,
> Enchaunt the world with such a sweet delight
> That their eternal songs (for ever read)
> May shew what great Elizae's reign hath bred."

[3] Daniel (*Musophilus,* in *Works,* I, 255) foretold as much:

> "And who in time, knows whither we may vent
> The treasure of our tongue, to what strange shores
> This gain of our best glory shall be sent,
> T'inrich unknowing Nations with our stores.
> What worlds in th' yet unformed Occident
> May come refin'd with th' accents that are ours."

described by E. M. W. Tillyard, the Cambridge scholar of literature.[4] The Elizabethans, he tells us, thought of a great chain of
being,[5] an ordered universe, arranged in a fixed system of hier-
archies, but modified by man's sin and the hope of redemption. Man
was subordinate to God, but the world and all in it and even the
heavens above were intended for man. At the head was God, and
below Him a multitude of angels in various ranks and subranks,
who waited on Him and were the guardians of man. Then came
man in all his various classes and subordinations. Below him were
beasts, birds, and fishes. Below them came trees and plants and
finally inanimate objects such as stones and metals.[6] Thus did God
express in variety the abundance of His glory. Nature he used as his
deputy or tool.

Order was everything. Break the chain of being at any point and
the result would be chaos. Shakespeare, in the passage describing
how the heavens themselves "Observe degree, priority and place,"
went on to say:

> Take but degree away, untune that string,
> And hark what discord follows.[7]

The fall of man had untuned those strings. Yet thanks to the
sacrifices of Christ man could hope for salvation. The fall had made
him subject to the stars and to the influence of Fortune, whose
effects upon the individual were never out of mind. But his situation
was not hopeless. Through the contemplation of the divine order, as
shown in the universe, he could come to know God aright. By education he could mitigate the force of the stars and survive the blows of
Fortune. It was a touch-and-go business, and the Elizabethans, as
Tillyard points out, could oscillate between the extremes of pessi-

[4] In his *Elizabethan World Picture* (London, 1948).

[5] See A. O. Lovejoy, *The Great Chain of Being* (Cambridge, Mass., 1936),
passim.

[6] Tillyard quotes the fifteenth-century Sir John Fortescue: "So that from the
highest angel down to the lowest of his kind there is absolutely not found an
angel that has not a superior and inferior: nor from man down to the meanest
worm, is there any creature which is not in some respect superior to one creature
and inferior to another." *Eliz. World Picture,* p. 24.

[7] *Troilus and Cressida,* Act I, Scene 3, 109.

mism and hopefulness about man and his fate. With all their interest in this world, they were intensely concerned with the next.

Their cosmogony included four elements: earth, water, air, and fire. These elements were mixed in infinitely varied proportions and were in constant struggle with one another. The food taken into the body was converted by the liver into four liquid substances, the four humors, which were to the body what the elements were to the earth, and had a correspondence with the elements. If these humors were rightly distributed within the body, a man enjoyed good health. But he might have, for example, too much phlegm and be phlegmatic.[8]

The men of the time delighted in other correspondences and analogies. The correspondences were countless, and they seem to us farfetched and fantastic, but to the Elizabethans they afforded interpretations of human beings and their behavior.[9] The Elizabethans assumed premises so different from ours that we can hardly put ourselves back into the intellectual realm they inhabited. Remember how the new psychologists within a single generation have made former judgments of men and situations seem incomplete, and then consider how much farther removed were the bases of judgment three and a half centuries ago. The adventurous and daring Elizabethans, still clinging to the last enchantments of the Middle Ages, puzzle us, until we remember that the next generation had hardly begun to doubt witchcraft. Were the Elizabethans more daring in action than in thought?

Their ideas had bearings ideal and practical. Tillyard says: "This renewed Platonizing created an enthusiastic idealism. . . . It is a

---

[8] The correspondences have been set forth by Tillyard (*Eliz. World Picture,* p. 63) in a table:

Elements	Humors	Qualities
earth	melancholy	cold and dry
water	phlegm	cold and moist
air	blood	hot and moist
fire	choler	hot and dry

[9] See Burton's *Anatomy of Melancholy,* a book full of traditions, moralistic aphorisms, notions, and folklore of the ancient and medieval world. There is hardly a better source from which to learn the ideas still prevalent in the Elizabethan world and that a little later.

habit of mind . . . at once fantastic and closely allied to action," [10] and uses Sir Philip Sidney as an illustration. But it had realistic applications too. The whole class structure of the time was regarded as part of the divine arrangement, exhibited in human nature as well as in God's cosmogony. The political structure was equally sanctified, and the King and all the subordinate authorities of state from privy councilors to petty constables were members of the hierarchy of power. Such a system allowed no place for government that springs from popular will. That way lay anarchy. The church, with its arch-bishops, bishops, and deans, fitted into the scheme. As for the individual, he was so affected by the stars and Fortune and the distribution of the humors in his body that he would appear to have had little freedom of the will. Yet many even of the early Eliza-bethans were losing faith in Fortune [11] and the stars.[12]

These ideas, implicit in the speeches of the men and women of the plays, in the poetry of Spenser and later of Milton, in Ralegh's *History* and in some degree in Hooker's *Laws of Ecclesiastical Polity*, were not soon discarded.[13] But new ideas did weaken the hold of the old concepts. Galileo's astronomical discoveries and the interest in science that began to be evident before the middle of the seventeenth century slowly rendered the old notions archaic.

They were losing their hold not only because of the attacks upon them, but because men were becoming more interested in other sub-jects. Through the new translations the Hebrews, the Greeks, and the Romans were speaking to the English as never before, and at the same time the latest Dutch, Swiss, German, and French writers on theology were being pondered by the learned in England.

[10] *Eliz. World Picture*, p. 41.

[11] See for example many passages in Lilly Bess Campbell (ed.), *Mirrour for Magistrates* . . . (Cambridge, 1938).

[12] The providence of a personal God was set against Fortune and the stars by the Reformers, who made attack after attack upon astrology.

[13] But they were coming under attack. Copernicus had made the earth a sub-ordinate planet; Machiavelli had assumed that men were bad and must be ruled by force and duplicity; Montaigne had made fun of the notion of man as the darling of nature. For a brief statement of the new attack, see Theodore Spenser, *Shakespeare and the Nature of Man* (2nd. ed., New York, 1949), pp. 29 ff.

The influence of the Bible needs little elaboration here, since it will be dealt with in later chapters. By 1560 the Geneva Bible made Scripture available to a wide public. Those who could read or listen, as soon as they had the Old Testament in English, had a great deal to think about that did not seem alien to their own experience: the folk tales, the precepts, and the codes of a pastoral people led by Providence; they learned of relationships in the family, of marriage, and of the duties of rulers and subjects. The Hebrew stories were already vaguely familiar from what the old priest had told them. The teachings of Christ and St. Paul took a long while to be thoroughly assimilated in all their philosophic implications, for the men of that day studied the Old Testament more attentively; eventually those teachings were to have effects beyond estimate upon the English.

Greek and Roman influences were second only to those of the Bible. The more intelligent reading public of England was poring over the classical writers, usually in the recent translations. There was less to read than nowadays and the translations afforded fresh materials. Men trained in the grammar schools and at the universities could read Latin easily, but even they took advantage of the translations. The reading gentry, who supplied most of the leadership, as we shall see, derived ideals of highmindedness, of endurance, of gravity, of reverence for tradition, and above all of moderation, from the ancients. It was stories of Greek and Roman characters that they remembered best and cherished longest. They had almost no novels in English as yet, and the collections of short stories in circulation were largely from Italian sources. In Plutarch and other ancient biographers and historians they found a treasure of narratives and episodes that showed men in crises behaving with heroism and disinterestedness, or the reverse. There were morals to be drawn from them, and the English of the time had almost a passion for drawing morals. Did not history teach by example? The example of Regulus was brought up in the House of Commons. As a prisoner of the Carthaginians he had been released on parole to go back to Rome and negotiate a treaty between Carthage and Rome, but he had stood up before the Roman Senate and advised it not to make the treaty. Then, in spite of the pleading of his friends, he had returned to Carthage and was said to have been tortured to death. Such high-mindedness deserved imitation even in smaller issues before the House of Commons.

So did endurance, which many Roman stories illustrated. That virtue was enforced by the philosophy of Stoicism which was invading England, and which, however pagan in origin, was not wholly repugnant to puritan gentlemen. The gravity of the leaders of the Roman republic impressed the English, who were themselves already given to gravity. Their own times called for that quality, and such men as Phelips, Digges, and Colonel Hutchinson [14] were exemplars of it. The *pietas* of the Romans, the reverence for progenitors and their traditions, was not alien to gentlemen who sat on Sunday in pews close to the graves of their fathers. Moderation, the *mediocritas* of the Romans, was praised by parents addressing their sons, by authors of books of advice, and by playwrights and proverb makers. With the leaders of Parliament it was a fixed policy. "A great wise man that knew the world to a hair," wrote Nicholas Breton, "would say that the mean was sure."

It was to be generations yet before the English with an empire on their hands would come to regard themselves as the modern Romans, but in the early seventeenth century the Roman *imperium* was not far out of their minds. Like the Romans they were members of a proud state, and their leaders carried themselves almost consciously as if in the Forum.[15]

The Reformation stirred up on the Continent a long and acrimonious controversy and thus accumulated premises and deductions,

[14] See Sir Charles Firth's edition of Mrs. Hutchinson's *Life of Colonel Hutchinson* (London, 1885).

[15] The settlers in the American colonies might have been supposed to be too near the instant need of things to have shown interest in classical works. But they carried books with them, and not only about theology and law. From almost the beginning a few of them had Latin books on their shelves. As leisure and means gave them more opportunities, the better minds in the new world sought out the Greek and Roman writers. The men of the late eighteenth century who made the American constitution were as familiar with the ancients as the members of the early seventeenth-century Parliaments.

pros and cons, which were quickly carried over to England and restated there in English terms. The combination in time of the interest in classical literature and of the new religion was fortunate. It could not but excite all good minds. Not only university fellows but gentlemen with bookshelves, clergymen who had continued their intellectual life, and lawyers who looked beyond the law were moved to meditate on God and man, on man's chief end, and on his freedom, his achievement, and his possibilities. Theology they read, but they did not overlook the pagan authors. Even the country parson, when he was expounding a passage in First Corinthians, was likely to quote from Cicero's *De Officiis*.

The intellectual ferment was bound in the long run to set men thinking along new lines. But there was a natural lag. The new ideas of the late Elizabethan and early Stuart period were about the old subjects, and some of them indeed were to be found in the church fathers. Men were still dealing with the Bible and its expositors and with the ancient thinkers, and in the old way. They found premises and then reasoned deductively from them. It was a habit taught them at the university. Moreover the majority of them had lingered so long at the university and were so grounded in the old books that they did not venture easily into new fields of inquiry. They were not prepared to use the method of observation about the world of nature, they were not even expecting—as we always are— to learn new things about that world, and Bacon's demand for observation of it was only slowly heeded. Furthermore they were not yet applying the method of observation to human nature.

It was to be a long while before the English attempted any general examination of human behavior.[16] It is disappointing, however, to find their writers making so little effort at the characterization of individuals. With a few marked exceptions the dramatists were not exploring the minds and motives of men and women, but developing Italian plots with little verisimilitude to life as the English knew it, and exhibiting stock characters in unreal situations. Shakespeare, it

---

[16] Some of them did read Montaigne, and his probing into human character in general must have seemed to them strange and new.

is true, could make the personages even in his historical plays living beings, but he transcended his own time. Some effort to depict human nature was made by the writers of books of "characters," but even those amusing delineators of types of men in vocations failed to go far below the surface. The biographers and historians were offering some analysis of men and occasionally telling a story that brought a Wolsey or a Sir Thomas More to life, but in general their characterizations seem rather cut and dried. They were indeed getting away from the use of careers as a means of drawing morals and giving instruction, but they continued to present men as ambitious and jealous and moved by pride and spite. Good men too crossed their pages, but the goodness had few ramifications.[17] Those who described their own immediate generation and depicted statesmen, courtiers, and members of Parliament they had known ought to have done better at characterization. The time was not far ahead when Izaak Walton and Edward Hyde, Earl of Clarendon, were to offer authentic portraits of the men they had watched. But with few exceptions those who wrote in the last years of Elizabeth and in the reign of James I failed to give significant interpretations of their contemporaries.[18] Even the members of the House of Commons did not probe into the prejudices and habits of thought of their fellows or of their leaders.[19]

If the studies of individuals and of their lives seem wanting in close characterization, it may be in part because the men and women of that time had less color and variety than those of our generation.

Can that be possible? It was the age of England's greatest dramatist, the age too of that powerful and original mind pushing out in

[17] The publication by Thomas North in 1579 of his translation of Plutarch's *Lives* gave an impetus to the interest in biography.

[18] Robert Naunton, in his *Fragmenta Regalia,* and Sir John Harington in *Nugae Antiquae,* showed some skill in characterization. Moreover John Chamberlain, in his letters to Carleton, slyly allowed men to speak for themselves and give themselves away.

[19] The interest in the close characterization of individuals is shown usually by rather mature people. Children are satisfied with heroes and villains and clowns, and so was the public that attended most Elizabethan plays.

new directions, Francis Bacon. Neither of them lacked color or variety, nor did the men and women in Shakespeare's plays want those attributes. Talented beings were common. The men who gathered at the Mermaid Tavern must have been birds of plumage.

Nevertheless the men and women of the seventeenth century seem as a body, even the privileged and fortunate, less complicated creatures than those of recent generations. Go to the National Portrait Gallery in London and spend the morning looking at the portraits of the late nineteenth and early twentieth century, and mark how much subtlety and sophistication and fineness of spirit are shown on many of the faces. Some of the men and women on those walls belonged in a highly civilized society.

Then go in the afternoon to the top floor of the same gallery and gaze at the paintings of the men and women of the time of Elizabeth and James I. You are in another England and among strangers. The men of that time look more like one another; many of the women might be Dutch; some of the nobles might be Spanish grandees. They are less English than the men on the first floor. But there is more to it than that. These men of the earlier time were simpler in every way. They were not fools; they could reason cogently and with power; they could be subtle. The difference between them and the men of a later day might be compared to that between a shrewd New Hampshire farmer and an old Bostonian.

It will be said at once that the painters of that day wanted the skill to set down on canvas all that was written on the faces, to indicate adequately the effects of experience and memory. Yet the Dutch artists who drew the English men and women did not miss much in a countenance and must be rated high among artists.

A reading of the letters, diaries, and autobiographies of the early seventeenth century and of those three centuries later does not weaken the impression gained from the portraits. We can study the letters written by John Chamberlain, by Sir Dudley Carleton, and by Sir Henry Wotton, pressing into the pages to get at the inwardness of those epistolary gentlemen and of the men they describe, and discover rather dim figures who hardly come alive. The autobiography of Lord Herbert of Cherbury is perhaps the most personal of such works and reveals a boastful knight-errant almost medieval, but his adventures are the stuff of old romances and leave us with little notion of Lord Herbert or of his friends. About all those seventeenth-century figures there is a kind of grayness apparent even to one long familiar with them. It may of course be our fault, with our limited knowledge of them and our limited imaginations, that we cannot reach to see them as they were. But I think not. We may grant that the men of that time had little gift for putting themselves on paper and yet suspect that even those who had a talent for exhibiting their own particular qualities failed somehow to show much light and shading.[20]

The ampler and more variegated personalities of our time could be accounted for in many ways. The explanations would add up to the fact that the complexity of modern life, which confuses us at times, makes after all for the extension of personality. Consider the characters in the best of modern novels, neither good nor bad, but with so many threads of so many colors and thicknesses woven into so many patterns, and then consider Shakespeare's characters, whose moral problems were comparatively simple and whose idealisms were few and limited. We have new sensitivenesses, new types of unselfishness, new forms of high-mindedness, of which neither our forefathers nor their imaginary creations ever dreamed.

They could be more immediately brave and more ready to take on the dragon; they were more certain where he was and what form he took. They had a philosophy more standardized and of a piece. Few of them had been at pains to make their own attempts at truth and unity. Their faith was more readily useful, their passions more immediate and more easily shifted, their aspirations more directed in a single line.

[20] We may ask ourselves, Is the difference suggested between our ancestors and ourselves a matter of lighting? The man of today has so much more illumination turned upon him, and he himself has become more skillful in carrying a candle before him. Might it not be that if we could analyze our ancestors as we do ourselves and our fellows, we might find them as complicated creatures as we, even if of less varied interests? I suspect that those who read the letters and diaries will think otherwise.

CHAPTER 4

The Nobles

Where is Bohun, where's Mowbray, where's Mortimer? Nay, which is more and most of all, where is Plantagenet? They are entombed in the urns and sepulchres of mortality.

When Lord Berkeley returning from London came down over the terraces of the Cotswolds to the hundred of Berkeley in the Severn valley, he was met by troops of tenants and retainers. His progress toward his castle was indicated by the peals of bells from the church tower of each village as he reached it. The noble was not the feudal potentate as he had once been, with a body of armed men and a fortified castle, but he was still a magnet of loyalty and a figure of state.

In London Lord Berkeley sat in the Upper House of Parliament, the House of Lords, to which he received an individual summons from the King, and was thus a peer of the realm. He was only a baron, that is, of the lowest rank of the nobility. Above him were the ranks of viscount, earl, marquis, and duke, but in the early seventeenth century there were few lords above the rank of earl. Lord Berkeley's position was higher than his title, for he belonged to one of the oldest great families in England; his ancestors had come over with William of Normandy and settled at Berkeley. Like other peers he would be succeeded on his death by his eldest son, who until then was a commoner; his younger sons remained commoners. He was representative of a class that was not a closed circle, but that was constantly throwing out younger sons into the middle classes.

The prestige of peers of whatever rank was still great. The general public looked upon them as men whose duty it was to stand round the King and be his advisers. Their devotion made him rich and strong and glorious to the world. In the words of a contemporary poet they were the eyes of the commonwealth.

They were not content with prestige. They would fain serve the state in some high capacity. Next to places in the Privy Council, they sought appointments as lords lieutenant of counties. In that post they had to see that the musters were held in the county and that the trained bands were equipped and drilled. Other offices were objects of their ambition, in the pursuit of which they would write letter after letter to the great in London. They aspired to the post of *custos rotulorum* in the county, the keeper of the records of the quarter sessions, a formal office of high dignity. They were no less eager for the presidency of the Council of the North or that of the Council of the Marches of Wales. Offices in the royal household, which would bring them into daily relation with a generous sovereign, were deemed worthy of their mettle.

Power or places that led to power they craved, but they were looking also for the means of increasing their wealth. In *A New Way to Pay Old Debts* Lady Allworth observes that those of eminent blood had been interested to gain honors, but nowadays they were more eager to study large additions to their fortunes.[1]

The favor of King James offered one of their best chances. There were crown lands to be had from him at old and nominal rents. Better, there were patents to be secured for the distribution of this and that commodity, patents that skimmed the cream from the profits made by businessmen and officials and raised the cost of living for everyone, but furnished the recipient with a handsome income. The begging letters to the King from men of ancient lineage were not such as proud men should have written.

[1] Act IV, scene i, in *Dramatic Works of Philip Massinger* (London, 1805) III, 555.

They needed the honors and wealth they could accumulate if they were to live up to what was expected of them. It was their duty and pleasure to play public parts as ornamental and generous figures. "Dignified and stately" they were to be then, as in Victorian days. It was stated that there should be a comeliness in the countenance of a nobleman, in his gestures and behavior. His clothes should be handsome, his pronunciation grave and deliberate. It should be his study, men thought, to do acts of bounty, piety, and charity. He should be a good landlord, a loving neighbor, a great compromiser (arbitrator), and above all a man of religious principles.[2]

The nobles who fulfilled these expectations were usually those less seen in Court and more often in their shires, such as the Stanleys of Lancashire and the Montagus of Northamptonshire. It was beginning to be said, however, by a new and critical generation that there was a falling off in the quality of the nobles. In the good old times there had been Talbots and their like.

> Nobility was then a name which bore
> Weight to its value.

The preachers were complaining that the nobles were not what they had been, but that they were ignorant, idle, and given over to sports, an accusation that might have been made in earlier times.

It was charged that they took advantage of their rank and regarded themselves and their retainers as exempt from the ordinary course of the law. A dowager countess wrote to her nephew, Robert Cecil, the great minister of state, that a distraint had been levied upon her land (probably for a debt she would not pay) by the justices of the peace. A lady of her quality was in no way subject to a letter from any justice of the peace. When justices in a Midland county were attempting to bring to time a bad man, they found that he had been allowed to put on the livery of a powerful earl and thus secure protection. In a sermon it was remarked that a great man's livery or countenance was enough to keep drunkenness from the

---

[2] See Sir Thomas Elyot, *The Governour,* Book II, chap. 2, etc.; Henry Peacham, *The Compleat Gentleman;* John Smyth, *The Lives of the Berkeleys,* II; Robert Bolton, *Works,* especially a sermon called "Four Last Things." These ideas about noblemen are to be found in many places.

stocks, whoredom from the whipping post, and murder and thievery from the gallows. Landed potentates could frighten justices and overawe juries, and had few scruples about doing so. Even the Star Chamber, when families of consequence came into its purview, moved with caution.

It was hinted that the manners of the nobles were bad. They carried themselves with an affected and artificial haughtiness, as some of them had always done. The grandeur and majesty of port which nobles enjoined upon their heirs easily degenerated into something like arrogance. Great lords had constant differences with neighboring boroughs and thought to bear them down with high-mightiness. They were arrogant with members of their own class. The Earl of Arundel was a better man than most of the Howard connection; he was the first English collector of continental sculpture and paintings, and his acquisitions are still to be seen. But it was he who in the House of Lords reminded Lord Spencer that the lord's ancestors had been keeping sheep when Arundel's may have been giving good service to the King. What was worse, he was insufferably rude to his inferior, the mayor of Chester. That local dignitary had failed to wait upon him and to welcome him to the city. Arundel summoned the mayor, abused and threatened him, and proved utterly unwilling to accept his explanation that he had not been informed of the coming of the great man. The Earl of Derby spoke up for the mayor, and Arundel relented at length, but ungraciously.

Pride and arrogance are often the weakness of those of high position with not enough to do. Unless the King bestowed offices upon them the nobles had in days of peace no real function, and even the offices he granted them might be largely honorary. The care of their various manors, usually somewhat scattered, was left to stewards. Too great personages they were to bargain with tenants over leases and fields. Their place was in Court and there they could tread the primrose path of dalliance and become restless magnificoes, who had lost the will to make any serious effort. In the hunting field they pursued conquests over deer shut up behind palings, and in London they won victories at tilting, or gained the favors of maids of honor.

The writers of the time were not unaware of the futility of many of the nobility. In Ford's *The Lovers Melancholy* Meleander is made to say:

> . . . range, range on,
> And roll about the world to gather moss,
> The moss of honor, gay reports, gay clothes,
> Gay wives, huge empty buildings, whose proud roofs
> Shall with their pinnacles even reach the stars. . . .
> Ye're fat in no felicity but folly.[3]

The huge buildings cost money and embodied in stone and timber the fundamental weakness of the nobility, their extravagance. They would repair old houses and add to them at the expense of two or three years' income; they would tear down buildings and erect more stately three-story mansions, which might involve the sale of one or two manors.

The servants still deemed necessary were a continuous drain upon them. The wages paid them were small enough, but they had to be clothed and fed and they knew how to live well at their master's expense. The nobles suffered from guests,[4] the casual well-born travelers who asked hospitality, and those who came and stayed and were not easily sent away. When Lord Berkeley found the "captains, scholars, poets, cast courtiers, and the like" a burden, he would suddenly leave his castle and go a-visiting, or stop at one of his small houses, or even become a boarder, taking with him only his wife and a few body servants.[5] He had at his hand a wise lawyer to see that he did not spend too much.

The hunting habits of the nobles cost them heavily. Good horses had to be picked up at fairs, hawks brought often from overseas, and great parcels of woods set aside for deer. The steward of Viscount Lisle in Kent made efforts to save money for his master. Did

---

[3] Act II, Scene 2. William Gifford (ed.), *Works of John Ford* (new ed. by Alexander Dyce, London, 1869), I, 46. Licensed 1628.

[4] Thomas Jefferson in Virginia was impoverished by casual visitors.

[5] See John Smyth of Nibley, *The Berkeley Manuscripts . . . a Description of the Hundred of Berkeley,* ed. Sir John Maclean (3 vols., Gloucester, 1883–85), II, 286, 411, *passim.*

the lord really need two great parks for entertaining his friends with hunting? Were the four hundred deer he had not enough? The mere palings for fencing in the deer cost large sums. Was not so much hunting perhaps a fashion that would decline?

The travel of a nobleman round the country and to London was no small item. The old country gentleman had moved on horseback accompanied by one or two servants. The great nobleman nowadays thought he had to have a coach for his journeys, especially if he were taking his wife with him, and she liked to go to London. A coach meant outriders and several servants in attendance who could, when necessary, pull it out of the mud.

The incidental expenses of a lord mounted up. As the Earl of Huntingdon progressed from his country house to London, he was expected in every town where he stopped overnight to leave money for the poor, to bestow shillings upon the servants of the mayor or of the leading officials who welcomed him, to reward the bell-ringers who had rung him into town, and to remember those musicians who had suddenly appeared before him while he dined. Like obligations fell upon his countess when she set out for the city.

The lord had to pay at every turn. But it was attendance at the Court that broke his back. The clothes of a gentleman in that time cost money, one suit something like $1,000 in our money, and the nobleman had to have clothes for various types of occasions. James reveled in a showy Court with entertainment constantly afforded by his nobles—it saved him expense—and one entertainment might cost £2,000 or, say, $30,000. He loved a round of jousts, masques, and fancy-dress balls; he liked to see the women wearing costly jewels. The exact value of the jewels worn by Lady So-and-So was talked about next day. It was the opinion of Ben Jonson, not an entirely disinterested opinion, but one no doubt widely held, that it was the duty of great personages to be studious of riches and outward magnificence, and such studiousness was not uncongenial to Herberts and Howards and their kind.

Naturally such nobles found themselves compelled to sell or mortgage some of their manors. The Earl of Shrewsbury, who died in late Elizabethan days, had been accounted for "cattle, corn, wool, lead, iron, lands, revenue and of ready money" the richest subject in England, but the old proverb proved true, "no dead man rich." The *State Papers Domestic* are full of the letters of lords and ladies asking to be released from old debts due to the Crown. They owed debts of long standing not only to the Crown but to their tailors and their butchers, and were always trying to settle for a fraction of their obligation. Most of them were spending beyond their incomes. It is a mystery economic historians are trying to explain that they did not lose all their lands. Some of them of course had many manors scattered over various counties and could go on running into debt almost indefinitely. As debtors they benefited by the decreasing value of money.

The nobles who attended Court in the reign of James I were impoverishing themselves, but they were also doing much to discredit their class. A more unsavory lot it is hard to come upon in the annals of England. The story of the Howards and of the Overbury murder will be told in another chapter.[6] The Howards were among the least estimable of families, but they kept the show going. Lords and ladies proceeded from one festivity to another; they played for high stakes; they drank to excess. Great ladies who were to take part in masques had to be carried out. Things went on in galleries and balconies that had to be hushed up. But the gossip reached sober Londoners and disgusted them, and disquieted country gentlemen when it came eventually to their ears. Had James determined to destroy the prestige of the nobility, he could not have managed things better.

The nobles must not be utterly condemned. They were caught in a current too strong for them. But there was more to it than that. They were the sons of rich and favored men, and such sons have been usually a problem to their parents and to the public. The heirs of great families had neither the bringing up nor the discipline to make them men of character and attainments. As growing boys they were likely to be fawned upon by servants and retainers who

[6] See Chapter 15.

taught them how to throw money around. In writing advice to his
son the Earl of Northumberland lamented his youth, when his
humor was to be "young, handsome, brave, swaggering, debauched,
wild, abetting all my young desires." The sons were often educated
by private tutors and chaplains more anxious to please than to correct. If a son of a peer went to the universitly, he was shown all
favors there. A few of them went abroad with tutors and gained
possibly some knowledge of the world and of the polity of other
nations, but learned much of less value.

It has been implied that there were nobles of more character than
those conspicuous at court. Such men performed services as keepers
of royal parks and forests and as members of commissions. They
traveled a certain amount, occasionally on an errand for the government. A few were intelligent enough to patronize poets and alert
enough to take small parts in promoting discovery and colonization.
One of them might fight a duel or exhibit some streak of sudden
wildness, derived no doubt from a moorland ancestor on his mother's
side, and then on another occasion might act with the judgment of
an elder statesman. Some slight mark a number of them left upon
their time, enough to have their lives recorded in the *Dictionary of
National Biography*. If they were less impressive than their fathers
who had served Elizabeth, it was because they had fewer military
opportunities in which to show the mettle and courage that had
been the tradition of their class.

A few nobles deserve by some quality of mind or achievement to
be remembered. An earl took part in the Virginia Company, cooperated with the opposition in Parliament, and patronized Shakespeare. Another earl, one of the richest in England, welcomed
Thomas Hobbes, the political philosopher, to his home and gave
him respect and leisure. A viscount refused to pay benevolences,
forced loans, and ship-money, sent colonists to the mouth of the
Connecticut River, and talked of going himself to New England,
but stayed in England and helped Pym and Hampden lay plans for
the Long Parliament. A baron, the eleventh of his line, was a member of the Council for Virginia and that for New England; presi-

dent of the Council of Wales; a friend of Gerard, the herbalist, and of Ben Jonson; and a wise and learned man. Another peer devoted himself to reclaiming fen lands.[7]

Wives there were among the nobility who proved an ornament to their class. It would seem that riches and rank may give to women some special grace not afforded to their husbands. Mary Sidney, Countess of Pembroke, is remembered chiefly because of the celebrated epitaph, but was really wise and fair and good. Penelope Devereux, sister of the unfortunate Earl of Essex and the Stella of Sir Philip Sidney, although her morals were not particularly correct, was a figure in the Court of Elizabeth and in that of the first years of James, charming and spirited enough to have her sins condoned. Anne Clifford, wife in succession to two great nobles, agonizing amid the gardens of Knole and Wilton over the neglect and unfaithfulness of her husbands, resisting the fearful pressures of King and Court to yield her Westmorland lands, and meditating upon Chaucer and Spenser, had a quiet old-English charm of her own. Lucy Percy, who married a Scot, in spite of her Percy father, became at length Countess of Carlisle and one of the first great ladies of English history.

A thoughtful man of the time might have guessed that the peerage was running down at the heels and would lose its influence. He could not have foreseen that the Civil Wars would give them again their military functions and chances to become leaders and even heroic figures. Other factors were to strengthen the position of the class. Old families, grown eccentric and ineffectual, died out, and new men with coronets emerged: men who served the government well, or improved their lands, or developed mines, or sent ships to the East. Still later, men who built an empire and governed it were ennobled. Such men of deeds often bred good heirs. What saved the nobility was a new nobility always coming on.

---

[7] They were Henry Wriothesley, Earl of Southampton; William Cavendish, Duke of Newcastle; William Fiennes, Viscount Saye and Sele; Edward Lord Zouche; and Francis Russell, Earl of Bedford.

CHAPTER 5

The Country Gentlemen

Like columns do upprop the fabric of a building so noble gentry do support the honor of a kingdom (engraved on the market hall at Leominster, 1633).

For nearly two and a half centuries up to the late nineteenth century the country gentlemen were the leaders of English politics and life. For at least three centuries before the Local Government Act of 1888 they were the kings of the countryside. They constituted the bulk of the membership of the House of Commons and supplied most of its leadership. In the shire they were the justices of the peace and had their fingers in many pies. More than any other group they set the standards and developed the codes of the English. They were not the men who made England rich and imperial, but they did the job of building good government and creating a humane and enlightened society.

Few of those English who came to the New World were of gentle stock, but they brought traditions of the class with them. When a lawyer grew rich and important in a New England village, he was often dubbed "the squire," as many gentlemen in England were called. In Virginia, as soon as the settlers had cleared bits of the woods and built houses, they set up plantations modeled on the manors they had known in England, and tried to live, as best they could, like country gentlemen. All over the South the plantation system developed country gentlemen who in their relations with one another, in the conduct of their families, in their interests in hunting and fishing and out-of-door sports, carried on an English way of life.

What was a country gentleman? Technically he was one to whom or to whose ancestors the Heralds' College had granted the right to gentility. That right depended of course upon the possession of a certain amount of property. A country gentleman had lands and tenants and a rent roll of significance. Occasionally he was recognized by the community and by his equals as a country gentleman even when the Heralds' College had failed to enroll him as such.

On his lands he had a house that was usually the largest in or near the village, often a two-story house with enough rooms up and downstairs to provide crowded space for a family and several servants. Such houses of seventeenth-century gentry can still be seen in the country, and are today often occupied by well-to-do farmers. In that time many gentlemen had recently built or were building larger houses, sometimes including the old house within it, often three stories in height and containing from sixteen to thirty rooms.

The country gentlemen were of many types and intermediate types. Of the rustic type, to be found in numbers in almost every shire, something has been said in Chapter 2. Shaftesbury's description of Henry Hastings' home is well known:

A house not so neatly kept as to shame him or his dirty shoes, the great hall strewed with marrow bones, full of hawks' perches, hounds, spaniels, and terriers; the upper sides of the hall hung with the fox-skins of this and last year's skinning, here and there a polecat intermixed, guns and keepers' and huntsmen's poles in abundance. The parlor . . . as properly furnished; on a great hearth paved with brick lay some terriers and the choicest hounds and spaniels; seldom but two of the great chairs and litters of young cats in them . . . he having always three or four attending him at dinner, and a little white round stick of fourteen inches long lying by his trencher, that he might defend such meat as he had no mind to part with to them.[1]

There were many gentlemen of more cultivation, who had per-

[1] W. D. Christie, *Life of . . . Shaftesbury* (London, 1871), I, app. XVI.

haps been to the university and were in some degree reading men. There was also the great gentleman with several manors and stewards to look after them, who in habits and outlook was little different from the noblemen described in the last chapter.

Other types can only be mentioned. There was the gentleman who held a position in the Civil Service in London or some other profitable office, and who had a country estate near London. There were gentlemen, largely in the North and West, who had mines and mineral rights and gained most of their income from them rather than from rents received from tenants. There were also gentlemen who accumulated capital, and, instead of buying more land, put money out at interest. In this chapter we shall deal with the standard type, the gentleman who lived on the land and received revenues from his tenants. Of course many such gentlemen had other sources of income.

Few gentlemen were what we call "dirt farmers." Yet most of them knew something about soils, in terms of that day, and what crops were best on what soils, and about marl and manure. Their woods were of special interest to them, and the replanting of land with trees took some of their thought. Many of them had on their manorial lands a "home farm," the planting and cropping of which was done under their own supervision.

Certain kinds of out-of-door work the lord of the manor did not think beneath him. It was custom, at least in certain parts of England, for the gentleman to take part in the haying. In a wet summer drying the cut grass and getting it under cover before rain involved fast work by all hands, and it was pleasant, clean work at that. The gentleman was also concerned with the orchards and gave special attention to the choosing of the fruit trees and to the grafting and pruning of them.

With the tenants the gentleman, unless he had a steward, was closely associated. Usually he knew the various terms upon which his tenants held their lands, and for how long, and how much each tenant had in each field. When a tenant suffered from bad harvests, or from other misfortune, it was his landlord who had to make the decision whether he should be given time for payment of his rent.

If he were a gentleman of modest acreage and living far from neighbours of his own status, he could hardly escape a certain intimacy with his tenants. His grandfather had known their forbears, and some of them might repeat to him sayings of his father. In the long winter evenings he and they might discuss fields and beasts. If on a late autumn day the gentleman wished to do a bit of coursing, he would find farmers, no longer rushed with work, ready to join him. If he went over to the alehouse or inn, he would see the farmers sitting on the bench, and would be told what last night's storm had done to the barley.

The wife of the lord of the manor looked after the flower garden and sometimes the vegetable garden, and might give special attention to an herb garden where she could raise plants useful in case of illness at home or in the village. She attended the dairy house and she supervised the household servants. Sir John Oglander tells us that his wife never wore a silk dress but when she went abroad. "She was up every day before me and oversaw all the outhouses; she would not trust her maid with directions, but would wet her shoes to see it done herself." Not all ladies could give so much time; they were too occupied with young children. Some left details of housekeeping to a gentlewoman relative; others depended upon upper servants. An occasional woman stayed long in bed and rose in time to cut flowers and issue general household directions.

Many of the Stuart gentry, but hardly a majority, were of comparatively new families. Their great-grandfathers had been given, or had been allowed to buy cheaply, monastic lands. Or their fathers or grandfathers had been yeomen who grew rich by good farming, or who made money as merchants in city or town, or by buying and selling wool, or by holding lucrative offices, or by the practice of law, or in other ways, and invested their savings in land, the best investment then.

The new family had refitted the old priory on the ground, or had taken its stones and built out of them a new house across the road,

or had erected an entirely new dwelling. There they hoped to remain, and they fell readily into the traditions and ways of their
neighbors who had been longer in the country. It took but little time
for a new family to regard itself as established in the shire and to be
accepted as such by those of longer residence. The gentleman with
one or two generations of landed dignity behind him began to dream
of the future of his family. If he had a likely son or grandson and an
unencumbered estate, the disabilities of age and the approach of
death were small matters. The continuity of his line reconciled him
to mortality.

Unfortunately the estate of a new family, or of an old one, was
often encumbered. All over England were gentlemen who had tried
to live up to their neighbours or in one way or another had overspent
themselves. The new scale of living was too much for men who depended upon their rents or were too considerate of their tenants to
raise the rents. In Lincolnshire thirty-four families are said to have
been declining and many new families rising, some from the yeomanry. Richard Whalley of Sussex wrote his sister in 1624 that
many gentlemen of great fortune, "who had opposed their parents,"
had "consumed their whole estates, even to one foot of ground, five
of them with much ado to get winding sheets; some died under
hedges." Whalley was no doubt exaggerating and was certainly
overlooking the real reasons for the decline of those he had known,
but his story might have been paralleled in other counties. John
Smyth from Gloucestershire, walking down Chancery Lane, used to
watch a man picking up shreds of rags and would stealthily slip
him a shilling, affecting with a natural courtesy not to recognize him.
He was a Wikes, a member of what had been a great family in the
county.

The turnover in gentle families was rapid at this time but was
nothing new. "Citizens devour country gentlemen," wrote Robert
Burton of the *Anatomy*, "and settle in their seats; after two or three
descents, they consume all in riot, it returns to the city again." The
American says, three generations from shirtsleeves to shirtsleeves,

and the Elizabethans had proverbs of their own to the same effect. On a brass in a Cheshire church is written:

> Why glory in the splendor of thy race? It fades apace.
> Why glory in the long line of illustrious forefathers . . .
>   traced back in unbroken descent?
> It came and went.

The gentlemen of any one county constituted a kind of social unit, in which there was a certain camaraderie. The gentleman met his cousins and his friends at quarter sessions and at the assizes, at markets and fairs. Heywood describes such a gathering at Barnet in Hertfordshire just north of London:

> This Barnet is a place of great resort,
> And commonly upon the market days,
> Here all the country gentlemen appoint
> A friendly meeting; some about affairs
> Of consequence and profit—bargain, sale,
> And to confer with chap-men, some for pleasure,
> To match their horses, wager in their dogs,
> Or try their hawks: some to no other end,
> But only meet good company, discourse,
> Dine, drink, and spend their money.

The same thing happened all over the realm.

The county was more than a social unit; it commanded intense loyalty.[2] To illustrate that loyalty we may be allowed to imagine a Sir Edward, who might have belonged in any corner of the country. Sir Edward was, let us say, a Norfolk man, whose forbears had long "seated" themselves on a certain piece of ground.[3] He spoke plain

[2] Sir John Oglander's first loyalty was to the Isle of Wight, like that of Nantucket men to their island, but he was enough Hampshire to feel a shade of distrust for those from other shires. To such devotion Americans are hardly accustomed. Yet Virginians and Carolinians will not allow one to forget from what county in those states they came, and I have met Massachusetts men who insisted that they were Essex County-born.

[3] Sir John Oglander's feelings about his own acres appeared in his instructions to his son: "We have kept this spot of ground this five hundred years from father to son, and I pray God thou beest not the last nor see scattered that which so many have taken care to gain for thee."

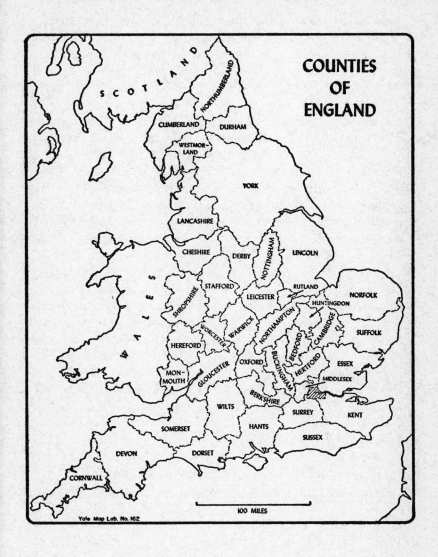

COUNTIES
OF
ENGLAND

SCOTLAND

NORTHUMBERLAND

CUMBERLAND

DURHAM

WESTMOR-
LAND

YORK

LANCASHIRE

CHESHIRE

DERBY

NOTTINGHAM

LINCOLN

W A L E S

STAFFORD

SHROPSHIRE

LEICESTER

RUTLAND

NORFOLK

HUNTINGDON

WORCESTER

WARWICK

NORTHAMPTON

CAMBRIDGE

SUFFOLK

HEREFORD

BEDFORD

MON-
MOUTH

GLOUCESTER

OXFORD

BUCKINGHAM

HERTFORD

ESSEX

MIDDLESEX

BERKSHIRE

WILTS

SURREY

KENT

SOMERSET

HANTS

SUSSEX

DEVON

DORSET

CORNWALL

Yale Map Lab. No. 162

100 MILES

Norfolk, as he liked to admit, and he had Norfolk sayings at the tip of his tongue. He hoped that his daughter would marry a Norfolk man, and that his son, when he came back from Lincoln's Inn, would be put on the Norfolk commission of the peace as one of the "quorum."

There was as yet no county hunt for him to attend, but men from one part of the shire might arrange a meeting for a two or three days' hunt. When he found himself craving companionship he might get on his horse and make calls on other gentlemen of the county, many of whom were his kin in some degree. Occasionally he would take his wife with him and make visits of two or three days.

Now and then Sir Edward would take the road to London. From Norfolk it was only about three days' journey (from Devon it would be a journey of four days, from Lancashire of about eight). He would go on horseback, accompanied by a servant or two. He would stop overnight in his own county with cousins or friends, and beyond his county at inns in the larger towns. When he arrived in London he would put up at the Sun in Cheapside, where his father had always stayed, and where other gentlemen of his county were accustomed to lay their heads. His arrival in town might be noted in newsletters. Various errands he would have to do. He had to testify for a neighbor in the Court of Chancery; he had to see his London lawyer about the title to a piece of land; he would call on a friendly nobleman who lived part of the time in the county; he had to buy a locket for his wife and some material for a new dress. If well known in the county, he would be presented to the King, and kiss his hand, and perhaps meet a few of the men round the King. He would be escorted to the great room in Whitehall to watch the sovereign dining in state, and have the royal favorite pointed out. On Holborn Hill he would be accosted by a man who pretended to be from his county and to have accepted hospitality from him, and who wished to take him across the way for a friendly glass of sack, but Sir Edward was no gull to be taken in by such tricksters. But he might run into a friend whom he had known at Clement's Inn, and the two would go off to the Three Tuns and talk of the days when they had heard the chimes at midnight. Eight or ten days, and he would turn homeward, unless as a member of Parliament he had to stay on for the session.

His London interval had been diverting but he was glad to be home. In his letters to acquaintances he would say that he desired a retired life. Not all of them felt the same way; some looked toward London and to becoming figures in the kingdom. One of his friends had become indeed a high servant of the sovereign, but professed to envy him. Sir Edward suspected that it was only when weary and in disgrace with fortune that his friend craved the quiet way of living. He himself loved the chimney pots of Norfolk and was afraid of any other world. He liked to arrange his gardens, to lay out walks and make fishponds, and above all to plant trees. His own house was hidden in a clump of trees set out by his father.[4] It was in a vale shielded from the wind, as retired as one could wish.

From London he had sent home by the carrier a few books. As a magistrate he was happy to have got hold of Lambarde's *Eirenarcha or the Office of the Justices of Peace*. He shelved it beside Crompton's older manual on the subject and Fitzherbert's *La Graunde Abridgement* of the Year Books. The newly printed edition of the statutes passed by the last Parliament he had picked up in Paternoster Row. Next to his lawbooks were some historical volumes, Holinshed in black letter, Hall, and Camden. He owned Gerard's *Herbal*, Elyot's *The Governour*, and the poems of Sidney. His collections might include works by Calvin and Luther and by the English William Perkins. He was pretty sure to possess writings of Plutarch, Cicero, Livy, and Suetonius, and possibly Diodorus Siculus. Such books, often with marginal comments by the seventeenth-century owner, comments that prove how carefully he had read them, can still be examined in country houses by those searching today for manuscripts.

Not uncommonly our country gentleman of the reading type allowed himself the luxury of antiquarianism. He collected manu-

---

[4] He might well plant a grove that cut off a view. It was only a few poets who took pleasure in the "delicate" or "delicious" or "unshrubbed" downs.

scripts of early chronicles; he gathered charters and deeds and coins. Presently he was writing about them to his friends of the same tastes, and loaning and borrowing manuscripts, and putting his secretary, if he had one, to copying from them. Even before the end of Elizabeth's reign the cult of antiquarianism was beginning to flourish, and it did not fall off in the next reigns. It has recently been pointed out that many ardent antiquarians were Kentish-born, but the species was to be found in almost every county. The letters they wrote to one another fill volumes of manuscripts in the British Museum.

Antiquarian or not, the gentleman, as he grew older, became increasingly interested in his own ancestry, and thus in heraldry. He employed retainers to make elaborate diagrams of his genealogy. On his walls he hung up shields showing the various quarterings of families that came together in his own. His family arms he had carved over the front door, and there they are to be seen to this day.

Not all of his time was taken up with such agreeable diversions. He had much else to do. His daughter Alice was about to be married, and he must negotiate a loan of ready money for her dowry. He must be laying in winter supplies, and he would go to the nearest town about that. The dairy house needed repairs, and he must look at the trees in his woods and see what could be cut. The old precepts his grandfather had written out for him would not do in this changing world. A gentleman nowadays could not live on his own; he had to buy many things away from home, sometimes even meat. He had to go in debt now and then for ready money if he were to do his duty as head of a family. The scene was shifting; he was not a feudal lord in a castle, but in some degree a businessman who must keep up with the times.

There were of course old duties and responsibilities that every gentleman recognized. He could do no less than uphold the church, as a national institution, and in his village. He would attend the parish church regularly on Sunday, sitting in the box pew near the brass tablet about his grandfather; he would read the lesson when called upon. He had seldom enough philosophy in his make-up to realize that the church stood behind the established order and taught the villagers to be satisfied with the state to which God had called them. More simply, he knew that the parson was on his side, or ought to be.

The parson might be his younger brother, or his own least-hopeful son, or a nephew. or the college friend of a nephew, and then all was easy between kin. But even if the parson were of a lesser breed, he might be useful in translating writs and helping him, as a justice of the peace, with law Latin. If the gentleman and the parson happened both to be of puritan outlook there would be close cooperation between house and parsonage; if of opposite opinions, there might be bickering.

It was his duty to be benevolent. Few wills of gentlemen but left money to the poor of their own village and sometimes of adjacent hamlets. Weddings, funerals, and christenings in the family were occasions on which the poor expected to be remembered. When a Lancashire wife narrowly missed death in childbirth, her husband made donations to the needy of five parishes. Such gifts had become almost a ritual. What was more natural was the kindness shown when a tenant or laborer was seriously ill.

The kindness of the gentry to their servants, most of whom came from the village, was personal. When a servant was to be married, it was a courtesy for his master to give him a wedding party and for every guest from the kin of the gentleman to bring contributions which would make up a small marriage portion. Lady Felton wrote Framlingham Gawdy that an old servant was to be married at such a time, "and what follows you know." The affairs of servants, their odd notions, their religious opinions, and their lapses from chastity were mentioned often in the letters of the gentry. They were not queer folk out of an obscure stratum of society, but personalities to be reckoned with.

To show hospitality was a duty country gentlemen seldom shirked. Herbert of Cherbury, that cantankerous knight from the west border, tells of his grandfather's "very long table twice covered every meal with the best meats that could be gotten." The neighbors used to say whenever they saw a fowl rise: "Fly where thou wilt, thou wilt light at Blackhall." All guests of good quality, no matter how unexpectedly they turned up, should be welcomed. For what were a gentleman's venison and grouse but to be eaten by his neighbors?

That was the notion of the good old gentleman who kept an old house at a bountiful rate. The makers of ballads liked him better than they liked the thrifty gentleman coming into fashion, who had bought the house when the good old gentleman had to sell. There was a new note in the literature of the time. In a play Sir Bounteous was made fun of for his overpretentious hospitality. Keen observers of their class, like Oglander, believed that kindred and allies should be always welcomed, but that parasites should be shaken off; and Robert Burton of the *Anatomy,* whose father had been a Shropshire gentleman, thought much the same.

It was the duty of the gentleman and his family to set an example of pleasing manners and affability. It was wise, wrote a father in a series of precepts for a son, to show a high humility toward inferiors, to bow the body and stretch forth the hand. But the obligation of affability is more often laid down in books on the ideal gentleman and his conduct than mentioned in diaries or letters. The playwrights give occasional portraits of gentlemen of kindness and consideration to everyone. Of John Hampden it was written that he had a flowing courtesy to all men.

It was the duty and sometimes the pleasure of the country gentleman to be a kind of family patriarch. This nephew was adding a few acres to his freehold and importuned his uncle to be his security. That nephew desired his help in getting a scholarship at Cambridge. This cousin wished money to pay for his apprenticeship in London.

His own sons were naturally his first interest. Their education in school and perhaps at the university had to be considered. The heir of the family, the eldest son, was given a preference from birth, and no younger brother would have disputed that right. He might be sent a year or two to the university, attending a college favored by men of his county. From the university he might go to one of the Inns of Court, where he could pick up enough law to serve him if he should become a justice, where he might savor the delights of youth in London, and where he might meet men of his class from all over England. That a young man should use the university and the Inns of Court as a means of making friends likely to be useful to him afterward was an accepted principle. The oldest son might finish off his education with travel on the Continent, but fathers were less enthusiastic than formerly about sending their sons out of England.

The marriage of the son had next to be considered. In such a matter the son could not follow his own devices. His wife must come from a family of good quarterings or, if not, with a great deal of money. The gentry sought daughters-in-law of birth and race (they were old hands at the breeding of fine horses and dogs). They did not demand beauty in her, but comeliness. She should be able to govern her household and servants. In all matters her husband's word was to be final, but she had the rule in his absence. She must defer to his judgment and obey him gladly.

The arrangements for a marriage [5] involved correspondence and meetings. The parents on either side might open the negotiations, usually with a family in the neighborhood or in the county. The quality and character of the possible young man or woman were the subject of discussion in letters.[6] Girls were like their mothers; close

[5] In Sir John Strode's advice to his son (C. F. Aspinwall-Oglander, *Nunwell Symphony*, London, 1945, p. 52), advice which may not have been original with him but possibly a copy of a manuscript passed around, he said: "Until thy marriage and ever after keep thy body unspotted by wicked women." Gentlemen occasionally boasted in their autobiographies that they had lived up to that ideal. But many a gentleman, respected in his time and remembered in ours, left one or more unauthenticated offspring. In a play, *The Returne from Parnassus*, the dull hunting squire hopes that he may have his wench in a corner without satire or epigrams. Of Henry Hastings, already mentioned, Shaftesbury wrote that he "bestowed all his time in such sports [hunting and fishing], but what he borrowed to caress his neighbors' wives and daughters, there being not a woman in all his walks of the degree of a yeoman's wife, or under, and under the age of forty, but it was extremely her fault, if he were not intimately acquainted with her."

[6] It was a saying of the time that a father should marry his children betimes lest they marry themselves. In general the gentry arranged the marriages of their children and the children accepted the arrangement. But wiser parents, who gave their children latitude to refuse marriages proposed, were not uncom-

inquiry should be made about the mother. As for financial arrangements, there was always bargaining. It was assumed that a young couple could not set up a household unless the parents made settlements upon them.[7] Those settlements were figured out closely; social status was weighed carefully against money.[8]

Once married, the heir to a country family recognized his first duty. It was necessary that he should have many children because the loss of children in childbirth and in infant years was appalling. If he were fortunate he might rear three children from ten births. Nothing was more desired by a country family than a male heir. That meant that the young gentlewoman who had married the heir had to devote the years from twenty to forty to bearing children. In Beaumont and Fletcher's *Scornful Lady* Loveless says to the lady: "What can you do in a household to provide for issue but lie in bed and get 'em?"

What happened to younger sons? In *Two Gentlemen of Verona* surprise is expressed that the lord kept his son at home:

> While other men, of slender reputation,
> Put forth their sons to seek preferment out;
> Some to the wars . . .
> Some to discover islands far away,
> Some to the studious universities.

Some did go off to the wars, with the English forces in the Low Countries or with armies of other nations. As for discovering islands, it was in the minds of many. George Herbert, the parson and poet, thought that a young man might well study mathematics and prepare himself for navigation and discovery, and possibly for plantations overseas. Sir John Oglander, facing toward the Channel,

---

mon. Occasionally fancy prevailed over portion, as Oglander puts it. The evil of enforced marriage, a theme dwelt upon by playwrights and pamphleteers, was recognized by many parents.

[7] Henry Oxinden of Kent married the fair daughter of a rich yeoman. Such marriages occurred now and then in every shire, but more often in ballads.

[8] If the eldest son of an ancient family were to marry the daughter of a merchant, it followed that the merchant's family should bestow a larger dowry in consideration of the better blood of the future husband.

thought a gentleman who wished to get on would do well to buy a ship.

Many possibilities were open to them. The studious universities were frequented by some. Those who impressed their tutors and made helpful friends might seek secretaryships to the great, whose fortunes they might follow, and gain eventually a foothold for themselves in the King's service. Other sons found places as pages in noble families where they might learn courtly ways and be recommended in due time for posts at Court or in the service of a dignitary. Still others became apprentices to London merchants, or factors in companies. The easiest way for younger sons to prosper was to marry the daughters of merchants, or better still rich widows, who were always coming into the market, and then set up as country gentlemen.

If many younger sons landed on their feet, there were hundreds who did not. They went to London with a lump sum in their wallet, bestowed upon them by a father or elder brother, and used it up in the clothes and display that might commend them at Court, and gained nothing thereby. Such a young man would write letter after letter home begging desperately for a remittance, and his long-suffering family might dole out small sums to him. His lot was hard; he had been brought up with some prestige and ease of living, and was ill equipped to go on his own in the city. Sometimes his last end was pitiful.

The daughters were possibly better looked after than younger sons. The least a gentleman could do for each of his daughters was to bestow a dowry upon her at her marriage, or to leave her in his will the money which would make up a dowry. A dowerless daughter was unthinkable. Sometimes a gentlewoman sent her daughter to London to do honorable service in a great house there, in the hope that she would marry into the London world; sometimes she sent a daughter to a nobleman's house in the country, with the same end of a good marriage in view. Most daughters were kept at home. A good-looking girl with a dowry of a thousand pounds or so might marry into the neighboring gentry. An ill-favored child, or one with a dowry of a hundred pounds, might stoop to marry a curate or a wool broker in the next town. Sooner or later, and usually sooner, before she was in the twenties, she did marry. The family saw to that. Unmarried women were rare in a time when wives, owing to the death rate among them, had a scarcity value. Occasionally a girl had bad luck. Doll Leake, a spirited but indigent relative, came to live with the Verneys in Buckinghamshire, and to help in the house, hoping no doubt that they would fit her with a good husband. They came near to doing so, but the promising wooer dropped her for a more advantageous alliance. Doll remained unmarried, a useful and beloved member of the Verney household.

With all that has been said about the country gentleman, there remains something elusive about the best of them. One thinks of Peter Wentworth, in mid-Elizabethan days, who stood up alone to criticize the Queen's invasion of freedom of speech, knowing well what punishment awaited him. One thinks of Reginald Scot of Scot's Hall in Kent, reading the more obscure authors that had by the generality been neglected, and listening now and then to the testimony against poor silly women until he dared publish his *Discoverie of Witchcraft* (1584). One thinks of John Winthrop in Essex, distressed by the dissolution of Parliament in 1629 and foreseeing evil days when the church must "fly to the wilderness," and making the hard decision to embark for Massachusetts. One thinks of John Hampden, saying hardly a word in Parliament, but meditating among the beeches on the Chilterns, and refusing at length to pay ship-money. All of them were men who had leisure for reading and thinking and who had been bred to courage. They were quiet men with some inward fire that flamed forth in action when the situation demanded it.[9]

[9] Lawyers and clergymen could also be brave, but not in the same way. The country gentlemen of whom I have been talking and their like had a way of thinking it over slowly with few words, like yeomen, and then taking a stand and sticking to it to the last consequence. They had indeed an old-English yeoman quality modified by the traditions of their class and by their reading. Reading was more important when books were few and pondered upon.

CHAPTER 6

The Clergy

A N ENGLISH clergyman of the Established or national Church occupies a position rather different from that of an American minister. He is appointed to a "living"; that is, he is named as rector or vicar of a church with an income attached to it. He is not, as usually in our country, supported by the congregation. He is named for life and cannot be removed except for grave cause, but he can be promoted to a better living. In the early seventeenth century his income was of several kinds. Lands were attached to the parsonage known as glebe lands, which he could lease or work with a servant or on his own. In addition he had the right to levy certain tithes, or tenths, from the farmers, tithes of crops, animals, poultry, eggs, garden produce. Some of the tithes might be commuted for money. A rector was entitled to all the tithes. A vicar had only partial tithes. At the time of the dissolution of the monasteries the tithes of "appropriated" churches had fallen to the Crown, which distributed most of them to laymen and left many livings with small incomes from tithes.

The collection of tithes was an embarrassment to the clergyman. It took time and involved business dealings with those to whom he ministered in a spiritual capacity. The parishioners often begrudged the parson his tenth hen and tenth calf, and found ways to circumvent him. He had a wife and children to support and he had to insist upon his rights. It was not easy to make demands upon those to whom one was preaching goodwill and forbearance.

In addition to his income from the glebe and from tithes, the parson received in rare instances a salary from the parish, and now and then a borough voted a minister of whom they thoroughly approved an annual sum. The parson had also fees for marriages, for the churching of women after childbirth, and for burials.[1]

The method of his appointment was different from that to which we are accustomed. With us the clergyman, except in churches with a bishop, is usually chosen by the congregation or by a committee of the congregation. In England today the bishops are responsible for many of the nominations to livings, but the Crown, Oxford and Cambridge colleges, and a few private persons have rights of nomination. In the early seventeenth century the Crown had certain livings in its gift and the bishops and the colleges had a goodly number, but most livings were at the disposal of lords of the manor or of other individuals, who were known as patrons. Those patrons occasionally sold the right to make the next nomination to a group of parishioners who had combined together so they might choose their own parson. At other times the patron sold the right of next nomination to a tradesman or yeoman who wished possibly to put in his son or a relative.[2]

A clergyman who had friends in power might be appointed to more than one living, to two, three, or more, and was then known as a pluralist.[3] He would derive the income from his several livings and employ curates at a small salary to take charge of the church or churches where he was not in residence. It was seldom a good arrangement. The curate was likely to be a man of limited education, and poorly qualified to preach.

The curate was not the only untrained clergyman. Many of those

[1] He had extra appurtenances in various places: the hay from the churchyard, the profit from the pigeons in the dovecote, etc.

[2] It happened often that the living went to a man who lived within the county and often not far away.

[3] In some cases a pluralist was one who managed to hold two small livings close together and could minister to each church.

who held livings were none too well prepared for their offices. Nicholas Breton tells a tale of meeting with a little old man in a gown and a corner cap, whom he saluted with a few Latin words. "My friend," replied the parson, "I understand not your Greek." [4] The story could easily have been true. The problem of the uneducated clergyman was one with which the church had had to wrestle since the Elizabethan Settlement. The mildly Protestant church the Queen had set up had to develop its own ministers and was handicapped in doing so. The future of the Settlement was uncertain; the death of the Queen might change everything. Moreover the new clergy were poorly paid. In consequence the more intelligent classes were likely to dissuade their sons from taking up the clerical profession. Meanwhile others were entering it, ignorant men of limited backgrounds, men who had never seen a university and were unfitted to preach. There had been a time, wrote a playwright, with exaggeration:

> When cobblers were made churchmen; and those black'd
> Smutch'd creatures, thrust into surplices,
> Look'd like so many magpies.

About all such ignorant and humble men could do was to read homilies. The church and Archbishop Whitgift were aware of the criticisms of the Puritans as to the quality of the clergy, and were doing what they could to better it; but, with the nomination of many of the clergy in the hands of laymen, found it no easy undertaking. The church did not relax its efforts and by the end of Elizabeth's reign was so far successful that the improvement in the character of the clergy was evident. Not only were they better educated, but they were more often men to whom the village might look up. The villagers could take pride in a parson who was a man of learning.[5] If he were gentle-born and showed it in his face and manners, they deferred the more naturally to him. If his income had

---

[4] *A Mad World, My Masters,* in A. B. Grosart (ed.), (Edinburgh, 1879), II, 8.
[5] A considerable proportion of the educated men who held country livings had worked their way through the university.

been so improved that he could live better than the average yeoman, he was the more esteemed by his parishioners.[6]

The church continued its efforts and by the time of the Civil War (1642) had a body of clergymen far superior to what it had been. Even then, however, it is probable that from one third to one half of the incumbents in country parishes were not university men and had no proper training. Many parsons and curates were of inferior intelligence and breeding; some of them had large families to support and lived little better than husbandmen. Such men might occasionally win approval by sheer goodness and kindness, but more often were of a kind who failed to command admiration.

The church had seen to it that the rector or vicar had a parsonage. Usually that building was not far from the parish church and was generally of about the same size and grade as that of a fairly prosperous yeoman, sometimes a little better. A vicarage included a hall, a kitchen, which might be detached, a study, and a bedroom and possibly other small bedrooms. The furniture would be oak tables and settles and cupboards, as in a yeoman's house, and a little silver and some linen. The parson had usually farm implements and stock worth as much as his household equipment.[7] As for help, the more fortunate clergyman had one or two laborers to farm the glebe; the less fortunate might work his fields or strips in the fields himself, with the aid of his sons. His wife in many instances had one helper in the kitchen.

The woman in the parsonage was likely to be of somewhat the same background as her husband. If he were a younger son of the gentry, she might have come from a neighboring country house or vicarage. In many cases she was the offspring of substantial yeomen. If her spouse were meanly born, she might be the daughter of a husbandman or of a shopkeeper and had possibly been a maid-servant. The wife had no special relation to the church. Elizabeth

[6] The old priest had enjoyed great respect in the village, but he had been unmarried and had no family to support. Yet he had been often underpaid.

[7] I am using here the conclusions of Miss Barratt of Bodley's Library, who has studied the clergy in three counties and who knows much about them in other counties.

had looked with no favor on married clergymen and there still lingered in Stuart days some notion that the wife of the incumbent was outside the ecclesiastical picture. George Herbert thought otherwise and declared that she should lead a becoming life as an example to the community. She was usually too busy with housework and small children to do much for the poor, but she did now and again visit the sick and attend childbirths.

The parson was seen often in the village and caps went off as he passed down the street. After all, he was the second gentleman in the hamlet. What the villagers thought of him is another matter. To them he must have seemed one who hardly earned the tithes they had to turn over to him. To carry on one or two services on Sunday, to church women, baptize infants, catechize children, bury the dead, and conduct marriage services, did not seem to hardworking yeomen and artisans a full time job for a man. They could hardly fail to see that he was often an idler and sometimes a little soft. Of a curate Shakespeare makes a character say: "A foolish man, an honest man, look you, but soon dashed; a marvellous good neighbor, faith, and a very good bowler."

In other words the curate was a decent and kindly man, a good fellow, and, best of all to many Englishmen, a sportsman, but not over bright and not able to stand up for himself. Vicars were usually better men than curates, but were not always men of force. The recent changes in the church had not encouraged the development of strong characters. The Elizabethan clergyman had learned to lift a finger to feel the way the wind was blowing. It might well blow another way. "Our Doctor differs not much from the weathercock in the steeple," said a speaker in a pamphlet, "sometimes he is all for ceremony, sometimes indifferent, sometimes against." Such trimmers did not win veneration.

The parson's esteem in the community was not increased by living under the shadow of the lord of the manor. Not uncommonly the squire had picked the incumbent for his pliability. He usually expected deference and sometimes obedience. If he chose he could make the position of the clergyman in the community less than dignified. In 1599 a gentleman of Tolleshunt in Essex walked up to the curate conducting services, struck him with his hand, and said: "Thou art a dunce and a bold dunce. I will make thee neither parson nor vicar. But I will not call thee knave."

What the community thought of the parson depended much upon his personality. In *The Magnetick Lady* Ben Johnson depicts a man of force:

> He is the prelate of the parish here;
> And governs all the dames; appoints the cheer;
> Writes down the bills of fare; pricks all the guests;
> Makes all the matches and the marriage feasts
> . . . draws all the parish wills . . .
> Comforts the widow, and the fatherless,
> In funeral sack.

A master of ceremonies this parson was, and village records reveal not a few like him. A parson would sometimes pick the church-wardens to be elected and then tell them what to do and how to do it. In many cases he kept the parish accounts because no one else understood such matters. He might press upon local authorities matters that needed attention. He was now and again listened to by the justices in quarter sessions; in the North he was put on commissions to determine about roads and bridges.

His usefulness and success in the parish did not mean that he was in line for a better living. There were many prizes in the way of livings, prebendal stalls, canonries, deaneries, and of course bishoprics, but a large number of them went to friends of favorites and of great men and to the kin of well-born families. An able man who had shown capacity for scholarship, or who was a remarkable preacher, or a writer of significant theological works, was fortunate if he attained great position in the church. Queen Elizabeth had an eye open for such men, but not James I. I can think of four men of comparatively humble origins who by their abilities gained bishoprics, two of them indeed archbishoprics. Many a talented man lived out his days in an obscure parsonage. Robert Herrick, whose poems about Julia and Anthea were and are still read, stayed long in his Devon backwater.

It will have been observed by the reader that clergymen differed widely from one another in background, in way of living, in training, and in functions performed. There was the rare clergyman who was almost perfectly fitted to minister to any parish. Latin and Greek he had been brought up to read and he had studied the Church Fathers and the old theologians and those more recent. Much else he knew: he had dipped into Chaucer and Spenser and perhaps Piers Plowman and had read Sir Philip Sidney; he had enough law at his command to help out the neighbor justice of the peace and to advise farmers as to their rights in their acres. If he had some acquaintance with medicine and gave the villagers the benefit of it, it did not diminish his influence. From a wide learning —still possible at that time—he had developed moderation and catholicity of outlook. At the same time he was a spiritual man and lived up to what he taught. An ideal parson that, and yet such men might have been found, and even in obscure parishes.

Equally admirable was the saintly clergyman. He recalled the scriptural injunction, "Feed my lambs." It was said of Richard Hooker that he tried to persuade rather than to frighten men into piety, showing reasons for what he asserted and using apt illustrations from the life familiar to his hearers. Of George Herbert it was told that the meaner sort of his parish would so love and reverence him that they would let the plow rest when Mr. Herbert's saint's bell rung to prayers, and would offer their devotions and then return to their plows.[8] Such a clergyman would often stay at Little Puddle against a good living offered him in London or at a cathedral, believing his task not yet accomplished. Love is his business and aim was said of the ideal parson. He would invite the poor to dinner; he would search out work for them, or hire them in his own fields. Epitaphs cannot be accepted as the last word, but many of them

[8] Izaak Walton, *Lives of John Donne, Henry Wotton, Richard Hooker and George Herbert* (London, 1888), pp. 265–266.

witnessed to the selflessness of the late vicar and prove at least that the notion of that type of clergyman was common.

There was the useful clergyman who made calls on all the families in the parish, blessing their houses and giving comfort to the sick. He would have heard about village quarrels and he might ask those at odds to dine with him and attempt to make them friends, or to settle their disputes, and thus prevent litigation. He would put in a word of advice to those who might require it. He had his eye open to discover a promising lad and would perhaps tutor him and encourage his father or a well-to-do uncle to send him to the university, or would interest the borough in doing so.

Less common was the clergyman devoted to his reading. Covetous of nothing but books, he might skimp his family in order to buy theological works. His sermons might be over the heads of his rural hearers, "good dull earthworms," or he might have the skill to make hard matters seem simple. One of the most learned men of his time talked to his parishioners so much in their own language that one of them told a stranger that their parson was a plain honest man, but "no Latiner." But learned men who were not pedantic were likely to be appreciated in the larger towns, and even to draw an audience from the more intelligent in the adjacent countryside.

The preacher with a gift for utterance and stirring up his flock was to be found all over the kingdom and especially in the towns. More often than not he was a Puritan in education and outlook and aimed at winning his parishioners to a life of Christian activity. Some of these brethren accomplished a great deal of good; others were little more than exhorters.

Occasionally we meet a clergyman who loved old customs for their own sake and because he knew that country people were much addicted to them and that to favor them was to win the hearts of his flock. He would make much of Easter and of the twelve days of Christmas celebration, of harvest festivals, and of May Day. George Herbert took pleasure in the perambulation of the parish [9] once a

---

[9] See pp. 241–242

year, when the parson and many of the parishioners would walk round the boundaries.

A more earthly clergyman was to be seen in many a hamlet. A good fellow, he would omit the afternoon service on Sunday to please his parishioners; he would make friends on the bowling green and at the alehouse, and would strive within limits to be all things to all men.

Literally more of the earth was the vicar who enjoyed gardening and farming and devoted himself to his glebe lands, raising grain, vegetables, and fruit for the family and for the market. Seldom except on Sunday was he out of his working clothes, and his attire did not go down well with yeomen who preferred a parson to look the part.

The quarrelsome clergyman who had trouble with his church-wardens and with those who paid him tithes, and who set the whole village against him, was to be met with in parishes here and there. So was the sporting parson who coursed and hunted with the country gentleman and missed no out-of-doors activity. Perhaps the most talked-of parson was the one who made too many visits to the alehouse and was suspected of worse weaknesses. He comes now and again into the records of the quarter sessions and boroughs, but he was not as common a type as puritan pamphleteers made out.[10]

By no means all of these types of clergymen came to the new world. Those who came to Virginia were good Church of England men. Most of the clergymen who took ship for New England were zealous Puritans and on the average better educated than the run of clergymen in England, but not more so than the clergy in borough towns and London. They did not have the lords of the manor to cast a shadow over them. In Massachusetts they became quickly the leaders of their towns. In Virginia they proved only less important than the owners of plantations.

---

[10] All these types and others shaded into one another. They were of course not unrelated to the economic position of the clergyman. A poor man had to farm his glebe acres himself. Only a parson with a good income could spend his time in the hunting field with the squire. The haunter of alehouses may have been a man driven to drink by poverty and boredom.

CHAPTER 7

The Yeomen and the Farm Laborers

PART I. THE YEOMEN

THE ENGLISH yeoman has been the pet of poets, chroniclers, playwrights, and writers of character books. Did not his long bow at Crécy darken the sky with arrows and demoralize the chivalry of France? More than the members of any other group he was believed to embody the old English tradition and to perpetuate it. His pride was the theme of playwrights. In the *Pinner of Wakefield,* George-a-Greene refuses the King's proffer of a knighthood for his services.

> Then let me live and die a yeoman still;
> So was my father, so must live his son.

In another play a yeoman is addressed as "Master" and answers: "No, gentlemen . . . spare the Mastership, call me by my name, John Carter . . . honest Hertfordshire yeomen, such an one am I."

The yeomen had need of no favors. Shakespeare makes York say that the King of Naples is not as wealthy as an English yeoman, and proverbs exaggerated his means in the same way. John Morshead of Devon, who had died back in 1557, was described by his gentle descendant as a worthy yeoman. "He always maintained a good house, a good plough, good geldings, good tillage, good rearing, and was a good husband [farmer]."

Though he took his part in the work, he was no mere ploughman or hind. He was the entrepreneur of the land,[1] who planned the use of the fields and supervised the men. "We will do this, or let us do that," he would say to his servants. The small yeoman, sometimes called a husbandman, and occasionally distinguished from the yeoman as constituting a class by himself, could afford only a little help and might be pretty much a "dirt farmer." At the other end of the ladder were the yeomen who had managed in a few generations, or possibly in one or two, to gather a good deal of land and to have better houses than the run of their class. Such men often graduated in the late Tudor and early Stuart period into gentlemen, and some of them into gentlemen of many acres. Even if they did not become gentlemen, the line between them and the small gentlemen was in places not at all hard and fast. Adam Eyre in the West Riding of Yorkshire was a yeoman, but was called on his tombstone a gentleman. In his life he consorted with a group of closely associated families, some of them small gentlemen and some yeomen. It is a kind of association to be found here and there in other counties.

The holdings of a yeoman varied greatly in size; they varied also in character. In theory and in old law he was one who had a freehold of 40s. annual value, and there were many freeholders among yeomen. But the term was used in the early seventeenth century in a broader sense, and we shall so use it. Most yeomen were men who held their lands from a lord of the manor for a rent, but on such old tenures from father to son that they felt they had a kind of property right in them. They held by various types of tenure,[2]

[1] A great deal of this chapter is a summary of what Mildred Campbell has said at length and better in *The English Yeoman under Elizabeth and the Early Stuarts* (New Haven, 1942). Here and there I have added a little from my own reading and I have profited from the writings of G. F. Hoskins, especially from his *Essays in Leicestershire History* (Liverpool, 1950).

[2] If the yeoman were a leaseholder, he might hold his land for one or two of three lives, or, as was becoming more common, on a short lease renewable at the end of the term, but with a possible increase in rents. If he were a copyholder, he held a copy of the manorial record which indicated his right to hold the land by custom on such and such annual payments and services, and that right was usually heritable. But copyholds for a term of years or at the will of the landlord were in use also, the rents and services not always fixed. There

but in all of them except that of freeholders there was an annual rent, and freeholders sometimes paid a small quitrent. If the tenure happened to be a long one, say for three lives and fixed, the holder had a great advantage in that the payments were based upon old and even medieval values of land, and hence with the decreased value of money had become in many cases little more than nominal.

It was a time when rents were being raised as soon as the terms of the tenures made it possible. The old lord of the manor wished to be considerate of tenants whose fathers his father had known, but his lawyer was urging him to gain more income from his land. Not only were benevolent men forced by the increasing expenses to raise their rents, but the new men who had made money were investing in land and, encouraged by their stewards and solicitors, were increasing the rents twofold, threefold, and more, that is, levying "rack rents." They had some right on their side. But the tenants were likely to feel aggrieved. They and their fathers had been long on the land and the rent they paid they regarded as little more than a symbol. Their complaints of the new rents fill the literature of the late sixteenth and early seventeenth century. The landlords, among whom was an occasional wealthy yeoman, were held up to the public as extortioners, grasping new men out of the towns, who were forcing off the land the men who had always worked it.

The position of the tenant farmer or yeoman was affected by the state of the lands, whether they were enclosed or "champion," that is, unenclosed. Unenclosed lands were those where there was one great field for peas, another for barley or rye or wheat, and still another field fallow. In each of these fields were parallel strips of land, say fourteen feet wide, which belonged to individual farmers and some of them to the lord of the manor. It was an uneconomical

---

were other tenures which cannot be mentioned here. The situation of the yeoman was complicated by the fact that he did not hold all his land by one type of tenure. This parcel of fourteen acres he held in freehold, this parcel of twenty-seven acres by leasehold, this parcel of six acres by copyhold, and other parcels possibly by other special tenures.

In most of the tenures, in addition to the rent, the heir had to pay on succession to the land a "relief," or "fine," a sum that amounted usually to one year's income, but that might be much more.

method of farming, but the old one, and for that reason hard to change. The tenant worked at a disadvantage. The man who had the strip next to one of his might be a slovenly farmer who allowed weeds to get the upper hand or who failed to clean his ditches and caused the strips of his neighbors to be flooded. Furthermore the farmer lost time in moving from one of his strips to another in a different part of the field, and he lost land in the necessary footpaths.

A great deal of enclosure had been carried out in such counties as Kent, Essex, Northamptonshire, and Leicestershire and was taking place in other counties. With enclosure Goodman Atkins gave up all his strips in the several fields and had his land consolidated into a single farm.[3] Enclosure proved an advantage to him, but not in every way. On the village common he and the other tenants had the right to pasture a certain number of horses, cattle, and sheep, the number proportioned to the size of the holdings of land. In the woodland he could allow his pigs to feed on acorns and the leaves from the low branches, and he could cut enough timber for the repair of his buildings. But the lord of the manor, when he consolidated his own strips in the fields into what became the "home farm," would sometimes help himself to more than was his due, part of the common and part of the woods; or if he did not do so at the time of the general enclosure, might later suddenly put up a fence, where no fence had been, as a token of possession.[4] Such encroachments, which reduced the pasture and the timber, were sometimes bitterly resented, and now and then the new fences were pulled down. The yeoman knew his rights on the land and was inclined to give up none of them.

The houses of the yeomen varied as much as their tenures and rights. A small yeoman, or "husbandman," might have a cottage of two rooms and add to it as he could afford it. The average yeoman was likely to have a one-and a-half-story house with a milkhouse, a malthouse, and other small buildings attached to the dwelling at the

---

[3] Even then his fields were held by various tenures, this by copyhold, that by leasehold, and another perhaps by freehold.

[4] Enclosures were made by wealthy yeomen as well as by lords of the manor.

side, or at the back. The well-to-do yeoman might have a good two-story house, perhaps half-timbered, or of brick or stone, depending upon the shire and building materials available. In Essex the houses were often rectangular and covered with weatherboarding such as was later used in Massachusetts. The yeoman's house was usually fairly simple and pleasing in line. The additions, made as the yeoman could afford them, did not always improve the appearance of his home. The house would contain a main living room, a parlor or second room, where there would be one or more beds, and several other rooms with beds. A yeoman had to crowd in beds and might have from four or five to ten beds in his house. There was sometimes a kitchen, although in smaller houses the cooking might have been done over the open fire in the great fireplace of the main room.

The inventories, as they are being published, give us clues as to the furniture in a yeoman's house. There would be large oak tables, stools, settles or forms, chests, cupboards, usually of oak, and a few hard-backed simple chairs. In the hall or large room there would be a recess behind the chimney for the fire irons and other utensils. The cupboards held the dishware, mostly of wood and pewter, but in the wealthier yeomen's houses there was beginning at the end of the Tudor period to be an occasional piece of silverware.

The number of laborers employed by the yeoman on the farm varied with his acres. A small yeoman might have no more than one laborer to help him, and perhaps a son. A well-to-do yeoman might have three or four workers in the field. He also took on as apprentices poor boys sent to him by the overseers of the poor. Such apprentices he was bound to keep in clothes and food until they came of age, and to teach them the skills of their calling. The daughters of the poor were also apprenticed to the farmer to help his wife in the work inside and outside the house.

The yeoman had work to cover the year. His seasonal occupations have been traced by Mildred Campbell. In the first two months of the year he had his fields plowed and harrowed and the manure spread; he set trees and hedges, pruned the fruit trees, and lopped the timber. March and April were the months to stir the fields again and sow the wheat and rye. In May gardens were planted and hop vines trained to poles and ditches scoured. It was also in that month that lambs were weaned and sheep watched lest they get the "rot." Sheep were washed and sheared in June. Then also the fields were limed and marled [5] and manured. In July hay was cut, dried, and stacked. Harvest came in August when extra help would be called in not only from the neighborhood but from townsmen who took holidays at harvesting. Threshing followed harvesting and winter wheat and rye were sown. During the autumn cider and perry were made in those counties where apples and pear trees abounded, as in the Severn valley, Kent, and Essex. By November the fall planting was finished and the time had come for the killing of cattle and hanging up their salted carcasses for winter meat. Straw would be laid down with dung, to be spread next spring on the fields. Meanwhile such stock as could not live out of doors in winter would be brought into barns.

The yeoman had at all times to be a businessman. He went to the annual fairs in his part of the country, and attended the weekly markets in one or two neighboring towns. There he bought and sold cattle, oxen, pigs, sheep, and horses, and sold various products from the farm. He had to know the prices offered at this market and that; he had to know what the "badgers" who came through the country were offering for grain and hay and other commodities. It might be a bad season and he might have to consider whether to hold his wheat for a rise, a practice discouraged by justices but constantly indulged in. Enterprising yeomen not only stored grain for a rise but would buy grain in quantities to sell at the higher price. Sometimes they acted as middlemen, or formed small groups for the sale of their commodities in the best market at the most opportune time. They could not escape the problem of transportation. The bad roads of the time meant that they could not afford to send grain long distances. Sometimes they engaged shipping or sold their stuff to buyers in port towns who conveyed it by sea to London or to other centers. When the justices of the peace at the instance of the gov-

---

[5] Marl was a mixture of lime and clay spread on the land.

ernment would stop the export of grain to prevent high prices of bread for the poor, there was likely to be an outcry from farmers, who could take a hard-bitten [6] and small-capitalist point of view.[7]

Many yeomen had, besides their lands, other ways of making a profit. In clothing counties, in Gloucestershire, Wiltshire, Norfolk, and Essex, and in many others, yeomen's wives and children received wool, spun and wove it, and turned it over to clothing men; such industry added to the family income. In East Anglia, from which so many yeomen went to New England, the majority of that class was probably partly engaged in one or another form of the clothing industry. Along streams they had fulling mills and in the east counties they had windmills to furnish power for this and that operation. An occasional yeoman presided over an alehouse, which sometimes replaced the land as his main occupation. Many a yeoman was also a tanner, painter, carpenter, or blacksmith.[8] In theory he could not take on such an occupation unless he had served an apprenticeship, and had a license to exercise the craft. Yeomen were always being presented to the justices for exercising a craft without having served an apprenticeship.

The wives of yeomen were hardly less important on the farms than their husbands. To thrive, the yeomen must wive, wrote Thomas Tusser, who in mid-sixteenth century made rhymes about farming that became proverbs. The yeoman's wife had to set a good table, "bread, beer, and beef, yeoman's fare . . . no kickshaws [fancy dishes], full dishes, whole bellyfulls." Her husband and the laborers who lived with the family would come home hungry, and there were the children and the female servants to feed. A good wife was always ready with extra fare if a neighbor dropped in.

[6] In a play (Richard Brome, *The Sparagus Garden,* Act IV, Scene 5), it was said that knavery was as rife in russet wool as in the proudest purple, and no doubt yeomen were often sharp businessmen.

[7] They were occasionally capitalists. Mr. Trevor-Roper tells me that he has come across instances where yeomen were lending money to their great neighbors.

[8] One has to be careful about yeomen as artisans, for many kinds of artisans were in court records denominated as yeomen, merely to indicate that they were of intermediate rank.

She had to watch and work at all the processes connected with milk and fruit, to make cheese and butter and jam and preserves for the use of the family, and to sell. Once or twice a week she would be off to market and sell apples, pears, frumenty,[9] chickens, eggs, bacon, and various kinds of garden stuff.

Her vegetable garden might contain melons, cucumbers, cabbages, radishes, skirrets [10] and salad herbs. Potatoes, that modern staple, were not much planted until nearly the end of the seventeenth century.

Her flower garden we know little about. By the middle of the century there were in gardens sweet William, lupin, white scabious, marigolds, life everlasting, London pride, and hollyhocks.[11] In yeomen's gardens were medicinal herbs such as the double fennel flower for eyes, camomile for headaches, white lilies for boils, and double feverfew against the shaking fever.[12] In the cupboard might be dried saffron, aniseed, elecampane, columbine, tansy, and various barks.

The yeoman's wife needed all the medicinal herbs she could raise. During her early married life she was usually looking after young children and expecting another child. The infants suffered many illnesses not then understood; physicians were far off and usually beyond the pocketbook of a yeoman, unless his child seemed about to die; hence his wife was usually the nurse and doctor for herself and for her children.

Between household duties and the bearing and bringing up of children she had probably a harder life than her husband. The epitaph of the wife of a Gloucestershire yeoman says:

> From my sad cradle to my sable chest,
> Poor pilgrim, I did find few months of rest.

[9] A dish made of wheat boiled in milk and seasoned with cinnamon and sugar.

[10] A kind of water parsnip.

[11] There might be a flowerpot in the window.

[12] Of goodwife Bedell (mother of Bishop Bedell of Kilmore) of Black Notley in Essex it was said that she was "very famous and expert in chirurgery, which she continually practiced upon multitudes that flock'd to her, and still gratis without respect of persons, poor or rich." T. W. Jones (ed.), *Life and Death of William Bedell* (Camden Society, New Series, 1872), IV, 2.

She was often too burdened with details to have general ideas or, even if highly competent, to be interesting. Her "whole discourse is what price barley bears or how her husband sold his last yoke of oxen," wrote the playwright Glapthorne. He gives a harsh picture of the wives of farmers assembled at a christening, eating bad food and drinking new ale, and talking of the last blazing star and of the new monster. At least one of them had evidently been reading the chap-books of the day.[13]

There were wives with better things to discuss. Even Glapthorne's women discussed also the danger from Spain. Many wives listened attentively to the sermons on Sunday and expressed their ideas about them. Some of them were versed in Scripture and brought their children up in the knowledge of it.

About the character of their housekeeping it is hard to find evidence. Richard Baxter, the Nonconformist preacher, whose father had been a yeoman, married above himself into a gentle family. "I had been bred," he wrote, "among mean people, and I thought that so much washing of stairs and rooms to keep them clean as their trenchers . . . was a sinful curiosity [undue fastidiousness] and expense of servants' time . . . but she that was otherwise bred had somewhat other thoughts." In *Henry V* Shakespeare makes the Duke of Bourbon say:

> . . . I will sell my dukedom
> And buy a slobbery and a dirty farm
> In the nook-shotten isle of Albion.

Shakespeare had seen many farms, and he was speaking of them, I think, with real affection. Their cleanliness had not impressed him. No doubt he was thinking of the barns and barnyards, but the farmer's wife was not likely to have been much neater than her husband.

The clothes of the yeoman's wife were plain. Yet yeomen's daughters contrived to get themselves up becomingly. As for the mother she was never criticized, as was the townsman's wife, for dressing above her station until in a later generation.

[13] By the reign of Charles I many yeomen's wives could read.

About the children of yeomen we have only bits of information. The oldest son succeeded his father on the land unless he took up another occupation. Another son might be apprenticed to a merchant in London or to an artisan or businessman in a country town; he might take a cottage on the farm and work for his father as a laborer, or become a laborer on the "home farm" of the lord of the manor, or enter service in the country house. A well-to-do yeoman occasionally bestowed some acres upon a younger son. The yeoman was likely to send his sons to the grammar school. If he were ambitious for his boys and could afford it, he might send one or more to the university. From the university the boy might enter the church or become a schoolmaster, or, less often, a lawyer or physician.

The daughters might help in the house or enter service with a neighbor's wife and learn housewifery; such service was not looked down upon. Presently they married. As working women in the house they had a better chance to find mates of their own approximate status than the daughters of the gentry, and possibly more opportunity to marry from inclination. But they, like others, were brought up to value money and to regard the home as needing an economic basis. Their fathers were supposed to lay up dowries for each of them, so that a large family of daughters might sometimes prove an embarrassment. The daughters married the sons of neighboring yeomen, schoolmasters, curates, and even beneficed clergymen, and no doubt also tradesmen, apprentices to artisans, and young laborers on their fathers' farms. Now and then, as we have seen in another connection, the fair daughter of the farm, if well dowered, might marry the gentleman's younger son, or even his eldest son.

It was said earlier that the yeoman was constantly praised as embodying an old English tradition. By many of his contemporaries he was looked upon as a rather dull fellow, interested in sheep and oxen and marketable commodities, and esteeming his church chiefly as a useful meeting place for striking bargains. He was often better than that. That he was in many cases a man of spirit and liveliness appears not only in plays but in the records of quarter sessions and in diaries. Religion offered him his intellectual outlet and he would discuss the old religion (Catholicism) versus the new, and offer opinions even upon transubstantiation. William Honiwell of Devon set down in his diary that at a dinner with his neighbors there was little talk to any effect but of arguments of Scripture.

Such yeomen were of course readers. Adam Eyre in mid-century built book-shelves and was always lending books. Yet in the time of Elizabeth hundreds of yeomen had put crosses against their names in documents they signed, not necessarily a proof that they could not read, but an indication at least that writing was not easy for them. To many reading may have seemed an unnecessary accomplishment. "We can learn to plough and harrow," Nicholas Breton made his yeoman say, "sow and reap, and prune, thresh and fan, winnow and grind, brew and bake, and all without book." [14] If he needed help, the yeoman added, he asked it of the parish clerk or of the schoolmaster, who served his turn well enough.

Not quite well enough. Every now and again a yeoman was tricked into signing a document which he did not understand. Furthermore, a yeoman who could not read and write could not keep accounts, and thus never really knew in any close way how things were going with his profits and losses.

The yeoman had a good opinion of himself and of his way of life. He prided himself on his simplicity of appearance and behavior, on his industry, on his skill, on his neighborliness, and on his thrift.

No fine clothes were on his back or in his chest, but russet garb, and a little better for church on Sunday. His language was equally simple, full of short, old English words and pithy sayings, and with a tang of country accent.[15] He made no ceremony of sitting down to or rising up from meals. The pudding was not brought in with a song. In eating his manners were probably even less formal than those of the more rustic gentry. In meeting people he might touch his cap to the squire or to the parson, but he made little of forms of greeting.

He believed himself to be more hard-working than other people, as farmers have always believed. Idleness, the disease of the English gentleman, was not his failing. Adam Eyre would recount in his diary what he had to do in a single day: to set a laborer at harrowing, another man at walling a gap, another at making repairs; he had to go buy a cheese and visit a neighbor and fix up the pigsty. He had also to be with the work folks, hewing wood till evening. In summer the yeoman was often up by three in the morning, and he was likely to be around the barn after supper in the evening. If he had a bit of leisure in the long English summer evening, he would walk over his fields, review the state of the various crops, and plan what to be done next day. He did not always give himself leisure on Sunday. The parson might tell him that it was wrong to work on that day, but the parson did not understand that it was sometimes necessary to get a crop under cover before rain.

He believed himself skilled in his craft. Robert Loder, the Berkshire farmer who kept accounts, and thus is blessed by historians, had his head full of ideas as to what to do and not to do. He was fully aware that he was a better farmer than most, unusually canny, wise, and successful. What fertilizers to use and on what soils were questions that involved judgment and experience, qualities that every yeoman recognized as his own special endowment. The improved husbandry of Devonshire had done marvels for that country because farmers there understood the nature of their grounds and used the helps most appropriate. The Somerset farmers took extraordinary pains, they said, in soiling, plowing, and dressing their lands. A Northamptonshire yeoman had found his lands much "out of heart," but had restored them by intelligent husbandry.

The farmers were not all as skilled as they deemed themselves. They were often stubborn men who suspected any new device or method and did things in certain ways merely because that was what their fathers had done. Country gentlemen had to prod them into taking proper means to keep their lands rich. In their leases the yeomen had many times to promise that they would fallow and manure the fields each tillage season.

The yeoman believed himself to be neighborly. In Adam Eyre's diary we see how often he was lending farm and kitchen equipment. Indeed we find the whole circle of farmers round Penistone in the West Riding engaged in helping one another out. They gathered together to raise the timbers for the neighbor's new barn. They sent food and cooked meats to those who had to provide a funeral feast. Dainty dishes were always being carried over to the sick and the incurable. Thomas Tusser advised farmers "To love thy neighbor neighborly." Nicholas Breton discussed neighborliness:

It is enough for us to give a cake for a pudding and a pint of wine for a bottle of beer, and when we kill hogs to send our children to our neighbors with these messages: My father and my mother have sent you a pudding and a chine, and desires you when you kill your hogs you will send him as good again.

In other words there was a give-and-take about neighborliness. "Thy love of thy neighbor shall stand thee in stead," said Tusser. Neighborliness was likely to pay off, but it was natural to people who lived deep in the country and did not themselves have all the necessary tools.

The yeoman believed himself to be thrifty, and in that respect contrasted himself with the country gentleman. Farmers who lived to some degree on the food they raised and who clothed themselves from the sheep they sheared, who engaged constantly in barter and who had a few coins in their pockets, were likely to overvalue gold and silver. Richard Baxter had known frugal freeholders who had much ado to raise as much as ten shillings in cash. The yeoman was often slow to make payments that were due, not always because he lacked the money, but because he hated to part with it.

His thrift in many cases amounted to hard-fistedness. George Herbert said that the besetting sin of the yeoman was covetousness, by which he meant stinginess. A country man, he declared, would often borrow and wear out his neighbor's spade to save buying himself a new one. Yet some of them could be generous and take in poor children and do uncalled-for works of charity.

Industry, neighborliness, thrift, those ideals of the yeoman were also ideals and traits of the English who went to New England, many of whom were yeomen.

The New Englanders soon went into business and often with success. That was to be expected of men of their background. Their ancestors had been more than farmers: they had had to buy and sell, to learn conditions and guess at what was ahead. Many of them had been in some degree connected with the woolen trade and knew how to make a little more money than their crops and dairies would afford them.

In England the yeomen did not stay on the land as long as the gentlemen. The eighteenth and nineteenth centuries saw them fading from the countryside, although they never wholly disappeared. Their part in the annals of their country may seem insignificant; they never became members of Parliament and seldom justices of the peace. Their indirect influence, however, must have been considerable. Most of the families who won to political power had yeoman blood in their veins and showed it sometimes by their earthiness and hard practicality.

PART II. THE FARM LABORERS

The laborers on the farms appear seldom in the records and we can learn little about them. They were hard-driven men, some of them little better off, so far as we can find out, than the serfs on medieval manors. They started work at dawn, had breakfast for half an hour at six, worked until dinner and then until supper at about six; in the summer they would carry on with chores around the barns until eight or nine. If unmarried the laborer lived with the farmer and was possibly not badly off as to food and lodging, though we know little about how small a room he may have shared. If married he lived in a cottage on a farm or in part of a cottage, shared by two or more families. Those cottages varied of course in size and quality, but in many cases were flimsy huts built of clay and branches of trees, and often without a chimney or any outlet for the smoke except through the door. Many cottages had one room or two and a loft. There were few windows. The sanitary arrangements do not bear description. George Herbert characterized the smell inside as sometimes loathsome.

There were few facilities for keeping warm, except the one fire in the fireplace and that was probably not always lit. The wife of the laborer and his children might gather a few pieces of wood or of dried cow dung and bits of furze from the heath. In bad winters the overseers of the poor might supply the cottages with a little fuel.

In theory and usually in practice, but by no means always, the laborer had four acres of ground in connection with his cottage; and there, if the soil was good, his wife and children could raise a few vegetables and perhaps some barley and rye for their bread, and have possibly a few fruit trees. The spades and other means of stirring up the soil he might have had to borrow.

The cooking arrangements in the laborer's cottage were necessarily primitive and irregular because of the scarcity of fuel. Meat was hardly known except when the father or son killed game he was not supposed to touch, or when the porter at the manor house gate distributed leftovers from the table of the gentleman. In some communities were laborers who lived on bread and cheese and beer purchased at the alehouse, and apparently did little cooking. How they could pay the alehouse keeper out of their poor wages is hard to say. Sometimes in winter the parish made allowances to poor families.

Their wages were inadequate. The farm laborer who was employed all the year round would get from 30s. to £2, let us say from $50 to $75 a year. But farmers in the early seventeenth century were depending more upon casual labor which they could get by the day or week, and which they paid from 3d. to 8d. a day, the larger sum being given to those who brought their own food. The casual labor by the day was needed from March to November. Thus farm laborers who were employed by the day or week would find themselves out of work from about December to the end of February. How the laborers, who would not have known how to lay up money against a wintry day, supported themselves in the cold weather we do not know. Possibly some of them became woodmen during that time and helped clear out underbrush and cut timber. In clothing counties their wives and children may have helped the family budget by taking on wool to spin and weave.

The sums paid in summer seem inadequate. The rates of wages for labor were set at quarter sessions by the justices of the peace, who did not understand the hardships of the laborer. Rarely indeed did the justices increase the wages; in most counties the wages were little more in the reign of Charles I than they had been in mid-Tudor days, though meanwhile the price of living had more than doubled.

Did farm laborers rise in the world? Had they any chance to better their condition? Now and then such a man did in some way manage to get a little land, and graduated into a husbandman or a yeoman. I suspect he did it most often by marrying a yeoman's daughter.

One wonders about the children of laborers and can only speculate. Possibly some of them became servants in houses and were much better off than their parents had been. No doubt some children were apprenticed to artisans and may have become artisans themselves and gained the status of a village shoemaker or blacksmith. Other children may have taken the road looking for work and perhaps found it in a nearby town, or perhaps have drifted from one occasional job to another. No doubt some of them filled the ranks of the squatters on the heath. One looks among the useful and slightly successful men of the time to find sons of farm laborers and finds none at all.

But we must always recall that the records are insufficient about such men. Even the churchwardens' accounts tell us almost nothing of them. Now and then in a list of pewholders we find that a farmer had a place at the end of his pew for one servant. I am inclined to believe that the farm laborers were seldom seen in the church. For one thing they did not have decent clothes for such occasions.

CHAPTER 8

The Inns of Court and the Lawyers

FROM late colonial days to the present the lawyer has played a leading role in the life of our country. No less a role was his in the England of the days before the colonists crossed the Atlantic. He had many functions, but above all he was the right-hand man of the country gentleman, preserving the titles of his land for him. His value was recognized: presents of venison arrived at his office in Chancery Lane; when he came to the country, he was treated with due observance.

Among lawyers the barrister is the one with whom we are most concerned. He was one who after long residence in one of the Inns of Court had been called to the bar, and he alone could practice before the King's courts. But there were also attorneys and solicitors who prepared cases for barristers and who practiced before minor courts.

The barristers were, many of them, younger sons of the gentry and occasionally eldest sons. They were also sons of barristers, of attorneys and solicitors, merchants, and well-to-do businessmen, and now and then sons of clergymen or physicians. Instances there were where even a yeoman's son was able to afford the expense of the long training at the Inns and to qualify for the bar.

The training was at one of the four Inns of Court, Lincoln's Inn, the Inner Temple, the Middle Temple, and Gray's Inn. Those Inns together with the Inns of Chancery made up something like a university. It was "the third university of England" and by the sixteenth century was already an established and characteristic English institution. It served the profession of law, but it was thought of also as a training ground for the sons of the nobility and the gentry and for those entering the service of the commonwealth. It was where

> Minerva's men . . .
> And finest wits do swarm.

When the American colonists in the eighteenth century wished to give their sons advantages, they sent them to one of the Inns of Court, usually to the Middle Temple.

The Inns were located on the western edge of the City, not a quarter of a mile west of St. Paul's, north of the Thames, and just west of where Fleet Stream used to join the Thames. The gardens of the Temple touched the river on the south, and beyond Gray's Inn on the north were green fields.

For all their importance the Inns were not corporate bodies. They developed no set laws but ruled by custom. They were not connected in any way with the state, and yet they had complete control over the education of the men who carried on the law. Each of the Inns had a governing body, the Benchers in Lincoln's Inn, the Parliament in the two Temples, and the Pensioners in Gray's Inn. That body was self-perpetuating, and consisted of established men in the law, who decided questions of allotment of rooms, instruction, the conduct of members, promotions in rank, and above all finance.

The students were supposed to live within the Inn, two in a chamber. Not all of them could be accommodated within the quadrangles; some lived at "ordinaries" outside, and awaited their turns to find rooms, or stayed outside for more freedom. Every student was supposed to partake of Commons or meals for a certain fraction of the year—from eight weeks to three months. Dinners were at noon and supper at six or seven o'clock. In hall the students were not allowed to wear hats, though caps were permitted, nor were they to appear booted or spurred or carrying swords.

A student coming to London for legal training might enroll for two years at one of the Inns of Chancery, at Clifford's Inn, Clement's Inn, or another, and then go home, like Falstaff or Shallow, to be a justice of the peace. Or he might proceed straight to one of the four Inns of Court. By the seventeenth century many men were going directly to the Inns of Court. If they did so, they had, during the first two years, few fixed exercises, but were supposed to do much reading and talking of law; they were called Clerks Commoners. After two years they became Mootmen or Inner Barristers. In five or six more years if they were fortunate enough to be called to the bar at the end of that time, they became Utter Barristers. The Inns were sometimes limited in the number of Utter Barristers they could name in a single year, and did not by any means choose all who had spent the required period. There was no formal examination, and there was not always a fixed number of exercises to be completed. The education was rather a flexible one, and the admission to the bar must have been based upon a general estimate of a man's qualifications.

An Utter Barrister was not through his training. For at least three more years and sometimes for four or five, he had to perform exercises and to assist in directing the studies of the younger men. In theory he could not plead before the general courts at Westminster until those years had elapsed, though in reality he sometimes did. In most instances he carried on law work in the offices of other men and probably prepared cases for them.

The details of the schemes of education differed much from Inn to Inn. There were moots, bolts, imparlances, putting cases, and readings. The moots were most important. Students were given topics in advance on which to prepare a pleading; two men, sometimes one of them younger and one further along, were set to argue an issue, and their arguments were then criticized by older men, by Readers and Benchers, perhaps by a Serjeant-at-Law, or by a great judge who happened to be in residence. In other moots men had to plead extempore; in others the student was required to recite the pleading from memory; in still others the pleadings were given in law French, which the student had to turn at once into English. Putting a case was a less formal procedure. As men were at dinner or supper one of the older men might put a case and draw out all those at the table as to what action should be taken and what pleading used. Young men walking about the quadrangles were encouraged to put cases to one another, and those who were skilful became known as put-case men. Law, said Serjeant Maynard, was a babblative art; men should study all morning and talk all afternoon. A plan for a new building in one of the Inns was opposed because it would cut down the walking space and so interfere with put-case men.

The most formal element in the education was the lectures given by the Readers. A Reader would be allowed half a year in which to prepare his lectures and then would give them over a period of weeks or days. The lectures would be devoted to the exposition of a statute, or more often to a series of statutes, explaining why the statutes had been passed, at what abuses they were aimed, and how they differed from earlier legislation. Before he was done the Reader would point out vague phrases in the statutes and indicate the ways in which those phrases might be interpreted.

It was a long training and men who had gone through it with attention and purpose must have been as thoroughly trained as anyone in England. Law Schools, said Maitland, make tough law.[1] One can see the effects as one scans the reports of the great judges. The debates in the House of Commons, where many members were old Inns of Court men, prove how good the training was. There were men who could gather together the arguments made in the House over a period of several weeks, point out the holes in each argument, and then go straight to the root of the matter. They knew exactly how to phrase a proposed bill so that it was perfectly clear.

It was the hope of wise old lawyers that the training in the Inns made not only for precision but for breadth of view. They urged the students to study history, and English history in particular, and to make themselves familiar with languages. Some of the best law-

[1] *English Law and the Renaissance* (Cambridge, 1901), p. 25.

yers and judges were men of broad scope. They had the wisdom that comes with experience of human behavior, and that accumulates when good minds apply themselves to what other good minds have set down in print.

Unfortunately the training was less rigorous in the early seventeenth century than it had been earlier, or so observers thought. It was noticed that attendance at the various exercises was becoming less regular. Young men found that by paying fines they could avoid the preparation of moots, and they were not always discouraged by those in authority who liked to see the funds of the Inn increase. It was said further that Utter Barristers and Readers were neglecting their duties. In this charge there was probably truth. From the last half of Elizabeth's reign there had been an enormous increase in the numbers of students, and especially of those who came to enjoy themselves. Where students intent on matters other than their studies flock in, standards deteriorate, and even teachers lose interest. Moreover, any formalized system of education tends to lose its initial impulse.

The Inns had much to offer besides moots. They were like clubs, which men joined because their fathers had belonged. Sir John's son not only met youths of his own kind but was thrown easily and naturally into contact with great lawyers and judges, and sometimes with national figures. Whether he learned law or not, and he could hardly escape absorbing a little, he caught the tempo of his time and breathed the air of a great center.

He might frequent Paul's Walk and hear gossip of the court and of Parliament and of what was happening in Germany. In his own Inn he was likely to hear about politics. In an unpublished diary of a student in Gray's Inn is evidence that the students talked public affairs and were critical of James I.[2] If the young man listened to older men in the Inns, he would have heard much against royalty. James was said to have told the lawyers that he would leave the hunting of hares and hunt them, and the lawyers resented his statements about them, his attacks on the law, and his bullying of the

[2] Simonds D'Ewes.

judges. Many of them favored Parliament as against the King, and were likely also to have puritan sympathies. Not all the young men would have agreed with such lawyers, but we may be sure they would have discussed the questions. They were studying the common law, and it was under fire.

The students had more frivolous interests. They thought the Christmas season, which lasted twelve days, demanded gaiety. Some of the gaiety was frowned on as unseemly, but a certain amount of decorous festivity was often provided for. At dinner the great meat dish would be brought in with state and music and much bowing. Then would come the singing of hymns and carols, and the Master of Revels would sing and call on others to join him. Dancing might follow and a Lord Chancellor might lead off with a few steps. All this was fun for the young men, and so were the celebrations when a Reader was appointed or a Reader became a Serjeant-at-Law. There would be a procession and perhaps a feast. Not infrequently the students were allowed a play. Shakespeare's *Twelfth Night* was played in the Middle Temple and the *Comedy of Errors* in Gray's Inn.

The students flocked to the theaters. At the foot of the Temples one could take a boat across to the playhouses on the Southwark side. That Inns of Court men and playwrights and actors consorted together has been abundantly proved. Shakespeare's plays are full of allusions to the law and to the men who studied law. It will be remembered that Falstaff had been to Clement's Inn (an Inn of Chancery) and so had Justice Shallow:

I was once of Clement's Inn, where I think they will talk of mad Shallow yet. There was I, and little John Doit of Staffordshire, and black George Barnes, and Francis Pickbone, and Will Squele . . . you have not found four such swinge-bucklers in all the Inns of Court . . . Jesu, Jesu, the mad days that I have spent.

Most of the Inns of Court men were like Shallow, and never became barristers. After a year or two they went home to become justices of the peace, undersheriffs, deputy lieutenants, and possibly members of Parliament. But the Inns had left a stamp upon them.

The best men usually took up practice. How did they set out to gain a practice? They might continue at the Inn, moving up from Utter Barrister to Reader. A successful Reader might hope to become a Serjeant-at-Law, and so be on his way to a judgeship. The ladder of promotion for those who had made a brilliant record at one of the Inns was a short one-piece ladder. They might attract the attention of one of the great judges and be invited to follow his circuit, that is, to accept cases before him as he went from the assizes of one county to those of another. Such men were in line for a career. Or the young lawyer might attract the attention, not of a judge, but of a great London lawyer who would turn over cases he could not accept to the young man, or who might whisper to friends, until word got round, that the young man was likely to be heard from.

Of course many of the lawyers gained their practice through family influence. Thomas Overton, let us say, came from a good Shropshire family, and, when he settled in Chancery Lane, what was more natural than that Salop gentlemen who came to London to get legal advice should visit Mr. Overton and retain his services? It was little different with Mr. Goodall who had come from Warwickshire. He had known attorneys in three towns in that county who had been friendly to his father and so sent him their business before the King's courts at Westminster. There were indeed barristers who cultivated attorneys in the hope of getting business, but the best of them avoided that method of gaining clients.

Men did not, as they do today, gain a large practice by having taken part in some *cause célèbre*. There was little publicity for barristers, except in the legal profession itself; though it is possible that lawyers who made famous arguments in Parliament, like Hakewill and Whitelocke, thereby gained fame which benefited their practice. As the reputation of a barrister spread, country boroughs and sometimes ecclesiastical corporations asked him to take on their business and paid him an annual fee for it. Indeed, now and then gentle families would retain a barrister at so much a year.

Some lawyers found the going slow at first. They were usually those who had been reckoned plodding students, and had only by intense application, and possibly by pressure from friends, been called to the bar. They could not tender their services to anyone, but had to sit gaping in their chambers until someone chanced to knock at the door. In the meantime they might make a living by working in the offices of more successful men, or gain clerkships, or small offices with fees attached. Sooner or later some of these plodders did rather well.[3] There was always use for men with stored memories. Mr. Waller was called "Index," and men went to him for information rather than interpretation. But old Index became a serjeant and was well known in Chancery Lane.

About country lawyers we know less than we could wish. It is evident that some men who had been called to the bar settled in corporate towns where they saw opportunities for business. Many of the country lawyers were probably not barristers, although they may have had a year or two at one of the Inns of Court or of Chancery. Much of their law they had picked up from other attorneys under whom they had served at first, some of it no doubt from manuals, and more from experience. They did paper work of all kinds: conveyancing, drawing of deeds, making of marriage settlements and land transfers. But they appeared also before borough courts and in quarter sessions. In those sessions they defended petty criminals and no doubt taught them the many methods of legal delay. Some of them knew the art of bribing juries. In *Ram Alley* the lawyer explains that he never practiced before the honored bench, but confined himself to quarter sessions where he had "good gettings."

If country lawyers and London lawyers with country clients served many classes, yeomen and tradesmen and occasionally even husbandmen, most of their work was with the landed families. In some instances the lawyer for a family was also its steward. Such a post was naturally profitable. Land was held by many kinds of tenures and leases that afforded opportunities for quarrels. Country

[3] In Webster's *Anything for a Quiet Life* (Act I, Scene I) Mr. Knavesbie runs into an acquaintance of Cambridge days, and recalls how he could not prove a scholar, but attained to be a petty lawyer, "and I thank my dullness for it."

gentlemen were often self-willed men, insistent upon what they believed were their rights and ready to go to law to maintain them. It was a litigious generation and lawyers benefited. The gentleman often paid the lawyer in long leases because he had not the cash at hand, and the lawyer knew how to make such leases grow in value. Moreover he was on the inside of family and community affairs and knew who was in straits and needed to sell quickly. He knew when and how to pick up at a bargain a good meadow here and a piece of woodland there.

In Warwickshire lawyers graduated rapidly into country gentlemen, some of them of course already younger sons. Dynasties of lawyers can be traced in that county. One of them might serve half a dozen families, and his son and grandson might continue to do so, even after he had quarterings over his front door.[4]

It was a convention in the early seventeenth century, as in other times, to speak ill of lawyers. They were ignorant of Latin and pretended to know more than they did. They persuaded landlords to increase their rents; they made quarrels in order to compound them; they went hunting with the penal statutes and found good men liable for infractions of forgotten laws; they leaped over hedge and ditch, as an Elizabethan poet put it, and taught the gentleman how to undo his tenants about boundaries and rights in fields; they undid the gentleman himself and got his manors from him, and then slept in purple and warm furs. Smyth of Nibley had grown rich by managing the affairs and legal business of the lords of Berkeley. It was whispered in the Vale of Berkeley that the fool of the Berkeley household had taken a string and tied the castle to the church, lest Smyth move it to Nibley. But Smyth, by his long hunt for lost documents and by his talent as a sleuth, had won back a whole parcel of manors for the Berkeleys and deserved even more than they had bestowed upon him.

The lawyers were probably not worse or better than other men of their time. They were more successful than most because they

[4] From conversations with Philip Styles of Warwick, the modern Dugdale of Warwickshire.

had a skill much in demand, and thus roused envy. It must not be forgotten that as students they had had ideals set forth to them by their elders. The leaders of the Inns urged young men to give counsel in good causes and to discourage those who had evil causes. They laid emphasis upon gentility as requisite for those entering the Inns because they hoped thus to enroll in the profession men of traditions of honor. Their hopes may have been often disappointed, but not always. One remembers the Abingdon lawyer who little esteemed the profits of his practice but was ready to give any man counsel, especially the poorer sort. One could name lawyers of that time whose general character makes us feel certain of their professional integrity. It was not merely the advice of his elders in the profession that weighed with the young lawyer. His whole training had made for thoroughness and precision of statement and must have tended to develop intellectual honesty and honesty of conduct.

CHAPTER 9

The Physicians

IT WAS a saying of the early seventeenth century that Dr. Merryman, Dr. Diet, and Dr. Quiet were the three best doctors. Expectant mothers were told to be quiet and cheerful. "It is the imagination," said a man of the time, "that doth the good and not the physic." However reluctant physicians might have been to admit as much, some of them recognized the effects of the imagination and were aware that it was not enough to minister to the body only. Dr. Merryman was not always able to do much for his patients, but we must remember that his successes were not likely to be recorded.

Dr. Diet was more in evidence. He ordered his patients to refrain from meats and heavy foods, nourished them on liquids, and often forbade them wine. Dr. Quiet confined his patients to their rooms or put them to bed, requiring the room to be kept at an even temperature.

Dr. John Symcotts of Bedfordshire, whose letter book and casebook have been recently published,[1] used the methods we have attributed to Dr. Diet and Dr. Quiet. He was aware also of the value of exercise, and he used laudanum and opium in distressing cases to cause sleep. Now and then he prescribed massage. He was not

[1] See F. N. L. Poynter and W. J. Bishop (eds.), *A Seventeenth Century Doctor and His Patients; John Symcotts, 1592?–1662* (Beds. Hist. Rec. Soc., 1951), XXXI. I have depended much upon Dr. Symcott's cases and more upon the admirable introduction.

wanting in a certain common sense, and the same may be said of many of his colleagues of the time.

They had some knowledge of the course of various diseases and when to expect the crisis. They made examinations of the patient, feeling his pulse, looking at his eyes, and making a guess as to his fever. The urine and the stools they examined, though they had no laboratory tests. They were on the watch to find spots on the body that might indicate certain types of disease, but usually without too close observation. Of course they questioned the patient as to his symptoms and the nature of the pain.

They were not without the help of books and writings. The classical works of Galen and Hippocrates were still their vade-mecums, but they had access also to a certain number of medieval works on medicine, and to sixteenth-century compendiums by French, German, and Dutch physicians. Many of them possessed in addition the recipes passed on to them by their professional colleagues and by laymen, whose assistance they were far from ignoring. Dr. Symcotts obtained some of his remedies from the women of his acquaintance who had ministered to their villages. If one of those women happened to be a countess, her remedy carried the more weight with the patient, and possibly even with the doctor.

The diseases of the time were described so vaguely that it is dangerous to make generalizations about their incidence. I shall have to confine myself to impressions from general reading, knowing how little these impressions would be supported by statistics, which are, and will always be, unavailable.

The first impression is of the dangers associated with childbirth. Physicians were called in only by the well-to-do, and in serious cases. Probably more than nine-tenths of all deliveries were made by midwives and neighbor women. The heavy mortality of women in bearing of children can be seen clearly in parish registers, and more graphically in the little statues in parish churches of a gentleman surrounded by four kneeling wives, three of whom perhaps died in that way, often in their early twenties.

The reader of the literature of the time observes how many

people, and especially women, died of coughs or of what was called a consumption. Tuberculosis killed many girls between the ages of fourteen and twenty. Women lived indoors much of the time in dark, poorly heated houses. A great many older men and women who suffered from various ailments died finally of the same disease. John Bunyan understood that, as his account of the death of Mr. Badman proves: "I cannot so properly say that he died of *one* disease, for there were *many* that had consented, and laid their heads together to bring him to his end. He was dropsical, he was consumptive, he was surfeited, was gouty, and as some say, he had a tang of the Pox in his bowels. Yet the Captain of all these men of death . . . was the Consumption, for 'twas that that brought him down to the grave."

People regarded the disease as a death warrant. Yet Dr. John Barwick, a well-known Anglican clergyman, was imprisoned in the Tower when so far gone with tuberculosis that a friend had made arrangements for his interment. A year later he was found by his surprised friends to be well recovered. Absolute rest—he had been refused all papers—had cured him.

There were many kinds of fevers. The "tertian," the "quartan," and the "quintan," intermittent fevers, may have been variations of malarial fever, and they occurred most often in low-lying country, "the nursery of ague." Some of the fevers were no doubt typhoid. Other fevers, attributed by the doctors to the lungs, were possibly pneumonia, but such fevers do not seem to have killed as quickly as pneumonia did, up to a few years ago. Smallpox was quickly recognized, and might take off two or three children in a family, and killed older people as well.

The reader of diaries and letters notes the number of men that were believed to be suffering from stone in the bladder or kidneys. The physicians gave them medicine to encourage the passage of the stones, but seldom advised operations, which were too dangerous. The heavy incidence of this malady is possibly to be explained by the addiction of the well-to-do classes to a meat diet.[2]

---

[2] Wenching, wine, and trenchering (overeating) led, thought Sir John Harington, to "running reins, an aching head, and grumbling guts."

Gout is constantly mentioned. Dropsy and cancer were more serious. But of course the only cancers of which people knew were external, and were seldom operated upon. I find no evidence that people thought of cancer as a death sentence, but of course they could not distinguish between a malignant and a "benevolent" tumor. Syphilis—the "pox"—and diseases of a similar nature were common in London and in other large centers, especially in Court circles. It may not have been uncommon in the country. The doctors used mercury as a remedy.

Of the two great maladies of old age, paralysis and heart trouble, we hear less than we would expect. Those stricken with what was called palsy rarely lingered long. Heart trouble was apparently not easily diagnosed. We do find middle-aged and older men and women falling over dead, but we never hear that they had been warned to be careful in their movements.

The bubonic plague, now known to have been spread by rats, was the terror of the English people. It hit London and large centers in 1604–05, in 1624–25, and again in 1637–38, but in many years of the first two-thirds of the century this and that village would be stricken and occasionally decimated. Physicians did what they could, some of them with great courage, but with little success.

Accidents were as common, I think, as in our machine age. Men fell from horses, often after leaving the tavern; they fell off ladders; they cut themselves with tools; they had mishaps on the narrow stairways. Surgeons had some skill in setting bones and bonesetters are occasionally mentioned.

It is not within the competence of the present writer to judge of the remedies prescribed. Behind them all was the theory of the four humors, described in Chapter 3. The four humors in the body were blood, phlegm, choler (bile), and black choler. On the balance between these humors depended good health; disease meant that the balance had been lost.[3] "To draw off the 'superfluous humors' before they could give rise to overt disease was a logical extension of the

---

[3] "This inundation of mistempered humor." Shakespeare, *King John,* Act V, Scene I.

accepted doctrine, and it was this idea which lay at the back of therapeutic measures like blood-letting." [4]

The expulsion of the evil humors involved harsh remedies. Blood-letting was prescribed by every physician, but some doctors were careful to limit its use if the patient were in a weakened condition.[5] Almost as terrible must have been the repeated purgatives and the clysters (enemas). Nor could ill men and women have enjoyed the emetics that were in constant use and that were no doubt beneficial to those suffering from indigestion, from a "surfeit," or from food poisoning.

Other remedies were less wearing. The sweating of the patient under heavy warmed blankets had often good results and the application externally of hot water did much to ease pain.

Herbs and plants were used and in many kinds of combinations. "Every morning," wrote Dr. Symcotts, "I gave her . . . a draught of wormwood, white wine, wherein sheep's trittles [dung] were infused, with a pretty quantity of eggshells powdered, and at other times in the day of white wine and small beer posset drink, wherein turmerick [root of an East Indian plant], dockroot, hartshorn, ivory, inner bark of berberis [barberry], etc. were boiled, and this made yellow with saffron." [6] Powdered minerals and chemicals were mixed with herbs, with asses' milk and orange juice, in hot liquid infusions. The attendants upon the sick must have been hard put to it to prepare the elaborate concoctions. We may guess that one or more of the herbs had some healing power. A few of those herbs are still the basis of medicines.

The physicians were not always assiduous in visiting their patients. Roads were bad and progress on them slow. If the patient were not seriously ill he might write his symptoms to the doctor, who might prescribe without coming to see him. If the patient were in great pain the physician would come and outline a course of treatment. If that treatment had no success the physician might come again

---

[4] Poynter and Bishop, *A Seventeenth Century Doctor,* p. xxx.
[5] Of another physician Dr. Symcotts wrote: "That noddy little thinks what an adventure it is to take blood from an old withered man." *Ibid.,* p. 43.
[6] *Ibid.,* p. 78.

and lay out another program and try other remedies. He might even accept a suggestion from the patient who had his own ideas. The doctor was likely to continue his care by correspondence unless the patient grew worse.

The casualness of physicians was no doubt due to their rush of work; there were not enough of them.[7] John Raach has listed the physicians in the province of Canterbury (that is, the thirty counties south of Cheshire and Yorkshire, not including London, and not including the eight northern counties in the province of York) and finds that between 1603 and 1643 there were 741 names.[8] By an elaborate calculation, based upon insufficient facts, one might guess that in all England there was one physician to about 8,000 people.

The medical men were naturally more numerous in counties close to the center; there were a good many also in some of the coastal counties, possibly because the foreigners who came over to practice settled there. One might suspect, as one looks over the figures by counties, a correlation between the number of doctors in a county and its civilization in other respects. John Raach finds that Kent and Devonshire had the most physicians (85 and 58 respectively) and that the East Anglian shires and Essex, Oxfordshire, Cambridgeshire, and Sussex were not far behind. Almost all the large boroughs had several medical men, Canterbury and Norwich being famous for them. Exeter, Bristol, Lincoln, Leicester, and Ipswich, each of them, had a number of licensed practitioners. But there were also occasional ones in country villages and in the houses of noblemen.

I spoke of licensed physicians. The doctors were licensed by the universities or by the bishops in whose dioceses they proposed to practice. Probably two-thirds of the physicians had their licenses from bishops. In London physicians were also licensed by the College of Physicians and Surgeons. That body, established in 1518, had for a considerable time as its chief function the licensing of

[7] There was complaint at the time that the realm had too few doctors.
[8] See John Raach, "The English Country Doctor in the Province of Canterbury, 1603–1643," unpublished thesis in the Yale Library.

physicians; it gave licenses only to graduates of universities, and, after an examination by "censors," an examination more rigid for those about to practice in London that for those proceeding to the country.

The licensed physicians were nearly all [9] graduates of one of the two universities.[10] At those institutions they were required to spend a long apprenticeship. In general they pursued for the B.A. degree the same studies as others, but with emphasis upon Greek. When they went on to the M.A. degree they were set at Galen and Hippocrates, the great classical writers on medicine, and were likely also to study some of the medieval authorities. If they continued for a degree in medicine they were expected to listen to lectures by the Regius Professor of Medicine and to see a few dissections.[11] They might hope in three years' study beyond the M.A. to qualify for the M.B.[12] and in four more years for the M.D. Some of the students would drop out after the M.A. and assist a doctor, and then perhaps come back for the M.B. Many might begin practice after the M.B.

[9] The College of Physicians granted what were called extra-licentiates to men, usually already practitioners in the country, some of whom were not university men.

[10] The ranks of those licensed were recruited from abroad. Some Huguenot physicians came over in the sixteenth century. Theodore Turquet de Mayerne became the favorite doctor at the Court of James I. In the records of boroughs we find mention of French, German, Dutch, and Italian doctors in England who were not always welcomed by the native physicians, but who were usually able to establish themselves.

[11] The students did not do the dissecting themselves. They could fulfill the requirements for anatomical study at second hand in two or three sittings. See Poynter and Bishop, *A Seventeenth Century Doctor,* pp. xv-xvi.

[12] It was provided at Cambridge in 1570 that men could omit the degree in Arts and receive an M.B. after six years of the study of medicine, taking an M.D. after eleven years. But students were allowed instead of taking the M.B. to receive the License of the University to Practice Physic (M.L.). Poynter and Bishop, xiv. At Oxford it was provided by the statutes of 1549 that the student had to study six years, to dispute twice, to respond once, and to see two anatomies before securing his M.B. To gain his M.D. he had to observe three or more anatomies, dispute twice, and respond once. Sir Charles Mallet, *A History of the University of Oxford* (London, 1924), II, 85. Under the statutes of 1634 candidates for the M.B. had to be M.A.'s and attend three years of medical lectures and take part in disputations. Candidates for the M.D. had to take lectures for four years more and lecture themselves on Galen. *Ibid.,* p. 325.

and later perhaps take an M.D. Some of the more ambitious would go abroad, to Montpelier, to Leyden, and in particular to Padua.

The long training required meant that recruits to medicine came largely from the well-to-do classes. John Raach has proved that more medical men came from the gentle classes than from any other, many of them, I suspect, from the small gentry. Next to the gentry the medical profession, including the apothecaries, supplied most sons to the profession.

As to how a physician gained his practice we know little. It is possible that a young man would begin as an assistant to an older man, and then become his partner and eventually his successor. But the dearth of doctors was so great that it could not have been difficult to find work to do. A young physician might settle in a borough where he would find patients among the well-to-do citizens, who made as much use of the medical profession as any group, and then, as he proved successful, extend his practice among the nobility and gentry in the adjacent country. If a noble or great landed family called him into attendance, possibly for weeks together, he might gain their confidence and thus find powerful friends in the community.

His practice was necessarily limited by the fact that many people could not afford to summon him. His standard fee was an angel, or 10s., something like £5 or £6 today, or say $25 or more in American money. The less affluent in towns and the yeomen in the country would hesitate to spend so much unless in a great emergency. They were the more reluctant when they had been told by neighbors that the apothecary had a wonderful remedy. A knowing woman in the next village was reported to have been successful with an infusion of certain plants in hot water. Why be at the expense of securing the learned doctor?

The very poor could not even consider the use of a physician. It is true that sometimes a kindly lord of the manor might offer to bear the expense if a farm laborer or one of his family were seriously ill. Moreover, in towns the borough authorities might appropriate an annual sum to be paid to a physician for looking out for all the poor.

Occasionally the overseers of the poor in a parish would offer the physician a lump sum if he would cure a poor ailing creature.

As a profession the physicians were not well spoken of. The distrust of their skill appears throughout the literature of the time. It was believed that they knew little about the causes of disease and less about the cure. They were blamed with sticking to old empirical principles they had been taught and with failure to try new methods. They did not make enough allowance for individual differences.[13] In their defense it may be noted that some of the best of them admitted the great gaps in their knowledge, as good physicians do today. God sometimes prospered their cures, they would acknowledge, and sometimes He did not.

The doctor was not always at pains to make his profession popular. An occasional practitioner might bring comfits and plums in his pocket for the children, and have merry tales for the elders. But the friendly soul whose presence buoyed up the patient and left the family relaxed is hard to find in the records. More often he was given to a portentous gravity, and now and then to obscene jests. Sir Theodore Mayerne and Sir Simon Baskerville were examples of men who had an excellent manner with patients. Too often we meet the doctor who held out little hope, urged the patient to make his will, and then by supreme skill rescued him from the pangs of death.[14]

One fails to hear of the beloved healer whom the community took to its heart. But on the other hand, listen to this epitaph:

> Stay! this grave deserves a tear.
> Tis Vaux, whom Art and Nature gave
> A power to pluck men from the grave,
> When others' drugs made ghosts of men,

[13] Their greatest faults, the want of close observation and the tendency to draw conclusions from a few cases, were not mentioned in the literature I have happened to read.

[14] Dr. Symcotts' assistant, Johnson, was frank with a patient: "You need not wonder that your cure is no further on foot, you may rather wonder that you was not in your grave long before this, and for the perfect cure . . . I cannot promise you that it will ever be done." Poynter and Bishop, *A Seventeenth Century Doctor*, p. 46.

He gave them back their flesh again.
Tis he lies here, and thou and I
May wonder how he found time to die:
So busied was he, and so rife,
Distributing both health and life.

Vaux must have had some special genius, like William Harvey, which could make up in some degree for the want of modern instruments and remedies.[15]

About the position of the medical men as individuals in their communities there is less evidence than could be wished. Undoubtedly physicians were looked upon by many, and notably by the ignorant, as rather queer, unearthly people, who dealt in a kind of magic, an attitude which medical men did not always discourage. Moreover they were not as a class greatly concerned with religion. It was observed that the more skill they had, the less devout they were. Too much they attributed to natural causes and not enough to Providence. Such men were always a little suspect. They were, I think, often outsiders, not quite an integral part of the natural good fellowship. Yet in some boroughs the doctor was a leading personage, and not disesteemed by the local worthies because he had money in his pocket.

The physicians turned over operations to the surgeons, a fairly well-organized group. In 1540 the Barber Surgeons and the Surgeons had been formally united, and in 1605 they had received a charter by which barbers were excluded from all surgical work except bleeding and the drawing of teeth. Dr. Alban B. Doran,[16] upon whose work I have drawn, says that the surgeons saw to it that the apprentices whom they took on were well educated. Eventually an apprentice, after taking an examination, became free of the company and could practice. The surgeons required their

---

[15] The age of observation was just ahead, and we may be allowed to imagine that an occasional physician in this time was using his eyes and ears and fingers and trying out new methods.

[16] C. T. Onions (ed.), *Shakespeare's England* (Oxford, 1917), I, 413–443.

Fellows to study anatomy, and for that purpose received four executed felons a year.

The surgeon's work was multifarious.[17] He had to deal with skin
diseases and ulcers, with hernia, and with stone in the bladder. He
performed amputations, but of course without antiseptics and
anesthetics. When operating he had the patient tied down and
sometimes had him made drunk. His operations for internal conditions resulted more often than not in death.

The story of the unlicensed and unprofessional healers can only
be touched upon. All over the country were a certain number of
practitioners who had no license of any kind but who, perhaps as
apprentices to doctors, gathered some medical lore. Sometimes a
clergyman, interested in the ailing members of his parish, and perhaps with some medical qualifications, had good luck with cures,
and became a part-time healer. Very common was the wife of the
lord of the manor, or of the clergyman or occasionally of a yeoman,
who had picked up some knowledge of herbs and made use of it in
the community.

The quacks and mountebanks, many of whom were foreigners,
figure largely in the diaries and letters of the time because so many
people went to them. Sometimes they were men who had left
another occupation and who knew little or nothing about the ills of
the body, but they would put up bills and advertise marvelous cures
and claim long experience. As they were found out they moved to a
new place. They deceived not only the ignorant but those who ought
to have known better. The quacks called themselves doctors and
hurt the standing of the medical profession. It was their kind that
caused men to say of doctors:

> . . . they make a churchyard fat,
> And make the sexton sing . . .

Apothecaries were to be found in every town and in many villages.
A few of them were men who knew their job. Many of them were

---

[17] I have an impression that surgeons were migratory, seeking work here and
there. Occasionally a physician took on a surgeon as his assistant.

little better than tradesmen, and pretentious tradesmen at that, who would reel off Greek and Latin names. Queer concoctions they made up, some of which were harmful, but they also devised sound remedies out of herbs and plants.

An effort was made to control their activities. In 1607 James I had granted a charter to the apothecaries and grocers, but in 1618 he gave the apothecaries the sole right to purchase and sell drugs, and to search the shops of grocers and stop the sale by them of any drugs. The apothecaries themselves were to be looked over by the College of Physicians, which was to see that they were not selling evil drugs or poisons, but this power was used chiefly in London.

There were three hospitals in London, two of them for the poor, St. Thomas's and St. Bartholomew's. Bethlehem, better known as Bedlam, was for the insane. For the middle classes and the well-to-do there were no hospitals. We find, however, that physicians took patients into their homes in order to look after them closely, and apothecaries sometimes did the same thing.

CHAPTER 10

The Businessmen

THE ENGLISH business classes included many types. There were the great London merchants connected with the Levant or the Muscovy or the East India Company, and the merchants of Exeter, York, Hull, and Newcastle and of other large towns, who together constituted the aristocracy of business and were the commercial statesmen of their time. Close to them in importance were the leaders of the various companies of London, such as the iron-mongers, the pewterers, the vintners, who were rich men and became aldermen and mayors. In country towns were wool brokers, grain dealers, coal shippers, butter-and-eggs men, and many others. In addition there were the mass of small shopkeepers in London and country towns.

In fortune and quality they differed widely, but had something in common. In high feudal days they had ranked as villeins or serfs, and to the great noble they were still an inferior breed to be patronized and put in their place. Even today, when we use the word "bourgeois" of someone, we express an attitude with a long history behind it. Great merchants of London were well aware that they were the pillars of the City and enrichers of the realm, as good men as any, but they had still to affect a deference toward nobles and courtiers. Their low esteem in the eyes of the Court was shown when Lionel Cranfield, a shrewd businessman of breadth of view and imagination, was given high office by James I, and the whisper went round, how could a mere merchant understand matters of state. The playwrights not uncommonly regarded the businessmen of London, the wholesalers as we would call them, as closefisted and avaricious, as men of a single purpose, allowing themselves no leisure and sticking to their offices to their dying day. Jonson makes Morphus say of a City man: " 'Tis thus, a dull plodding face, still looking in a direct line, forward: there is no great matter in this face." [1] The men in country towns who had made money seemed to their betters pompous and underbred, to be forgiven their manners only when they had bought land and set themselves up in the country. As for the little tradesmen who sat in front of their shops in London or Leicester and cried out to passers-by, "What lack ye, what lack ye?" they were the proletariat of the business world.

The rise in the world of the businessman had been usually a matter of a few generations. The East India merchant had a father and a grandfather not unknown in City circles, and a great-grandfather who had possibly been a shopkeeper or a yeoman's son. The merchants and the well-to-do of country towns had fewer generations of businessmen behind them. The father of the wool broker had been a shopkeeper and his father had come from a nearby village. As Breton puts it, the son of What-lack-ye was become the only right-worshipful.[2]

Men might indeed mount all the rungs of the ladder in one lifetime. The son of an artisan or of a yeoman might take the road to London, become an apprentice, marry the widow or daughter of his master and succeed him, go from one form of business to another, and conclude his career as a rich man and an alderman or mayor of London. The plays were full of stories less probable but not without basis of fact. Ben Jonson pictures

> Some foundling in a stall, or the Church porch;
> Brought up t' th' Hospital, and so bound prentice,

[1] *Cynthia's Revels,* Act II, Scene 3.
[2] Grosart, Breton's *Works,* II, *Wits Trenchmour,* 16.

> Then master of a shop, then one o'th'inquest;
> Then breaks-out bankrupt, or starts alderman.[3]

Heywood in *Edward IV* makes the mayor, just knighted, tell of his beginnings as a foundling, and with pride. The plays picture also the successful businessman in the country town whose father had been goodman Humble, a yeoman.

Such men won their positions by their special knowledge and shrewdness. The great merchants of London and of the exporting towns were probably among the most knowing people in the realm. They had to have intelligence as to what was going on in other nations; in their own country they had to know what measures were coming up in Parliament, who counted in the Privy Council, who had the ear of the sovereign and might accept a few hundred pounds to get something done.

The merchants and dealers in country towns were seldom so well informed. But the best of them were likely to know what was happening in nearby towns and at the other end of the shire, and listened to news from Blackhall, the cloth market in London.

They did not always seem as intelligent as they were. Few of their letters and diaries have been published, but such letters as we have show that they had little facility in writing or in stating matters in an orderly fashion. They had nevertheless some gift of getting at the main point. A mayor of Liverpool would compose a letter to a minister of state which would reveal an understanding of local conditions and of the relation of those conditions to the national picture.[4] About economic matters in particular, town authorities were often wiser than great men in London.

They had ability, practical ability, of a rather high order. They made good mayors and aldermen. They were less conservative than country people and more ready to take up new ideas. They might decide that the town should go into the brewing business and gain the profits therefrom and at the same time provide good beer.[5] They

---

[3] *The New Inn*, Act IV, Scene 2.
[4] Historical Manuscripts Commission, *Hatfield MSS.*, XI, 465–467.
[5] John Taylor, A Discovery by Sea, *Works* (Spenser Soc., 1869), I, 188–190.

might lay plans for bringing water from springs miles away by conduits.[6] They might order a census of all the beggars within the borough in order to determine a policy about beggary.[7] They might suggest an annual sermon "to move the hearts of the auditory to extend liberally to the poor." They anticipated fires and brought from a distance the newest type of fire engine.[8] Not only did they undertake new enterprises but they looked after everyday details with efficiency, not with efficiency as we think of it, but with more than that shown by churchwardens and justices of the peace. They were better than village authorities in keeping the streets clean and free for traffic. They saw to it that the debts of the town were paid, though not always at once.

Their experience must have developed breadth of view and some humanity. They had necessarily a wide acquaintance. Some of them had in their earlier days been factors for their companies on the Continent and had known men of other nations; others had traveled over England and had come upon men of every breed and had learned to meet them easily and to get along with them. In their own towns, at dinners of churchwardens and borough officials, at the feasts of guilds and companies, they had learned a certain bonhomie; indeed at such gatherings they seem now and then to have allowed themselves a good deal of fun.

They had a certain culture that is too easily underrated. In the town of Stratford-on-Avon, which has been examined microscopically by Shakespeare scholars, was a group of the fairly well-to-do citizens who constituted an interesting circle. We know that Exeter, Norwich, Shrewsbury, and other towns had similar circles. More than any other class they were lovers of music. When citizens gathered in a London or Exeter tavern they would at once call for the musicians to wait upon them and to entertain them while they

---

[6] As at Exeter, Ludlow, and other places.

[7] *Cheshire Sheaf,* 3rd ser., XIX, 29. The same thing was done in Norwich.

[8] B. H. Cunnington, *Annals of Devizes 1555–1791* (Devizes, 1925), II, 98; John Latimer, *Annals of Bristol in the Seventeenth Century* (Bristol, 1900), p. 216. These examples are of 1641 and 1647, but I think I have seen fire engines mentioned as early as the 1620's.

dined. In many a country town the "waits" or town musicians were fostered by the authorities and were in constant demand for this and that occasion. Some of the good burgesses themselves had skill with an instrument or could join others in a song.

They were fond of the theater. In the Elizabethan time various groups of actors were always touring the country and putting on performances in small towns as well as large. Some of these companies were turned away by town officials, but the King's players or those of a noble earl were likely to be welcomed and to be paid for out of borough funds.

The citizens found they could learn much from the plays: the pageant of English history, the careers of English heroes, and a body of moral ideas and ideals. Even the manners of the Court were to be picked up from listening to the actors. The citizen in Jonson's *Poetaster*, who was entertaining courtiers at his fine townhouse, says: "At your ladyship's service," and then in an aside remarks: "I got that speech by seeing a play last day, and it did me some grace now." [9]

But the fundamental element in the culture of the businessmen was their religion. They were, as we have seen already, largely puritan. The governing bodies of boroughs voted money for "lecturers," who were to preach at special times.[10] Moreover, they honored their clergyman, especially if he were of the same outlook as themselves, and, like New Englanders later, looked upon him as their natural leader. Such sermons as he and other clergymen published they bought eagerly. They read the Bible and talked about it in their homes and discussed what it meant. They bought all sorts of collections of religious extracts and stories, narratives of how this man breaking the Sabbath was struck by lightning and how that woman on her knees in prayer escaped the fire that consumed her house.

[9] The playwrights were willing to please the bourgeoisie, who were among their best patrons. A great merchant, Gresham, was pictured on the stage in a highly favorable light. In *Eastward Hoe,* Act IV, Scene 2, a merchant is addressed: "I hope to see thee one o' the monuments of our city . . . and thy deeds play'd i' thy lifetime by the best companies of actors, and be called their Get-Penny."

[10] See the chapters on Puritanism (Chapters 13 and 14).

Lozenges of Sanctified Sincerity such mélanges were called by a playwright,[11] and with some justice. Their taste in reading was not of the highest, but they lived nevertheless in a world of thought about religion and moral conduct. It is not an exaggeration to say that they had a culture of their own, the culture of the heart, as Sir Walter Scott called that of the religious families in Scotland. It was a culture that lasted long in England and was to be carried to the New World.

Like middle-class people everywhere, they valued respectability; they wished their neighbors to speak well of them. Young men who hoped to get on should not be seen playing dice, nor in the company of those of doubtful reputation. It was the mark of sound judgment to appear hard-working, to preserve at all times a grave demeanor, and to express oneself with caution. The offices they undertook as aldermen and mayors were eminently respectable, and they took pains to surround them with dignity. A man who became a mayor or bailiff had at once to give up any post as retainer of a lord or take down the sign from his shop. The great London alderman forgot for the time his warehouse or leather business. He was looking ahead to still greater dignity, "to see ten men ride after me in watchet liveries with orange-tawny caps." [12]

With the aspiration for dignity and pomp went exclusiveness. In many boroughs there was an inner group of families of means who governed. They all knew one another and were often intermarried; a son succeeded his father as alderman and cooperated in the affairs of the town with his father-in-law and uncle. Such an oligarchy had its advantages. The men who controlled, let us say, Dorchester in Dorset, had a continuous policy; they were familiar with the problems of the town; they understood its relationship to and rivalry with Weymouth, the port a few miles away; they were acquainted

[11] *The Malcontent*, Act III, Scene I, in A. H. Bullen (ed.), *The Works of John Marston* (London, 1887), I, 255.

[12] Thomas Middleton, *A Tricke to Catch the Old One*, Act IV, Scene 4, in A. H. Bullen (ed.), *The Works of Thomas Middleton* (Boston, 1885), II, 323. All classes loved the trappings of dignity. Francis Bacon, as he moved through the street to assume high office, was accompanied by hundreds of men.

with the gentry in the surrounding country and knew their prejudices and foibles, and which of them would be fit representatives of the borough at Westminster.

They were a narrow group and not uncommonly kept the smaller businessmen out of things, and occasionally drew protests from them. In other boroughs, however, all sorts of artisans were elected "freemen" and attained to offices which drew them slowly into the inner circle.

The burgess aristocracy of a town was seldom far removed in interest and acquaintance from the nearby gentry. It was an old story that a country gentleman who could afford it had a town house in such a center as Exeter or York or Norwich. By midseventeenth century there was here and there in the larger centers something like the later "season," when gentlemen leased houses for a few months in the late winter and early spring and moved in with their families. The rich at all times and places tend to flock together, and we may be fairly sure that lords of manors and affluent merchants living in the same town saw something of one another. We may imagine that the sons and daughters of both groups met, for marriages between town and country resulted. Mrs. Hutchinson [13] in relating the story of her courtship gives us a picture of a circle of young people at Richmond near London that reminds us of the circles at Bath described by Jane Austen. The Richmond coterie included lesser courtiers and young people of some wealth, who were being married off or marrying themselves off. Such groups, we may suspect, existed in other places; they are not the type of thing that finds its way easily into the narratives of the time.

Certainly it was a custom often observed that gentle families arranged the marriage of their oldest son to the well-dowered daughter of a London or country merchant. One has only to read the epitaphs of country gentlemen to learn how often their wives came from the business world. [14] In many a home with old quarterings a

---

[13] C. H. Firth (ed.), *Memoirs of the Life of Colonel Hutchinson* (New York, 1885), I, 79–93.

[14] Sometimes men in the business world married the daughters of the gentry.

daughter of a mayor or alderman came into the family at least once in every other generation. Those women brought not only money into the family but new blood,[15] that of enterprising people.

For the businessmen more than those of any other class possessed drive and imagination. They developed the great companies, they laid the foundations of empire, and they were to establish the commercial supremacy of their nation.

Even a small-town successful artisan might marry above himself. John Shakespeare, a glover in Stratford-on-Avon, married Mary Arden, the daughter of a farmer of gentle ancestry.

[15] Neither the gentle family nor the merchant always welcomed such marriages, according to the playwrights, who tended to exaggerate social differences. In Beaumont and Fletcher's *Beggar's Bush* (Act II, Scene 3, *Works,* Cambridge, 1906, II, 230) great fun is made at the expense of a rich merchant who is proposing to marry the niece of a gentleman. In the *Shoemaker's Holiday* (Act III, Scene 5) Simon Eyre urges his daughter to marry no courtier; they are like silken fellows, painted images. "No, my fine mouse, marry me with a gentleman grocer like my Lord Mayor, your father, a grocer is a sweet trade; plums, plums."

CHAPTER 11

The Schools

BEFORE the break of Henry VIII with Rome there had been many schools in England. Some of them were old establishments like Eton and Winchester; others were connected with cathedrals and monasteries, or with town guilds; and a few were independent. In many places the chantry priest, paid by an endowment to pray for the souls of the dead, also taught boys.

The dissolution of the monasteries and the convents was followed by an attack upon the chantries; the incomes devoted to them fell into the hands of the Crown, although a portion of the endowment was still set aside for schools. But many schools had to be closed and others had to continue in a small way. By the end of Edward VI's reign (1553) and that of Mary (1558) the realm was in serious want of schools.

The Elizabethan government was not unaware of the situation and was the more eager to encourage the foundation of schools because it feared that youths unless educated would cling to the "old religion." They hoped that grammar schools would be a means of inculcating the reformed faith; that proper teachers, of sound religion themselves, would move the children "to do reverence to God's true religion, now truly set forth by public authority."

The Crown did little to provide the necessary money. But here and there wealthy churchmen, zealous to promote Protestantism and to teach boys to read the Bible, set up schools. No less benevolent were businessmen who had done well in London or in one of the larger towns. During their lifetimes or at their deaths they left money—or their widows did—to create charitable foundations in their native towns, the main object of which was usually the establishment or reestablishment of a school.

The town authorities themselves did much. They would set aside money or lands the income from which was to be used to found a school or to put on its feet one that had decayed. More often they would vote an annual sum, say thirty or forty pounds, to pay a schoolmaster and an usher. The incidental expenses of the school would be covered by fees which the fathers of the boys, many of them "freemen" of the borough, were expected to pay.[1]

So many schools were set going in Elizabeth's reign (1558–1603) that by its close few towns of two thousand inhabitants or more were without one. Larger towns such as Bristol, Gloucester, Worcester, Salisbury, Oxford, Lichfield, Plymouth, Rochester, and York boasted of two. Some very small towns had schools, and here and there were parish schools taught by the curate, and in a few cases by the parish clerk.

The schoolmaster was licensed by the bishop or by his subordinate. Until the last two decades of Elizabeth's reign no close watch was kept on the religious opinions of schoolmasters, unless they were of Romish leanings. But when Whitgift, a born disciplinarian, became Archbishop of Canterbury (1583), he set out to enforce upon schoolmasters conformity to the Anglican service. In the reign of James I the bishops scrutinized with care the loyalty of schoolmasters to the forms of the church, and when Laud became Archbishop (1633) those who had any taint of Puritanism found themselves without posts.

It was the aim of the grammar schools to instruct boys of from seven or eight to fourteen or fifteen to read and write and speak Latin; some of the better schools taught them Greek as well. Occasionally enough arithmetic was given them, usually late in the

---

[1] Sons of the poor were usually admitted without fees.

afternoon, to enable them to keep accounts.[2] Here and there attention was paid to the teaching of handwriting and a writing master was sometimes brought in for a few weeks. But Latin was the meat course and salads and desserts were few. The methods employed were much at the discretion of the schoolmaster, but the scheme of work and even the timetable were often set down in the statutes for the school. All that can be done here is to indicate a typical series of stages in the teaching.

The approach was grammatical. Boys were started with the eight parts of speech, put through declensions and conjugations, and, at the same time, made to memorize a considerable number of Latin equivalents for English words. With words at their command and cases and tenses, they were in some schools set at reading Latin sentences arranged in an English order. To facilitate the making of sentences they were required to get by heart Latin sentences culled from the classics, and especially verses, the "roundness" or euphony of which would make them easy to recall. Much of this teaching of beginning Latin was done in the first two years by the usher, a subordinate of the schoolmaster, usually chosen by him. In many cases the boys in the upper forms helped with the teaching.

Disputations about grammar were often used. The boys would pose questions to one another about nouns, conjugations, moods, and tenses, and be answered. The principle of competition among the lads was tried; on a certain fixed hour of the week, they could choose leaders and the leaders would then pick boys for their sides.

Of the more advanced work the master himself took charge. He would try on the boys the method of double translation, the translation of a passage from Latin into English, and then two or three days later the turning of the same passage back into Latin. In this way it was hoped that boys would learn to write good Latin prose: choice Latin, picked phrase, Tully's every word.

As soon as possible the boys were turned loose on Latin epistles, and then asked to compose epistles themselves, letters of "chiding,

---

[2] With the Roman system of numerals still largely used, arithmetic was a less involved subject than today.

exhorting, counselling, praying, lamenting, some of them epistles to friends, some to foes, some to strangers." In the art of writing they were often given the *De Copia Verborum* of Erasmus, or the text-book on rhetoric written by Apthonius of Antioch in the late fourth century.

Meanwhile the master was supposed to see to it that conversation in the school was carried on in Latin and to punish those who lapsed into English. To facilitate skill in conversation the boys were asked to take part in Latin colloquies in which they discussed assigned topics with one another. Before doing this they were given prepared colloquies to read, most of them of continental origin, dealing with the activities of boys, and admirably adapted to awaken their interest.

In many schools the boys, no doubt toward the end of their schooling, were encouraged to put on plays of Terence and Plautus. The performance of a comedy was believed by one writer to be a means of ridding boys of "subrustic bashfulness and unresistible timorousness."

One of the harder ordeals of the grammar school, but one not used everywhere, was the prepared theme or oration. After the youths had familiarized themselves with the more famous of Latin orations, they were told to put together orations themselves. They had to make an exordium or formal introduction, a narration or argument, a confirmation or showing of proof, a confutation or answer to arguments that might be brought up on the other side, and a conclusion or summing up. In addition to orations there were declamations where two boys engaged in debate over some formal proposition, usually abstract. The composing of Latin verses, perhaps the hardest ordeal of all, was required in some schools.

The various exercises in writing Latin constituted a tough discipline. As a training in orderly thought it was unsurpassed. The pupil had to determine the most effective arrangement of words in a sentence and the exact relation of dependent clauses, and he had to marshal sentences in close-fitting sequence. To do so involved careful analysis of precisely what was meant. The student was forced to make fine distinctions and to think with exactness.

In the best grammar schools, and indeed in many others, the student was in his last years put through a good selection of the writings of the ancients. He read much of Cicero, the *De Officiis*, the epistles and orations, and sometimes the essays on friendship and old age. He dipped into Ovid, Terence, into Sallust and Virgil. He was given some medieval Latin works and compendiums to study. The *Distichs* of a so-called Cato of the third or fourth century A.D., metrical couplets on edifying subjects, were much used. Occasionally the pupil read in the Christian fathers and might be assigned writings of Erasmus and Sir Thomas More. Thanks to the Revival of Learning and to the printing press he had a chance for more variety of reading than the student of a few generations earlier. But the best teachers were chary of using too many authors; they believed in the study of a few books "learned most perfectly."

With a few books or many the student gained facility in reading the language of learning. He was equipped to profit from the accumulated wisdom and observation of the ancients and of the medieval world. He was fitted to communicate with men of other countries, and to become a member of the international world. His training would prove indispensable if he went into public service. Incidentally he was prepared for the university, if he looked in that direction. What was perhaps most significant was that the best students could hardly fail to acquire a somewhat Roman outlook upon life.

Such training was not all for the best. Since students could not procure many of the texts the teacher found it often necessary to read the books to the class, with the result that the boys tended to memorize what they heard and missed much of the meaning.

The weakness of the system appeared also in the topics assigned for writing and speaking. The boys had to use hackneyed themes out of old tomes, to quote this and that ancient or medieval maxim, to use stories and metaphors familiar to generations. Moreover they were encouraged to keep little books [3] in which they copied from their reading choice phrases, proverbs, synonyms, and figures of speech which they might work into their compositions. They were not expected to draw on their own experience and to develop their own notions and interpretations. They had further to rely solely upon deductive methods of reasoning. It must have been tiresome to build their little structures of thought on old lines and out of old bricks.

The effects of such a system for good and ill can be detected in the writings and speeches of the time. Preachers would marshal their arguments in perfect array; their sermons would be masterpieces of deduction; they would indulge themselves in allusions to classical stories from Rome and Greece that helped their hearers little. Those who took part in the debates of the House of Commons were even more dependent upon the ancient writers. Some of them could reason with sequence and force and, when they chose, could bring in a classical example that went home. But others, such as Sir John Eliot, showed the unhappy influence of their school training in their overabundant illustrations from the ancients, in their preference for long euphonious Roman words, and in their addiction to elaborate similes. Like schoolboys, they managed to make lengthy orations and say little. Perhaps the schools can hardly be blamed for the many, if usually less known, writers who had learned from their early lessons to depend upon latinized words and clauses, and who buried in long, involved sentences thoughts and ideas that have to be searched out. With the less intelligent the grammar school training did not always make for clearness.

The influence of the grammar schools in creating a latinized English language as against the idiomatic speech of the people appears in the plays and prose of the time. Shakespeare could make his more dignified personages use a latinized English. The mighty lines of Marlowe, the rolling verse of Massinger, the stately prose of

---

[3] The teachers believed that the keeping of such books by the boys taught them discrimination and judgment in their reading. One result, I suppose, was that grown men often kept such "commonplace books."

Clarendon and that of Milton with its long rhythms, exhibit a feeling for classic forms gained in early life at the grammar school, and no doubt also at the university. The language they wrote was unlike that spoken on the street and in the tavern. The racy English in the plays of Dekker and Heywood, in the roaring comedy of Shakespeare, in the testimony of yeomen at quarter sessions and in Star Chamber, and in the short sharp words of angry pamphleteers was the tongue of everyday men, some of it still to be heard in the southern Appalachians. The men who had been through seven or more years of Latin, and who had allowed their education to become part of them, could write and sometimes speak and think in that language. As a result they wrote English in a Latin way. That latinized English remained for nearly two centuries the instrument of scholars and essayists, and of some scientists, theologians, and statesmen.

Intellectual discipline was by no means all. The boys had to repeat prayers morning and evening, to recite the Lord's Prayer and the Ten Commandments, and to memorize catechisms. Sometimes they were assigned the Latin New Testament to translate and were often given textbooks of scriptural history, and then examined as to what good deeds they found commended and what sins condemned. On Sundays they were in many towns escorted by the master to the parish church and questioned on Monday morning as to what they had heard. In such ways and others they were made familiar with Christian ideals and with the forms of the church.

About moral behavior in general and about good manners they learned much from the books they studied, from Lily's grammar, and from the many collections of extracts from Latin writers. The colloquies already mentioned, in particular those by Erasmus, Vives, and Corderius, were full of precepts and advice as to courteous and becoming conduct in everyday affairs. Even the doggerel couplets the boys memorized were directed to encouraging good manners. It was a complaint of the Puritans, one not wholly justified, that the boys were taught a pagan morality.

It was recognized that boys gained something from association with one another, but little thought was yet given to making use of that association for the development of a type of character. The teacher used monitors to help him with discipline, but he set the boys no task of governing the school in order to bring out leadership. In the great "public schools" of the nineteenth century the boys were expected never to give one another away, but the teacher in the early seventeenth century encouraged them to do so, and sometimes used secret monitors or "spies."

Yet Mulcaster of St. Paul's School had some notion of extra-classroom education. He thought that sons of gentlemen, "whose ordinary greatness is to govern our state," should be brought up, not by private tutors at home, but in the grammar school, where they were subject to the hearing and censure of all. A boy ought to be acquainted in early life with other boys, since he would have to live with them in manhood. That theory was in line with the practice of the time. Sons of gentlemen, except those of the very rich and of the great nobility, were taught in grammar schools, often in small ones, along with the offspring of parsons, yeomen, mercers, and masons.

In consequence there was no such segregation of classes as later. The man who had spent the formative years of his life in the grammar school of three hundred years ago was not likely to forget any of his fellow sufferers, even if meanly born; he was not as cut off from the doings and thoughts of other groups as were the upper classes of the nineteenth century. Oliver Cromwell, a cadet member of a great family, attended a little school in Huntingdon where he met boys of every kind, and showed years later how well he understood and how highly he valued the virtues of yeomen. The letters of country gentlemen prove on what friendly and natural terms they were with all kinds of people in their communities, as they had been since school days.

The teachers of the nineteenth century schools were to emphasize the playing fields as part of a boy's training. In the early seventeenth century little was said about bodily exercise and play. Thursday afternoon was usually set aside as a holiday and a few masters encouraged the use of games and even suggested those suitable. Exercise is mentioned by the schoolmaster, John Brinsley, in his book on his vocation. He tried to believe in it, if used with moderation, but begrudged the time taken from work.[4] The ingenious (the talented) would really find their best playing in learning. Mulcaster with more vision thought that schools ought to have space around them so that the boys could have "some train in exercise," and recommended dancing, wrestling, fencing, and other diversions. Neither founders nor governors nor masters exerted themselves to provide facilities for play. Many schools were housed in a single room in a building on the street, right up against other buildings, and without any playground. The children played on the street or on the common or in the churchyard.

The problem of finding and pushing talent was with schoolmasters then as now. Richard Mulcaster declared that God had been marvelously munificent to the poor in bestowing ability upon their sons. Doubtless he was thinking of the better type of artisans. But he observed also that the middle sort of parents, "which neither welter in too much wealth, nor wrestle with too much want seemeth fittest of all . . . to bring forth that student which must serve his country best."

The progress of a talented boy to the university was facilitated. In some grammar schools an endowment existed by which one or two boys were given a few pounds a year toward their expenses at the university, usually at a designated college. Moreover, colleges at both universities awarded scholarships to youths from such and such schools. In some boroughs the mayor and councilors or aldermen might vote three or four pounds a year to boys from the local school toward their university expenses. If no other methods of sending a bright boy to the university could be found, the teacher, or more often the clergyman, might persuade a prosperous citizen to act as benefactor. The annals of the early seventeenth century are full of delightful stories of how boys of talent were given their chance.

[4] *Ludus Literarius, or the Grammar School* (London, 1627), 299–302.

What about the younger children who had to learn to read and write English? In theory grammar schools accepted only those who could read and write, and a few of the best grammar schools were able to live up to that theory. In practice many of the grammar schools, and especially those in the control of borough authorities, had forms for the "petties" where boys, and often girls, learned their alphabets. In many schools the "petties" were taught by the usher; in other places the parish clerk taught the small children; in still others the older boys, perhaps under direction of the usher, were set at instructing the younger. In small parish schools the teaching of the alphabet was sometimes the work of the master who had no usher to help him. He might also start the older boys in Latin and then encourage them to go away and "table" (board) at the grammar school in the nearest town.

In addition to grammar schools and petty schools there were small private schools carried on in their houses by obscure men and women, some of them foreigners who had settled in England, where they taught little children to read and write and possibly to do sums, and were paid by fees from parents. That such schools were often kept by men and women with little gift for teaching is evident from many biographies. Fortunate were those children taught their ABC's by their parents, who at dinners and suppers, or as they sat by the fire, might "find it a very pleasant delight."

What mattered most in schools was the quality of the teachers. In any profession quality follows at a distance the rewards offered in money, and especially in social estimation. Schoolmasters were paid from £10 to £25 a year, occasionally less and sometimes more, and ushers from £5 to £8 or possibly £10 a year. Extra remuneration the schoolmaster might gain from entrance and other fees, and he was often given part of the school buildings for his dwelling and occasionally a garden and an orchard. A number of schoolmasters would "table" boys from out of town and derive income thereby.

He did about as well as the poorer country clergyman, but his calling had by no means the same prestige. In the borough he was a figure known to all but not one honored. Alexander Aspinall, master of the school at Stratford-on-Avon, served as an alderman, but election to such a post was unusual.

"Our calling," wrote Mulcaster, "creeps low and hath pain for a companion, still thrust to the wall, though still confessed good. Our comfort perforce is that these things be good things, which want no praising, though they go a-cold for want of happing [covering]." Men did not crowd into a profession that crept low; indeed the profession received too many who could not stand up in the world.

The results were often unfortunate. It is an old story in the auto-biographies that the hero was sent from one school to another because he was learning little. The dissatisfaction of fathers comes out in borough records, which show that rulers of the town were often moved by their complaints.

The complaints were often justifiable. The governors of a school or the borough authorities seeking a master regarded an M.A. or a B.A. degree as a guarantee of merit, and were often let in for less than the second best, someone who had made little mark at the university. Such men when they became teachers were unable to inspire interest among their pupils and in many cases overstayed their welcome, or went from one school to another. They were likely to make up for their want of knowledge and skill by the assertion of authority, and to use the rod and ferrule more than was necessary.

A better type of schoolmaster used the post as a means of making a living until he could find something more to his taste. Perhaps he had made his way through the university and was in debt or unable to proceed further until he saved money. After a few years in the classroom he might become a secretary or a steward, or a country lawyer. It is just possible that Shakespeare, not a university man, was a schoolmaster for a time in his youth. It is certain that James Shirley, who wrote plays and some remembered verse, was one. The usual fate of the schoolmaster who did not continue in the vocation was to become a country parson.

The best type of schoolmaster was usually a well-trained university man who knew his Latin and Greek,[5] but who possibly had few influential friends to push him, or happened not to be ambitious. Such a man settled down with a will to the exacting business of coaxing youth into the mystery of Latin. Sometimes he managed to make the Romans living beings and by merry and facetious comments to catch hold of the imagination of his pupils: sometimes he contrived to make learning an amusing game in which friendly competition among the boys led them to outdo themselves. Shakespeare understood that point about teaching: "No profit grows where is no pleasure ta'en."

Occasionally the teacher made his work a pleasant game for himself and so for the pupils. John Brinsley, who taught for years at Ashby-de-la-Zouche in Leicestershire, had set himself to "seek out the best ways of teaching by inquiring, conferring, and practicing constantly all the most likely courses which I could hear or devise." [6] He followed his boys as other men followed hawks and hounds. Trained as a clergyman, he had turned his attention to teaching, but on account of his Puritanism was finally forced to give up his work. He counted himself "the unablest of many thousands," but was happy in the good he believed would come to church and commonwealth.[7]

There were indeed schoolmasters who had never seen the inside of a college quadrangle and who had picked up such Latin as they knew from the grammar school. They gained posts as ushers and sometimes as heads of small parish schools, and occasionally established their own schools for small children. Now and then one of

---

[5] Occasionally a college at Oxford or Cambridge, as St. John's at Cambridge, had been given by the founder of the school the right to choose the schoolmaster.

[6] Brinsley, *Ludus Literarius*, p. 3.

[7] Donald Lupton, in his satire *London and the Country Carbonadoed* (*Harleian Miscellany*, London, 1808, V, 327–328), said few good words for any and not many for schoolmasters. But there were those, he wrote, who stayed with their mother, the university, until learning, discretion, and judgment had ripened them for the managing of a school. Such men he loved and honored. They taught the cradle to speak several languages and fitted men for places of public note.

them, after a few years' teaching, went on to the university, and, upon gaining a B.A., became the head of a grammar school.

With all the weaknesses of teachers, the grammar schools of the early seventeenth century accomplished not a little. They trained boys in the orderly progression of thought, and they found out talent and sent it on to the university.

The education of women suffered from the dissolution of the convents. For three generations following, there were few places where girls could be taught. Occasionally they were tolerated in the schools for the "petties," but were seldom allowed to stay beyond the age of nine. Here and there may have been a small school for girls taught by a woman, but of such schools we have little information.

It was not until the reigns of James I and Charles I that we begin to hear of private schools being established in and around London for young women. Although receiving the daughters of the well-to-do merchant classes, those schools looked to the nobility and to the gentry for their clientele. Several of them were run by refugees from the Continent, who thus capitalized on their knowledge of languages. The girls were taught singing, playing of instruments, and often dancing, and nearly always French. Fine sewing and embroidery were almost always part of the curriculum and sometimes enough arithmetic for everyday use.

The old custom, mentioned in an earlier chapter, that the daughters of the gentry were sent to serve in the house of some noble lady was still in use, but less often than earlier. More commonly the daughters of both gentlemen and nobles were taught by private tutors, perhaps by the parson or the chaplain. In *The Taming of the Shrew* Baptista says of his daughter Bianca:

> she taketh most delight
> In music, instrument, and poetry.
> Schoolmasters will I keep within the house
> Fit to instruct her youth.

It is probable that such women as Dorothy Osborne, a widely cultivated woman, and Brilliana Lady Harley, a Conway born and therefore gifted, had been thus brought up at home.

The run of gentlewomen were less fortunate. Even those highly competent in their households and obviously talented would write a hand and exhibit a spelling that betray want of schooling. That great lady, Anne Clifford, who had known the best and most interesting people of her time, and who read the poets eagerly, labored over her handwriting and spelled curiously.

The wives of yeomen and citizens in towns could seldom have had tutors at home, but in some way by the reign of Charles I a considerable number of them were able to read and write. They may have attended those small private schools of which we know next to nothing, or have been taught by their fathers.

That girls had an education so far inferior to that of their future mates meant that they were seldom fitted to be intellectual companions and explains in some degree the subordination of the sex.

CHAPTER 12

The Universities

THE ENGLISH universities differed from those on the Continent in appearance. Scholars from across the Channel spoke with admiration of the buildings of Oxford and Cambridge; one of them ventured to say that a single English college was better equipped than a continental university. It was remarked in a college play at Cambridge that the buildings were fitted to be the abodes of knights, lords, and lawyers rather than of clerks', weavers' and butchers' sons. In another play the attraction of Oxford was described:

> The town gorgeous with high-built colleges,
> And scholars seemly in their grave attire.[1]

When Englishmen went to the New World they were too poor at first to erect universities such as they had known, but in time they took over the English conception of how a university should be housed.

There was an air to the English universities. The masters were often men of the world, and the fellows of gentle birth. A new type of students, the sons of the gentry and nobility, was beginning to be seen in the quads.[2] Learning and gentility were becoming associated;

---

[1] *Friar Bacon and Friar Bungay,* in J. P. Collier (ed.), R. Dodsley, *A Select Collection of Old Plays* (London, 1825), 3rd ed., VIII, 210.
[2] Mr. Mark Curtis, in his forthcoming book on the universities, makes much

the notion of such association was to be carried over into the universities of New England and Virginia.

The students were increasing in numbers. In 1622 Oxford, with eighteen colleges and seven halls, had 2,850 students; Cambridge, with sixteen colleges, had 3,050 students. Although there were only the two universities, the proportion of university men to population was many times greater than at the beginning of the nineteenth century, before London and the provincial universities were started.

The universities and the colleges within them were well provided with income. It would be a long story to tell how their endowments had been left them, by royal ladies, by peeresses, by ministers of state, by great ecclesiastics, by London merchants, and by gentlewomen. In 1575 an act of Parliament improved the financial position of the colleges. Their endowments were almost wholly in land from which they derived rents. By the new act it was provided that one-third of those rents should be paid in corn and malt at the fixed price of that date. But the price of corn and malt was steadily rising, so that the colleges received one-third of their income in commodities which were constantly becoming worth more. It was a further help to the colleges that nonscholarship students were coming in increasing numbers, paying for their rooms, their "battels," or food, and for their tuition.

The organization of the two universities had much in common, though with infinite variety of names. Each university had a chancellor, usually a great nobleman or statesman, who represented the university in its dealings with the government and had considerable oversight of it, especially in the initiation of policies. The vice-chancellor, who was appointed for a year from the group of heads of colleges, had with the mayor control over the town, looked out for the government of halls, enforced the statutes of the university, kept its courts, and performed other duties such as licensing wine-shops. Much of the control of the institution was in the hands of bodies of elder statesmen. The professors had the duty of reading

---

of this development. See also J. H. Hexter, "The Education of the Aristocracy in the Renaissance," *J. Mod. Hist.*, XXII (1950), 1–20.

lectures open to the university and, while each one was associated with a college, were university officials.[3]

The universities were offering various degrees. The B.A. was given after four years of study, and the M.A. after three more.[4] Advanced degrees could be taken in civil law, medicine, divinity, and music. By the Laudian statutes of 1636, Oxford students could attain a bachelorate of civil law or medicine [5] after three years beyond the M.A., and a doctorate in those subjects after four more years. Divinity required a longer time. The requirements imposed by the Laudian code were probably not very different from those at Cambridge.

The length of training for advanced degrees meant that many men stayed around the universities a long time; they must have acquired an academic outlook not easily shaken off. Their intellectual training was thorough; it resulted in professional men of high attainments. But it was so largely based upon medieval and ancient thought that it tended to make men conservative and even doctrinaire, unfitted to take up new ideas and unfriendly to experiment.[6]

Many of the men who continued for advanced degrees became fellows and took part in the teaching. Even those who were not fellows but resided in college were usually expected to take some small part in instruction.

For the B.A. degree the backbone of the training was rhetoric and logic. The study of rhetoric was based upon Quintilian, the Latin writer, and upon the Greek treatise of Hermogenes of Tarsus, who lived in the second century A.D. In addition students were put through Cicero's orations as models of style, and also as useful ma-

[3] As scholars the professors were not at this time comparable with the best on the Continent.

[4] The two standard works on the universities are J. B. Mullinger, *The University of Cambridge* (3 vols., Cambridge, 1873–1911), and Sir Charles Mallet, *History of the University of Oxford* (3 vols., London, 1924–27).

[5] About the requirements in medicine, see also chapter 9.

[6] The charge made at the time against university men when they came to London was that they were inexperienced in the ways of the world and easily taken in.

terial for the training of statesmen. In logic the lectures were usually an exposition of Aristotle and his many interpreters. A whole body of dialectic had grown up around Aristotle, and had been the staple of university training in the Middle Ages. It had not been wholly abandoned. The students had to prepare themselves for examinations, which were public disputations in the "schools" (where lectures were given and examinations held). Two "sophisters," as candidates, arrayed against one another, debated a Latin thesis in the presence of a critical audience, who would vote on their degrees. The business of attacking and defending the thesis involved the old scholastic dialectic, an ability to use readily the medieval refinements upon Aristotelian logic and to use them quick-wittedly.

For this ordeal students had been prepared by many practice disputations in their colleges in the presence of their tutors, and by listening to disputations by older men versed in the intricacies of logic. Of such a disputation between Samuel Collins and Dr. John Williams it was said: "No greyhound did ever give hare more turns upon Newmarket heath than the replier with his subtleties gave to the respondent." George Gascoigne, in his friendly wishes for the universities, hoped

> That logic leap not over every stile
> With curious quids, to maintain argument.

Logic did leap over the stile. Lord Herbert of Cherbury, reflecting upon his university experience, thought that a half year of logic would have been enough. Thomas Hobbes was bored with Oxford scholasticism, and John Milton, looking back on his training at Cambridge, complained that the students were drawn into fathomless deeps of controversy when they were expecting worthy and delightful knowledge.

Though Oxford and Cambridge were slowly shaking off some of the medieval preoccupation with logic, they were putting it too early in the course, in the second year, when students were not ready for it, and making them continue its use until they undertook their disputations at the conclusion. But the students could also get courses in the Greek and Latin writers and in the church fathers and in philosophy. In the last-named subject they read Aristotle's works in metaphysics and in natural and moral philosophy.

As intellectual centers the universities were still greatly concerned with theology. All studies in the liberal arts were considered, however, proper prerequisites for the course in theology. The teachers had long been training students to be clergymen, and they were still at it, though in a less degree. To them the logic and rhetoric which they imposed upon their pupils were methods of arriving at the truth about divinity and of expounding it.

The breach with Rome had reinforced the interest of university men in religious discussion. That breach demanded fresh thinking and a reexamination of the church fathers and a careful study of the scholars on the Continent who were formulating Protestantism. That was work for university men. For two decades of Elizabeth's reign there were still fellows around the colleges who were Romanists at heart and were awaiting dangerously a change in the government. The case against the old theology, the case for those who followed Calvin in theology or in church organization, had to be stated, and was being stated. Lastly, the case made by others for the compromise religion of the Elizabethan Settlement had to be justified. That justification carried scholars back to the church fathers.

Such work was the proper function of universities. They were to be leaders in finding out truth, and theology was the beginning of truth. J. B. Mullinger, in *The University of Cambridge,* says that in a petition presented to Parliament in 1584 one of the important articles dealt with the "endowment of research." The petitioners wished to give senior members of the university leisure to read and meditate upon theology. From such study and thought they ought to be able to set at rest forever questions such as Augustine, Aquinas, Luther, Zwingli, and others had raised. How touchingly hopeful they were!

None were more so than the Calvinists, even if they had on their hands the thorny problem of reconciling predestination and free will. They were working out, particularly at Cambridge, a whole body of Calvinistic philosophy with the help of the new logical methods of Ramus.[7] They had hopes that they were leading the way for the English church, hopes that were to be dashed by James I, by Charles I and Laud. But they did set forth a body of doctrine which the New England clergymen were later to elaborate.

More important than the university were the colleges. The heads of Oxford colleges were called, variously, president, provost, master, warden, dean, rector, and principal. At Cambridge most of them were called masters, but there were a president and a provost. The head was surrounded by what we may call senior fellows, though different terms were used in different colleges. Each college administered its own affairs without much interference from the university. The master and fellows had always with them the problems of their property, the lands scattered over England from which they derived rents. They apportioned money for the various expenses, awarded scholarships to students doing well and to future students

[7] A new approach to theology was developed in France by Peter Ramus. In 1526, when he was twenty-one years old, he had, with a boldness resembling that of Luther, attacked Aristotelian logic. Within a few years after his death, in the massacre of St. Bartholomew's Eve, his views had won wide support in Cambridge; they were taken up by Richardson of Queen's, by Temple of King's, and by Bownham of Christ's.

It is impossible in this note to explain Ramus. Perry Miller, in some forty pages of his *New England Mind* (New York, 1939, pp. 111–153), has attempted to set forth the logical theory. Ramus sought to simplify the methods of logic, to make logic more teachable. He wished, says Mullinger, "to exemplify as far as practicable the employment of the natural reason in the acceptance of facts, or in arriving at conclusions, without recourse to those artificial processes which Aristotle, or rather his commentators, had prescribed as indispensable aids." It is to be added that Aristotle himself was seldom given to students, but the medieval expositors of Aristotle who had elaborated his logic. Ramus believed that to understand the functioning of reasoning one had to choose those most able to help in discussion, and that the reasoning of such men ought to give the exact image of the nature of reason. "Science ought . . . to study the lessons that are innate in select minds and transmit them in their most natural order."

Select minds Ramus insisted upon. That put him in line with the Renaissance and the new Humanism. His logic was opposed to the scholasticism which had become part of the great tradition. Today his dichotomies themselves sound scholastic. But he did more than any other thinker to prepare the ground for Bacon's method of observation, and for Descartes.

who looked promising; they determined upon new buildings, and upon the repair of old ones.

In addition to senior fellows were fellows called by various names, but equivalent to what are now called junior fellows. They took part in teaching but in most instances had little share in college administration. Like senior fellows, they were given lodgings and food in the college. It was from their ranks that appointments were often made to senior fellowships, but many junior fellows never attained to senior fellowships and left the college. Any fellow who married was required to resign his fellowship.

The fellows were chosen by the heads of colleges and the other fellows, though pressure was often brought to bear upon them by the Crown or by some great man for such and such an appointment. Usually they elected a talented young man who had just taken his B.A. or M.A. from their own college, making him at first a junior fellow. But in some colleges they did not hesitate to look outside, and even to raid the other university.

Ability was not the only consideration in choosing fellows. Of a certain warden it was said that he had a liking for fellows of a goodly personage. Other heads of colleges would choose nephews and sons-in-law, but such nepotism, although common, was frowned upon. What was more common, and quite natural, was to pick fellows who would continue the college tradition.

Piety had once been deemed a requisite in a fellow, but learning was beginning to be more regarded. Students were flocking to the colleges, and their need for intellectual direction had to be met. Probably nine-tenths of the fellows were still in orders, but they were usually clergymen who could qualify in the new situation.

It is perilous to divide fellows into types; they were not only members of colleges that had certain special traditions, but individuals. Yet a few types appear often enough to be mentioned.

The fellows who had strong and pronounced opinions left their mark for good or ill upon policy and figure in the annals of the college. The men of open minds and broad tolerance were rare in those controversial days or, at any rate, were seldom mentioned. We think we can detect now and then men of fineness and generosity of spirit, but such qualities usually escaped the recorder.

More often than not the fellows were men of some modest achievement. They published sermons, engaged in religious controversies, and wrote disquisitions upon this and that. A fellow of Christ's, Cambridge, was said to have been a melancholy man but an excellent commentator on Corinthians. The translators of the King James Bible were largely fellows, or those who had been fellows, Hebraists and Hellenists scattered around the colleges. The achievement of John Preston is interesting to Americans. As a fellow at Queen's, Cambridge, he had attracted the attention of Buckingham, and, had he not been so thoroughgoing a Puritan, might have mounted high in the state. He became Master of Emmanuel College,[8] Cambridge, the graduates of which had much to do with the beginnings of Harvard, and his closely reasoned arguments for Calvinism were carried to New England, and constitute his monument. The achievement of Robert Burton is better known. Living quietly in Christ Church, Oxford, he ministered to a parish in the west part of the city, and pored over old folios. He wanted nothing, he said; his treasure was in Minerva's tower. He gave us *The Anatomy of Melancholy*.

Many a fellow left no mark in print but gave his time and devotion to the college, its routine and ceremonies and properties, and could think and talk of little else. Others were not so hard-working. We may guess that many became, like some in universities today, fussy, old-maidish bodies, taking it easy after forty, and living "like drone bees on the fat of the college." They might prove quarrelsome, and join in a movement against the head of the college, or be drawn into one of the factions that made college politics a continuing game. Thrown a great deal together, they easily accumulated aversions, and when it came to their turn to make commonplaces (small sermons) in chapel, they would choose a text

---

[8] About the influence of Emmanuel College on Harvard, see S. E. Morison, *The Founding of Harvard College* (Cambridge, Mass., 1935).

and condemn certain sins in a way that the sinner could not be mistaken.

Occasionally a fellow was a disappointed man, who had dreamed of greater posts and perhaps just missed them. He might be saved from becoming a soured spirit by a great devotion to the college or to his faith. Others found it easy to sit in the seat of the scornful, to employ dialectical skill in contradicting associates, or to turn serious matters into mockery or make mockery seem serious. The type was to be found still in senior common and combination rooms forty years ago, and has not become quite extinct.

Better men with a deep religious sense maintained a pastoral relation toward their students and left their impress upon them. From the letters of the time we learn that many a student continued throughout his days to show in his life and conduct the spiritual influence of his college tutor.

Few fellows carried on what we would call research. Yet here and there a curious mind was playing with algebraic formulae, or collating manuscripts to determine a text, or searching through ancient and medieval writings to find answers to questions or to support a point of view. It could not have been otherwise where talented men were gathered together.

The fellows had usually five or six pupils, but occasionally a successful tutor might incur the jealousy of his colleagues by having as many as fifteen. He might gain a reputation among certain families who patronized his college and be sought by fathers for their sons.

In many colleges the fellows gave on set mornings stated lectures on rhetoric and logic, on Greek and Latin writers, and on the church fathers. Some of them used summaries rather than the works of the masters themselves and thus offered their students what was called a "compendiary" education. The effect of such teaching may be recognized in dilettante writers of the time who had learned how with superficial study to make an impressive display of learning.

Wiser tutors gave their pupils what they would need afterward. The new type of student who was not interested in becoming a scholar or a clergyman, and who cared little about taking a degree, did nevertheless often crave knowledge and was willing to take pains to acquire it. Richard Holdsworth of St. John's, Cambridge, would assign his pupils such books "as might serve for delight and ornament"; Joseph Mead of Christ's, Cambridge, would ground his students in humanity, logic, and philosophy, and then set each one his daily task of reading according to his particular needs.[9] At the end of the day he would call them together in his room and ask, *"Quid dubitas?"* ("What are you in doubt about?") and would then resolve their questions.[10] A tutor might give a young gentleman books to read which would prove useful to him when he became high sheriff of his county, or he might, probably with no ill intention, set him at works on the ancient tyrants which the gentleman would quote years after in the House of Commons.

The fellow in many cases took charge of the finances of the pupil under his charge, paying his bills to tradesmen and to the college, and doling out money for his extras. In this way he could prevent him from buying more clothes than he needed, from haunting alehouses, and from attending the plays and bearbaitings of the time. However carefully the tutor managed the boy's moneys, he found himself usually out of pocket because he had advanced the money to pay the "battels" and other bills. Letter after letter he would send off to the father, asking repayment, and waiting sometimes a long while for his money.

But the tutor did often manage to be on friendly terms with the family,[11] and regarded such a relationship with pleasure. Lady

[9] I owe these references to Holdsworth and Mead to Mark Curtis.

[10] He would conclude by engaging in prayer with them.

[11] The responsibility of the tutor for his pupil is illustrated by a story about John Preston. When he was still a fellow of Queen's, Cambridge, it came to his ear that one of his pupils, Sir Capel Bedell, an orphan of a very fair estate, was frequenting the home of an ecclesiastical official in Cambridge, Dr. Newcome, and was friendly with Newcome's daughter, "a very proper, wellbred gentlewoman," and was "resolved to have her."

Preston found that he needed to take the air at Saffron Walden and invited Sir Capel Bedell to go with him. By chance he spent the night at the house of old Sir Arthur Capel, the grandfather of Sir Capel Bedell. After the young gentleman had gone to bed, Preston stayed up late in gossip with the grand-

Harley was always sending presents to her son's tutor and inviting him to visit them. The fellow might continue over years his relationship with a former pupil, or he might find that when the pupil had come into the family lands he would take pleasure in snubbing the man who had once governed him.

The fellows were fortunate when they stuck to their forte of finding out good minds. Then as now they were scouts for talent. Football coaches in American universities search no more eagerly for good dodgers in an open field than fellows looked about them for promising young men. The best of them loved a scholar, and when they found one pushed him ahead as fast as possible.

Fellows had incomes that varied much, part of it from the college in the form of food and lodging, and for this and that service, part of it in fees from pupils. Many of them could live fairly well, enjoy a little travel, and add to their libraries. They had a certain security and were likely to retain their posts for life, often past their days of usefulness.

The heads of colleges had by the late sixteenth century become important in the government of the university; in their own colleges they were personages. The Elizabethan government preferred heads of colleges with power, upon whom they could hope to impose their policies without having to deal with the fellows. With power and dignity went spacious lodgings in the college, an ample salary, and a position in the country. The head had been elected usually by the fellows, but not infrequently under pressure from the Crown, and was chosen as one who would be able to speak for the college and give a kind of continuity to college policy. He set the tone of the college, although not without the assistance of the fellows.

A gentle background, or connections with the government, or service to the church or to scholarship, were not looked upon as

father. Sir Arthur was as subtle as the tutor. He asked his grandson to stay over with him, and then persuaded the boy to drop his studies and engage in travel, a diversion seldom rejected by the gilded youth of the time. The rest of the story does not concern us, but it is interesting that Dr. Newcome made great trouble later in ecclesiastical circles about Preston's Puritanism.

undesirable in such a post. Nor was the grand manner unbecoming, such as graced an Elizabethan master of Trinity College, Cambridge, "a splendid, courteous and bountiful gentleman."

The head of a college had to keep a watchful eye on the students; it was best that he should be often in the quad to know their comings and goings. According to gossip, a master might sometimes peep through a keyhole to discover whether the boys were at their reading, or might publicly shear a boy who had allowed his hair to grow fashionably long. There was to be a later Oxford that rejoiced over eccentrics, and seventeenth-century Oxford was not different.

The students came up to the university at a slightly earlier age than today. Boys of fourteen and fifteen were not unknown, but most of the undergraduates entered the university when they were sixteen, seventeen, and eighteen, and some were nineteen and twenty. They were of several categories, not always sharply marked off. In general, at the top were the fellow commoners or gentlemen commoners, the sons of noblemen and great country gentlemen. They dined at high table with the fellows, had commodious rooms, and in many colleges were released from some of the academic requirements. A fellow commoner might bring a servant or two with him, and now and then employed a special tutor to coach him. Anthony Ashley Cooper, who became the first Earl of Shaftesbury, kept both servants and horses at Oxford, and was allowed what expenses and recreations he pleased. He entertained the better sort, and allowed needy students when in distress to eat at his expense.

The commoners were more in numbers. They paid lower fees, were often the sons of economical gentlemen or businessmen, and sometimes received scholarships that paid part of their expense. At the foot of the ladder were the battelers, who came to college with little money, received scholarships sometimes, and in many cases performed various kinds of service as sizars, taberders, etc. They did errands for fellows, carried water, waited on tables, and were themselves served in the kitchen.

The family backgrounds of the students were almost as various as in the world outside. We have seen that the gentle classes were flocking in. So were the sons of well-to-do businessmen in London and country towns. There were more of them, I should guess, than of any other group except sons of clergymen. But the sons of trades-men were also managing to come to the university, and now and then the sons of yeomen.[12] I have never heard of the son of a farm laborer at either university.

It is hard to find more than hints as to the natural groups which boys formed. The good talker was not uncommon. He was always amusing, consorted with his own kind, the "wits" of the university, and was occasionally taken up by the gilded youth. Sometimes he had been advised to cultivate his betters and found it pleasant to do so. In contrast was the quiet boy who devised his own amusements, pored over maps, dallied in bookshops, or roamed the countryside. There was the larger group of boys who worked diligently. They had to do so, because their parents, thrifty gentlemen on small manors, or more thrifty businessmen, gave them skimpy allowances which allowed nothing for diversions. Furthermore, a young man who aspired to a good living and preferment in the church, or to get under the wing of a great man and gain a start in diplomacy or government, knew that he had best win favor with college authori-ties. Even the students who toiled late might allow themselves a lapse now and then and take part in one of the outbreaks connected with the results of a disputation in the "schools," where two colleges arrayed against one another had carried the disputation into a street brawl. Or they might get into a row with townsmen.

The sporting young men were not as conspicuous as in a later day. They spent a good deal of time in fencing and dancing schools, coursed and hunted, played tennis [13] and bowled, and found out the other young men of their own kind. It was said that they studied in jest and played in earnest.

What the boys talked about in their off hours is seldom recorded. We may be sure that they talked religion, for everyone did. We hear

---

[12] On taking a degree they became automatically gentlemen.
[13] The old tennis in an enclosed court and not our lawn tennis.

1. JAMES I

2. SIR EDWIN SANDYS, parliamentarian and a leading figure in the Virginia Company

3. LADY OGLANDER, wife of Sir John Oglander of the Isle of Wight

4. Nottingham and the Trent, one of the earliest English landscape paintings, belonging to Lord Middleton, by J. Siberechts

5. A Farmyard with Figures, showing a yeoman coming home, by Francis Barlow
(Courtesy Crown Copyright)

7. INIGO JONES, architect, producer of masques and Surveyor-General of the Works, painting after Vandyck (Courtesy National Portrait Gallery, London)

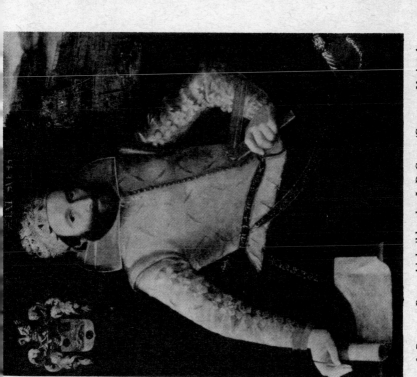

6. PHINEAS PETT, shipbuilder, by J. DeCrety (Courtesy National Portrait Gallery, London)

8. A reading country gentleman. Tomb of Sir Thomas Lucy 2nd in Charlecote Church, Warwickshire. Note the books (all in Carrara marble) in shelves at the back.

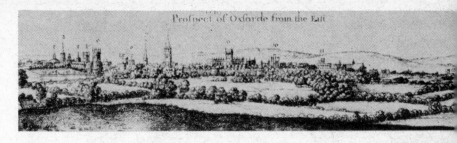

9. Prospect of Oxford, by Wenceslaus Hollar

10. A Small Landscape, engraving by Wenceslaus Hollar. Note the fence, and what may be hop fields.

11. An Old Ruin, by C. de Jongh, who made the wash drawing, circa 1628-30, a rare contemporary picture. On the left is part of an English village (probably in Kent)

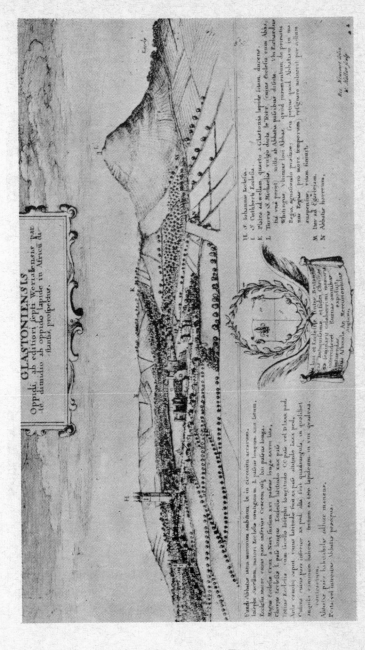

12. A Somersetshire Prospect, by Wenceslaus Hollar

13. A Devonshire Prospect, by Wenceslaus Hollar

14. A Marriage Fete at Bermondsey, from an Elizabethan painting at Hatfield House
(Courtesy of the Marquis of Salisbury)

16. Sir John Glanville, lawyer and Speaker of the House of Commons, by an unknown artist (Courtesy, National Portrait Gallery, London)

15 The House of Commons. From a unique print of the House of Commons in 1625, in the Manuscript Room of the British Museum

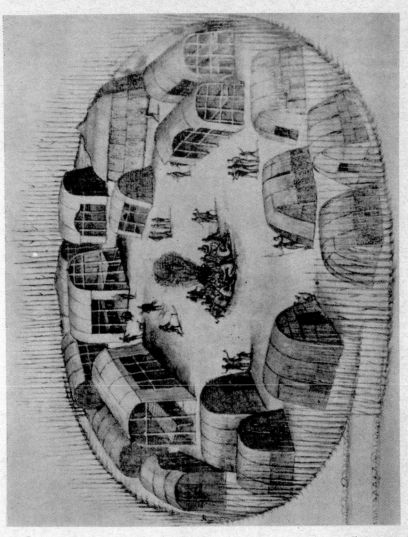

17. An Indian village in Virginia. Copy of a water-color drawing by John White who accompanied **Ralegh. Circa 1585-86**

18. The Thames at Richmond with the old palace in the distance, by
Vinckboons (Courtesy Fitzwilliam Museum, Cambridge)

19. Hunting scene, by Woolton. Late seventeenth-century painting of a
romantic landscape (Courtesy Leggat Brothers)

20 A Haying Scene in the Cotswolds, early eighteenth-century painting of a family property. (Courtesy of the President of St. John's College, Oxford, and of *Country Life*)

21. Windsor Castle from across the Thames, by Wenceslaus Hollar. A country town is in the foreground and to the right.

22. The Royal Exchange, engraving by Wenceslaus Hollar

23. Canterbury and surrounding country, by Wenceslaus Hollar

of a few of them who followed politics, and knew what was happening at Whitehall and Westminster and even in the Lowlands and Germany. As always there were, especially at Cambridge, young men of literary ambitions, who discussed poetry and plays, and were trying their hands at writing them. Did they discuss love and marriage, as in fraternity houses today? If so, the letters they wrote do not show it. Marriage was more than an incident in their future lives, but one their parents had to worry about.

Their daily routine we know better. A college bell wakened them at five in the summer and at six in the winter. Breakfast was usually a light meal and included frequently a draught of beer. Dinner was at eleven and supper at five. Students were not expected to leave the college before dinner except to attend lectures, and, when they did leave in the afternoon, could proceed only in pairs, or in larger numbers. They had to be in by eight or nine o'clock in the evening, and were punished for later arrival, but they climbed over the walls then as now. That they worked long hours in their rooms would appear from the bills they incurred for candles.

The arrangements for housing the students seem primitive to us. A fellow of the college would have about five students who would make up his "company"; he would sleep in the large room, now the student's sitting room, and the five students would sleep on trundle beds underneath and around his bed. The little rooms that are now the bedrooms of students were then used as their study rooms. In this way a hundred and fifty men could be housed in one small quad, which was about all the space that many colleges had. The students and fellows dined in the great hall, a small hall by the standards of today, the fellows and fellow commoners at the high table, on a dais, and the other students at tables around the hall.

Athletics were casual. Football was deemed a hurtful and unscholarly exercise, and often forbidden, but was played. Shovelgroats (shovelboard) was mentioned. Archery had been encouraged by Elizabethan tutors, in accordance with national policy, but is seldom mentioned. The students played at running, jumping, and pitching the bar. At both universities swimming was forbidden and carried on continuously. Probably the standard exercise was the same as it was to be in Matthew Arnold's day, walking. The students walked all over the outlying country.

> Ye fields of Cambridge, our dear Cambridge, say!
> Have ye not seen us walking every day.

And Cowley went on to suggest that there was not a tree in the country unknown to the students.

The graduates of the universities looked back upon their careers there with pleasure, but possibly with less sentiment than we today. Yet Simonds D'Ewes leaving Cambridge set down in his diary: "So, then farewell, dear mother! farewell, dear schools!—farewell, happy lectures!—farewell, faithful friends!" It was the poets he had read while at the university that Marlowe remembered. It was books that George Herbert recalled:

> Thou didst betray me to a lingering book
> And wrap me in a gown.

Thomas Freeman, who came from Gloucestershire, wrote of men's devotion to their own place of origin, but concluded, "My love is Oxford." Many were equally devoted to Cambridge. When Milton sang of storied windows richly dight, he was thinking no doubt of a famous chapel there. Abraham Cowley regarded his life there as a splendid poverty but one with comeliness and beauty.

Former students looked back upon university life with the more affection because afterward they were many of them cut off from such comradeship of talent. Those who practiced law or medicine in London or who took part in affairs of state did not suffer from the want of good men with whom to talk. But a great number of graduates became clergymen in country villages. In a play a future parson laments his imprisonment:

> 'Mongst russet coats and mossy idiots,
> Ne'er shall I hear the Muses sing again,
> Whose music was like nectar to my soul.[14]

---

[14] J. B. Leishman, *The Three Parnassus Plays* (London, 1949), p. 141. *The Return from Parnassus*, Part I, Act I, Scene I.

The graduates had had something done to them that was more than intellectual. A change came over a boy from a "mean" background as he lived in college with others of another kind, and fell under the influence of men of breeding. In a play one of the characters marvels

> . . . to see a ragged clark . . .
> Some stamel weaver, or some butcher's son [15]

become on graduation a sweet gentleman. The son of the weaver learned what availed him much, whether he was to stand before kings or in some country pulpit.

A generation ago it was said that one of the purposes of Oxford and Cambridge was to enroll men of every class and to transmute them into men whose bearing and poise might fit them to serve the church, the state, and the public. That idea was not as clearly put forward in the seventeenth century, but it was implicit in some of the writings. "Manners makyth the man," the old Wykehamist motto, was on the walls of New College.

[15] *Ibid.,* p. 295.

CHAPTER 13

Elizabethan Puritanism

RICHARD GREENHAM, a graduate of Cambridge University and a fellow for some years of Pembroke Hall there, became in 1570 the rector of Dry Drayton, not far from Cambridge, a living with a good income. A Puritan who objected to the wearing of clerical vestments and who was opposed to the nonresidency of clergymen, he was nevertheless careful to avoid all occasions of offense. Intent upon his work, he would rise "as soon as he could well see" to conduct an early service for those going to the fields. He liked to walk over the farm lands and talk religion with the plowmen. He would go into Cambridge and discourse with young men preparing for the ministry. But what made him most remembered was his practical charity. Not only did he sell to the poor straw and grain at far below the regular prices, but he induced the tenants of the village to hire a common granary and lay up grain for the poor. As he rode over the country he was on the lookout for any wandering man who might need help and would send his servant over to give him money. So much money did he give away that his wife sometimes lacked means to pay the harvesters.

Greenham represented Elizabethan Puritanism at its best, in its gentle, otherworldly, and benevolent aspects. Men of his type, devoted and selfless, were not uncommon among the puritan ministry, and their lives afford us a contrast to the world of Drake and Essex, of the Royal Exchange and St. Paul's Walk, of merchant adventurers and roaring apprentices. It is pleasant to leave London and come upon quiet men in country vicarages living for an ideal still dimly understood by the world.[1]

Puritanism was an ideal and a way of life. It was far from static; it underwent considerable changes and it had had an extraordinary continuity. The student who attempts to formulate a definition will find himself perplexed and bogged down with adjectives. It is best rather to attempt a descriptive account of the rise and progress of the movement.

We may start with the radical wing of the Protestants in the reign of Elizabeth, from which Puritanism was to emerge. That wing wished to carry the Reformation far and to put an end to Romish forms and ceremonies. They found it hard to accept the compromise imposed by the Queen and known as the Elizabethan Settlement. To maintain her throne Elizabeth dared not move too far Protestantward lest she offend her Catholic subjects, who might be persuaded to support Mary Queen of Scots in her claims to the English throne and might receive help from continental powers. Nor could she afford to alienate the Reformers who gave her support. The middle-of-the-road position she adopted was the only one politically possible.

But her policy had to be carried out in a kingdom where advanced Protestantism was on the march. The return of the "Marian exiles," that is, those clerics who had fled to the Continent during the regime of Mary and had come under the influence of the Reformers at Frankfurt, Strasbourg, Zurich, Basle, and Geneva, brought numbers and talent and zeal to the Protestant cause. Some of the exiles hoped for great changes, and were ignored by the Queen. Others looked back to the Protestantism of Edward VI and

[1] It is to the biographies of puritan ministers, and of laymen too, that the student should turn who would understand the forerunners of American Puritanism. Those biographies were many, for the Puritans were given to recording the virtues of their worthies as examples to posterity. The reader comes to know about the admirable traits of the Puritans and about those less agreeable; for however sympathetic a biographer may be, he usually tells more than he intends. See, for example, Samuel Clarke's various collections of lives of Puritan divines.

of the Second Prayer Book, and asked only to put an English face upon the church. The more moderate were willing to accept the Elizabethan Settlement, putting up with a certain amount of ceremony and trusting that the episcopal authorities would look with a blind eye upon those who failed to conform in every respect. What they, and those also who wished to put an English face upon the church, were most intent upon was an ideal of practical piety and of the creation of a godly nation.[2]

The zeal for practical piety was no new thing. In the reign of Henry VIII, William Tyndale, the translator of the New Testament, and John Frith, both of them destined to be martyrs, had been zealous to see the Gospel preached in simple terms to the people. They grounded their faith upon the Bible and upon the individual interpretation of it, but had been less eager than Luther and Calvin for a clean break with the past. Their program had been not unlike that of Wycliffe, who in the late fourteenth century sent out young men in long russet gowns, "evangelic men," to preach wherever they could gather an audience.

Thus a Protestantism of preaching and practical piety had a considerable history behind it. In the time of Elizabeth its supporters came to be known as Puritans. As a party the Puritans first showed their strength in the Parliament of 1566 on the question of the succession. They continued to be a power in the House of Commons; they had friends in the Privy Council; they were gaining support in the towns and not a little among the gentry.

They were so strong because much of what they believed was in line with the spirit of the time in England. Men were reading the Bible in translation and taking to heart its injunctions, and gaining thereby a new zeal for active and personal Christianity. Had it not been for the opposition of Elizabeth and of her "little black husband," Whitgift, the Archbishop of Canterbury, and for the vigorous anti-puritan policies of James and Charles, it is possible that, as

---

[2] I owe something in this paragraph and that following to conversations with L. J. Trinterud. See his "The Origins of Puritanism," *Church History,* XX (1951), 37–57.

the danger from Spain and a Catholic revolt in England receded, the Established Church might have gone in a puritan direction. Some of Elizabeth's bishops leaned that way, as far as they dared. It is not surprising. Much of the religious revival which we associate with Puritanism had roots in the medieval English church and even farther back in the church fathers. To understand the religious feeling of the late Tudor period we have only to examine the strict moral regulations imposed upon towns by their rulers and supported by much public opinion and at times by the ecclesiastical authorities. Thus it is hard to draw a sharp line between Puritanism and the naturally religious impulses of the sober-minded English of the time.

But names are useful even if sometimes slightly misleading. It was the Puritans who gave form and cohesion to the religious tendencies of the time. They may be divided into those who came to be known as Presbyterians; those who were called Brownists or Separatists, and later Independents and then Congregationalists; and the much larger group who desired neither to make over the church nor to leave it, but who were nevertheless puritan in outlook.

Those to be known as Presbyterians had adopted Calvin's notions of church government. They believed in a system by which each congregation should elect representatives to larger bodies, and those bodies to a central body. In such a scheme, republican rather than democratic, the power derived from the men at the bottom, from the church membership. The Presbyterians had no wish to break off from the English church. On the contrary they aimed to make it over on their own lines, and thus to do away with the great power of bishops. They managed to erect a kind of skeleton Presbyterian system in some of the eastern counties, but were soon put down.

The Brownists or Separatists were less numerous. From early in the reign of Elizabeth, and indeed before, there had been small bodies of men who believed that the godly should covenant together to worship God in the simplest possible way. Each congregation was to settle its own body of doctrine and each member was to be a judge of the faith and works of every other. The minister was not essentially different from other members of the congregation. Some of those who held these opinions remained within the church, hoping for a better day. Others set up quietly little groups that worshiped together in secret. One of those groups left England for Leyden and a few of them came at length to Plymouth on the north side of Cape Cod.

The larger body of Puritans were those who, neither Presbyterian nor Congregationalist, wished to remain within the church. They were willing to tolerate bishops, although they had no fondness for them, and they had no great urge to make over the church. Like Mr. Greenham they desired to see nonresidency abolished, believing that every parish should have its own preaching clergyman and that no cleric should be allowed to hold several livings at once. Many of them hoped that this and that ceremony might be made permissive rather than obligatory, so that men of many minds as to details might worship God together.

The several types of Puritans had more in common than might be at once apparent. All of them desired a ministry of learned and godly men preaching in every village the gospel of conversion and repentance. Their preachers within and without the church were accustomed to deal with such topics, as were indeed some of the non-puritan wing of the Church. The Puritans stressed more than others what has been called in our country "the old-time religion," a religion of everyday effort for a godly life.[3]

The Puritans believed that the Bible had been given to provide a pattern for life and that it should be followed in every detail. Every sentence or phrase, even in an obscure part of the Old Testament, might offer a clue as to the intentions of Providence about human conduct. It is amazing what incidental statements they could turn up in narratives of the Scripture to guide them as to their duties.[4]

[3] The non-puritan clergy were many of them pious men (see Chapter 6). They relied less upon their sermons to win people; their own lives were sometimes examples to their flock. Their piety was less active, less self-conscious, more restrained and formal, with less emotional drive behind it. The prayers they read from the Prayer Book were less intimate expressions of the soul, but could hardly have been bettered.

[4] The non-puritan Anglicans had equal respect for the Bible. In that work

They did not dismiss the use of reason. Every minister, they held, should be learned in Greek and Latin and, if possible, in Hebrew, and accomplished in logic. With those tools he could examine the original texts, and by the use of reason draw the right deductions. Once the text had been determined aright every word had meaning for man.

The Puritans believed in a daily walk with God. This life they compared to a walk or journey or pilgrimage,[5] long before John Bunyan wrote his *Pilgrim's Progress*. The men who set out from Leyden and landed at Plymouth "knew they were pilgrims . . . but lift up their eyes to the heavens, their dearest country, and quieted their spirits." [6] To walk with God meant to have a mind filled with thoughts of the spiritual life, to give much time to reading the Scripture and to prayer. We were to pray continually, wrote John Preston. God, he said, was not changed by our prayers but we ourselves were changed.

The puritan diaries offer illustrations of that life of prayer. Margaret Lady Hoby in the North Riding kept a daybook [7] which shows us her routine. Long hours before breakfast she was at prayer. Three or four times a day she was on her knees, and, when not there, was likely to be reading the Bible. John Bruen, a Cheshire gentleman, whose daily round has been described by a contemporary,[8] rose between three and four in the morning to spend an hour or two in prayer. Later he would gather his family for morning prayers and the singing of psalms; then he would read a chapter of the Bible to them, and then pray again, bringing before the Lord the requests

God had revealed to man as much as was necessary for salvation. Richard Hooker stated the case for the church in his classic *Laws of Ecclesiastical Polity*. Not every verse and word in the Bible was significant, he thought, for conduct. To search the Bible about small matters was to derogate from the authority and dignity of the Scriptures. We should look to the general meaning. God had given us an outline of His will, to be filled in by the traditions of the church and, by the use of reason and of natural law, the agents of God.

[5] The notion of a pilgrimage can be found in medieval writers.

[6] The life of the Christian was often compared to a warfare. The hymn "Onward Christian Soldiers" expresses a common puritan idea.

[7] Dorothy Meads (ed.), *Diary of Lady Margaret Hoby* (London, 1930).

[8] William Hinde, *Life of John Bruen* (New York, 1857).

of various members of the family. The same routine was gone through in the evening; at that time Bruen gave religious instructions to the family, which included of course the servants.

It is not to be supposed that every puritan family was as devout. But many families had prayers twice a day and much reading of the Scriptures. Those more pressed with their daily labors were likely to be less regular in their devotions, unless they were in trouble.

The Puritan was not afraid of offending the Almighty by asking for His interposition in personal matters. At the same time he expected that God would give indications of His will toward him and was on the lookout for signs of God's pleasure or displeasure. When he took one of two roads and learned later that highwaymen had been waiting on the other, when a tree fell close to him but without touching him, or when his horse stumbled and threw him but without hurt, he marked his escapes as signal mercies and proofs of God's favor. When he had an illness in the family, or misfortune of any kind, he examined his life to recall what sins he had committed. When Ralph Josselin, an Essex minister, lost his ten-day-old child, he speculated in his diary on what had been his shortcomings. His mind, he decided, had been given up to the unseasonable playing of chess, and he resolved to be more sparing in that recreation. Some vanity in his thoughts he recalled; perhaps he had been puffed up by praise of his sermon. He had been negligent, he feared, in instructing his family.[9] This diary belongs to the reign of Charles I, but such self-examination was characteristic of earlier Puritans.

The zealous Puritan watched the health of his soul, as some of our friends watch their blood pressure. Like some medieval Catholics,[10] he believed in meditation—his spiritual advisers were

[9] *Diary of . . . Ralph Josselin* (Camden Society, 3rd ser., XV, London, 1908), pp. 46–47.

[10] The connections between Puritanism and the old church before the Reformation merit more examination. It is in the local records, in churchwardens' accounts, etc., that the changes of the Reformation can best be seen. Occasionally one observes that the families who had been zealous in all the activities of the parish church before the Reformation were a generation or two later among the earnest puritan families of the now reformed church. Devout families they had been, and their sons or grandsons had now embraced Puritanism. But

always encouraging it—but his meditations tended to become self-conscious. He recalled those gracious days when he had known himself to be in communion with the Everlasting and those dark days when the face of God had been turned from him. Richard Rogers of Wethersfield near Braintree in Essex kept a diary [11] in which he recorded the ups and downs of his soul; he found old and new corruptions; he was unsettled and unprofitable.[12]

The Puritan believed in the careful use of time. At his back he heard always time's winged chariot. Much time ought to be reserved to the use of God and the remainder should be devoted to one's calling. In that calling it was his duty to earn a good living and support his family. The more earnest Puritans frowned upon such pastimes and worldly pleasures as interfered with their occupation. Much casual evidence could be adduced to indicate that they were the best of workers. An examination of almost any center where skilled men were turning out cloth and other commodities, where business was humming, would show that by the last years of Elizabeth the inhabitants were largely puritan. Whether their activity was the result of their form of faith, or whether the more active of the artisan and trading classes took up with a religion of zeal and effort, would be a question deserving consideration.

The case of the east counties seems to point both ways. The people of Essex, Suffolk, and Norfolk were among the most up-and-coming citizens of the realm. A good stock originally, the population had been augmented by Flemish and Huguenot craftsmen of ultra-Protestant backgrounds. For that reason and others Puritanism

conclusions about such matters must await much publication and analysis by local historians.

[11] See Marshall Knappen, *Two Elizabethan Puritan Diaries* (Chicago, 1933), a book that deserves reading by students of early American history.

[12] The worries of Josselin and Rogers may leave the modern reader a little cold. He must never forget their sincerity. But there was often an unpleasant display of zeal among Puritans. When the Banbury butcher and the Northampton shoemaker paraded their spiritual moods and quizzed others as to theirs, they were likely to find themselves figures of fun in their communities and to be satirized by the less godly. The canting weaver and the unctuous glover rendered the "Precisians," or extreme Puritans, ridiculous to many. See Thomas Nash's many gibes at them in his writings.

flourished in those counties, and they were also hives of industry. It was that part of the country from which ships were filled for Massachusetts Bay.

The Elizabethan Puritans are often represented as disapproving all forms of diversion, a notion little borne out by the literature of the time. Many were devoted to music and made much of it in the home. Some of them in towns were as fond of singing madrigals as they were of godly sermons. Dancing, if between the sexes, was frowned upon by some puritan writers, but many middle-class puritan families sent their children to learn dancing. As for bowling and such sports, the puritan gentlemen and yeomen took their turns at such diversions with others.

Some of the interference with the pleasures of the individual commonly attributed to puritan intolerance [13] was the result, as already hinted, of the law of the land and of administrative policy in country and town. The statutes forbade the use of dice and cards in the alehouse. They forbade men to spend more than an hour at one time in such resorts, or to indulge in excessive drinking. In some counties the justices of the peace were active in suppressing church ales because those celebrations led to drunkenness and worse consequences. The borough authorities were usually unfriendly to the traveling companies of players, and would prevent their performances, unless they were members of the Queen's company, or that of a great nobleman. Those borough rulers may or may not have been puritan; they were afraid that the poor would spend too much money and spend it outside city walls.[14]

Puritan opposition to the theater was not yet clearly evident. It is true that before the end of Elizabeth's reign puritan voices had begun to be heard in criticism. John Rainolds, the admired president of Corpus Christi College, Oxford, was opposed to stage plays be-

[13] In this and the next paragraphs I owe much to Marshall Knappen's *Tudor Puritanism* (Chicago, 1939), but something to my own reading of puritan literature.

[14] It could not be said, however, that those administrative policies of the boroughs were uninfluenced by the moral yearnings of middle-class townspeople, who were ready at all times to be their brothers' keepers. These moral yearnings made them readily susceptible to puritan preaching.

cause men had to wear women's clothes in the female parts. But he took a stronger position than most Puritans of his time, who were inclined to point out abuses in the theater, but were not yet ready to condemn it. After all, the morality plays put on by the church were not far in the past.[15]

About the Sabbath it cannot be said that the Elizabethan Puritans differed from the non-puritan Anglicans in theory. The subject was one about which opinion had not yet crystallized. In the reign of Henry VIII, John Frith had been opposed to sabbatarianism. It was said by some that holiness on one day rather than another was a Romish superstition; others thought that Christ had spoken out plainly against the Jewish Sabbath, and that the Fourth Commandment did not bind the Christians as it had bound the Jews. Such an influential Puritan as William Perkins took a fairly moderate view of the obligations of Christians on the Sabbath.

There was, however, a growing support for the opinion that the whole of the Sabbath should be given up to religious duties and works of mercy. The Rhineland Reformers, whose effect upon England was considerable, were taking up that point of view. A rigorous exposition of it was soon to appear in England. Launcelot Andrewes, then head of Pembroke Hall, Cambridge, where Puritanism flourished, and later himself to be one of the saints and glories of high Anglicanism, gave in 1580 a series of lectures on the Commandments and took a strong line on the observance of the Sabbath. He quoted St. Augustine, but could also have quoted medieval Catholic writers. In general, however, the theological writers, puritan and otherwise, had not a great deal to say about the duties of the Sabbath until the last decade of the Queen's reign. The account of what happened then belongs in the next chapter.

[15] Marshall Knappen (*Tudor Puritanism*, p. 440) makes the point that the Puritans were less critical of the plays of the time than of the acting profession. It was not always made up of devout and prayerful men. Between the playwrights and the "Precisians" there was a kind of war. The playwrights were always making fun of them; sooner or later the Precisians were likely to think less than well of the playwrights.

CHAPTER 14

Puritanism Under the Early Stuarts

THE STORY of Puritanism under the first Stuarts might easily have been different and have come to a happier conclusion. Had the Crown only been willing to give some small degree of toleration to the Puritans, who by the end of Elizabeth's reign had become modest in their requests, it might have prevented that great fissure in English life which revealed itself in the Civil Wars and was evident for two centuries afterward. The Church of England might have become a comprehensive body drawing all groups to it and gathering within itself the best of English religious idealism. But these are might-have-beens, in the use of which the historian should be economical.

The Puritans, harried in the last years of Elizabeth's reign, had hopes from the new King, James I, who had been brought up on Calvinist doctrine, and they made immediate overtures to him. In October, 1603, James called the Hampton Court Conference to discuss ecclesiastical matters and invited four of the more moderate spokesmen of the Puritans to state their case. The meeting in the early weeks of 1604 availed them little. James had had enough of Presbyterianism and realized moreover that the Calvinistic form of church organization fitted ill with royal power. During the Conference he heard language that stirred memories of his unhappy education under the Presbyterian George Buchanan. He plumped against the Puritans. Puritan ministers were to accept the ceremonies and trappings of the church or give up their livings. Even the reasonable demands for a learned clergy, for the doing away with pluralities, and for the abolition of nonresidence were rejected.

About three hundred clergymen had to surrender their livings. Here and there a minister who had support in his community, or was protected by an important figure, was able quietly to evade the use of such ceremonies as he disliked. The larger body of clergymen of a puritan tradition conformed, but many of them went on teaching puritan doctrine.

The conforming puritan clergy included some of the most talented men in the church, men who had made records at the universities and had tarried there long enough to ground themselves in Greek and Hebrew. They were eager to set an example of Christian living. Not a few of them refused better places and wider recognition in order to shepherd their country flocks.[1]

They were busy preachers and have left behind them large accumulations of discourses. William Haller and Perry Miller have rummaged carefully and understandingly among these sermons and their conclusions are of interest, for the thoughts of Perkins, of Preston and Dod, and of others were carried to New England.

These men did not discuss the abuses of the time, enclosures, patents of monopoly, and corrupt administration. They stuck close to the Bible and what it taught; they were concerned with election and grace, with God's covenant with Abraham, and with man's duty. About heaven and hell they had less to say than might be expected; they were dealing with the Christian's pilgrimage through this world. Texts they expounded, and then fell upon the "application." They preached practical divinity, encouraging their hearers in the godly life or beckoning them toward it. They were not "affectionate" preachers, as the Scottish ministers of two generations later, who would set their audiences a-weeping, but they did charge their words with emotion. In the main the sermons seem to have

---

[1] But a few of them received lectureships, which were often better paid than the places they had held before.

been worked out logically and in orderly fashion. If many of them were pedantic and wordy, others were phrased in simple and direct English.

For the preachers were intent on being understood by the common people. Their illustrations and figures of speech were drawn from the field and from everyday life. William Perkins had urged the men he sent out from Cambridge to speak simply, and John Preston had given the same advice. It was said of Mr. Capel that he would stoop so low as to speak to the poor country people in their own dialect.[2]

Yet they had some hard matters to set forth. Foreordination or predestination, which in Elizabethan times had been accepted by most churchmen, was now upheld particularly by the Puritans. It was no new doctrine; it was as old as St. Augustine (354–430), and had been supported by St. Thomas Aquinas (1225?–1274?). It was hard to oppose in logic. No limits could be set to the power of God. Therefore He must from eternity have known and foreordained the future. He must have determined the course of every man's life, and whether the man would embrace salvation and in consequence be saved, or reject it and be condemned to everlasting punishment.

The good Puritan believed that at his conversion he had received grace and become one of the elect. Lady Harley, who wrote letters to her son at the beginning of the Civil Wars, recalled that she was one of "the dear elect," [3] and that assurance fortified her in all her troubles. Mrs. Hutchinson, who lived in about the same decades, tells us that her husband was thankful to God, who had been pleased to choose him out of the corrupted mass of mankind. But the realization of his good fortune did not produce "a carelessness of life in him, a thing generally objected against this faith." His assurance did not cause him to relax and indulge in the pleasures of this world. Rather it "excited him to a more serious and strict walking." It was likely to do so. The elect had the Almighty on their side. In

[2] Samuel Clarke, *A Collection of the Lives of Ten Eminent Puritan Divines* (London, 1662), p. 252.

[3] Not all Puritans were so certain of their election; a few of them worried themselves into illness, lest they be not among the elect. One reads of pious souls, more often women than men, who went into melancholia.

the war with the forces of evil they were in the long run sure to prevail. Thrilling it was to be the chosen of God and to work in cooperation with Him. It roused them to exert themselves to the utmost.[4]

The doctrine was all very well for the elect whom God had chosen for his own, but hard on all others. Hence some of the Puritans developed the theory of the Covenant. It was not wholly a new idea; it was to be found in the writings of William Tyndale.[5] But Perkins, Preston, Sibbes, and Ames developed the notion and their ideas were carried to New England and worked out still further there. Perkins had declared that if the most infinitesimal element of faith was in the soul, that was the work of God's spirit. Man could start the labor of regeneration as soon as he began to feel the merest desire to be saved. This lessened, says Perry Miller,[6] the area of man's inability to win grace and gave the preachers a chance to encourage him toward his regeneration.[7]

It was a theory that took the curse off predestination and gave the sinner grounds for hope. Whether the average Puritan thought much about predestination may be doubted. He assumed his own election and let it go at that. But the theologians wrestled mightily with the problems of foreordination and continued to do so in New England up to the middle of the eighteenth century.[8]

To their task of winning the unredeemed and of ministering to those within the fold the Puritans brought purpose and enthusiasm.

[4] Foreordination offered a philosophy to its adherents. God created things themselves and their circumstances and times. All history flowed from His decrees.

[5] See L. J. Trinterud, "The Origins of Puritanism," *Church History,* XX (1951), 37–57.

[6] I am following Perry Miller closely. See "The Marrow of Puritan Divinity," *Publications of the Colonial Soc. of Mass.,* XXXII (1937), 247–300, especially p. 255.

[7] John Preston stated the theory: "Thou shalt believe, thou shalt take my Son for thy Lord and Savior, and thou shalt likewise receive the gift of righteousness." When the man realized the goodness and mercy of God, his opinions, his disposition, and his affections were altered, and his heart melted toward the Lord and became soft and tractable. Out of an ingenuity and willingness he came and served the Lord with alacrity and cheerfulness.

[8] See the writings of Jonathan Edwards.

They believed with all their hearts, and that belief was contagious. Dr. Edmund Staunton used to greet his associates in the morning: "Come, friends, what shall we do for God this day? How shall we trade with our talents for the furtherance of his glory?" They were impatient to get on with the Lord's work, forgetting that good verse in Scripture, "He that believeth shall not make haste." No occasion did they overlook to bring saving grace to the attention of their fellows. When a puritan minister sat down at an inn table he would engage the man across from him in conversation and work around to an inquiry about the state of his soul. When the eager Staunton met with others he would divert their merry and idle tattle into a serious and profitable discourse, introducing some "heavenly argument." From heavenly argument the Puritan could turn to rebuking sinners, even those of quality. Such men lived in a state of continuous excitement and conveyed that excitement to the more impressionable.

The puritan layman was hardly less intent upon God's business. In a play Mistress Aurelia complained that her Dorcas, as she dressed and curled her, sought to talk religion with her. Country gentlemen would quote St. Paul to their servants and tenants. Ignatius Jurdain, a puritan merchant from Exeter, was riding back from a meeting of Parliament in the company of a man of honor when the gentleman invited him to pass by the inn and lodge for the night at his house. Jurdain had heard the gentleman swear and stipulated that he would not stop with him unless the gentleman would promise that neither he nor his wife nor his servants would swear while Jurdain was in the house. The man was good-natured and agreed. Then Jurdain demanded further that next day, which was the Sabbath, there should be a sermon not only in the morning at the parish church but one in the afternoon. His long-suffering host accepted the terms.[9]

The zeal of Thy house hath eaten me up, said the Psalmist, and many of the Puritans could have echoed that boast. But the burden of winning England to their point of view fell upon the ministers.

[9] Clarke, *Ten Eminent Puritan Divines*, pp. 468–469.

That campaign went on steadily from the end of the Hampton Court Conference (1604) to the Long Parliament (1640).[10] Frustrated in their aspiration for a simpler and more Protestant national church, they set out to preach an evangelical Christianity, a religion of prayer and the reading of Scriptures, of meditation and self-examination.

The puritan clergy not only preached but had their sermons published. Other sermons taken down in shorthand were transformed into manuscript copies and passed from person to person, and were often caught up by printers and published. In those days men bought sermons with the avidity with which today they buy detective stories.

Whenever a puritan worthy died, the sermon at his funeral was likely to give an account of his or her daily walk with God. It was in the reign of Charles II that Samuel Clarke began publishing the lives of puritan clergymen and laymen and found a ready market for them. But even as early as the reign of James I the records of puritan lives, even the spiritual diaries in which good Puritans recorded their experiences, were circulated.

The "lectures" were part of the campaign. From Elizabeth's day on, the Puritans had been arranging lectures on Sunday afternoons and on weekdays in churches and elsewhere.[11] Some of the lectures were endowed and often well endowed. Men would sometimes give their services as lecturers in towns adjacent to their parishes. We catch glimpses of Cambridge fellows planning a series of lectures in the country round about. Dr. Harris and his brother-in-law took advantage of every festival and fair in their part of Oxfordshire to make the Word known. "Oh what a fair of souls was then held at Hanwell and Banbury by these two brothers! How did religion then

[10] It is the great contribution of William Haller that he has traced this campaign and shown its effects.

[11] The scheme of lectures was perhaps an outgrowth of the "Prophesyings" which had been developed in Zurich as early as 1525. Those Prophesyings were originally for the training of clergymen, but the English lectures were, says Trinterud, for the edification of the people. See his "Origins of Puritanism," p. 46.

flourish and professors thrive like the calves in their stalls!" [12] Borough after borough would vote money to support lecturers, who would supplement the work of the local clergyman by giving sermons at other times than his, and sometimes in spite of his opposition. Of the Earl of Huntingdon in late Elizabethan days it was said that he wasted his patrimony in support of "the more fervent sort of ministers."

Where were the bishops and archbishops during this campaign? Why did they not put down the lecturers? Sometimes indeed they did. In other instances they seemed afraid to antagonize the authorities in important towns and even less anxious to cross swords with well-known country gentlemen. But when William Laud, who was relentless about deviation in ceremony, and who feared neither mayors, country gentlemen, nor noblemen, began in the reign of Charles I to show his hand, the lecturers found their opportunities severely limited. All preachers of the slightest puritan leaning had to walk quietly lest they be haled before the Court of High Commission.

By that time, however, the Puritans had done their work; they had won a great deal of support among the more religiously minded people of England. The inclination of the solid citizens of the towns toward Puritanism, recognizable in Elizabeth's reign, was even more evident in the reigns of the first Stuarts. Francis Osborne reported that the more conscientious gentry were styled Puritans, by which he means no doubt those more interested in religious matters, and that statement could be supported at length. That some of the yeomanry, following the lords of the manor, had embraced Puritanism would appear from the records of local societies. As for the humbler classes, the Puritans had not as yet awakened to the possibility of evangelizing them. [13]

---

[12] Clarke, *Ten Eminent Puritan Divines,* pp. 284–285.

[13] Eventually the puritan preachers touched the ignorant classes. At Cartmel in Lancashire John Shaw preached in 1644 to thousands of people, as he said, who were very ignorant and yet receptive. One man who listened to him had heard of Christ only through a Corpus Christi play. No doubt many such people had never seen the inside of a church. By the reign of Charles II the Nonconformists were reaching some of them.

As the Puritans won more support in the country, they might have been expected to water down their opinions in order to make them more acceptable to the wider public they were reaching. It was not so. The driving zeal in the Calvinistic faith caused them rather to intensify their attitudes.[14]

The attitude of the Puritans toward the Sabbath had undergone a change in the direction of greater strictness, a change already evident in the closing years of Elizabeth's reign. The lectures of Launcelot Andrewes, already mentioned, had probably been heard or read by the good Richard Greenham of the same college in Cambridge. In 1592 Greenham brought out *A Treatise of the Sabbath*. No book of the age, wrote Thomas Fuller, made greater impression on people's practice. The Sabbath, asserted Greenham, was to be given up to spiritual exercises, meditations, and conversations, and to works of mercy. No work should be done on that day except the care of beasts, feeding them and watering them and milking the cows. Men were to be allowed to prepare meats for their own sustenance, but must engage in no feasts. As for harvesters and those sowing seed who, in times of rainy weather, might wish to take advantage of a fair Sunday, Greenham would have none of it. About shepherds and drovers he was a little uncertain, but thought that in any case they ought to attend church.

Greenham's son-in-law, Nicholas Bownd, used his father's notes and published in 1595 a large book, *Sabbatum veteris et novi Testimenti, or the true doctrine of the sabbath,* which amplified Greenham's views, and became the textbook of Puritans on the subject. By now the Church of England was evidently prepared to take a lenient view of the observance of the Sabbath, for Archbishop Whitgift called in copies of Bownd's book and summoned ministers before the ecclesiastical courts for preaching its doctrines. From this time on sabbatarianism became an issue between Puritans and High Churchmen.

[14] They were afraid of the return of Catholicism. People used to come to the reverend Mr. Carter and ask: "What do you think? Shall we have Popery again or no?"

The Stuart period saw the Puritans deeply committed to a Sabbath of wholly religious activities. The zealous Ignatius Jurdain, as mayor of Exeter, was able to stop the mills running and to put down the selling of fruit on that day, and his policy was pursued by other mayors and aldermen.

The matter of the use of Sunday afternoon became presently a controversial one between Puritans and their opponents. In 1616 James I on his way down from Scotland was waited upon in Lancashire by a delegation of servants, laborers, and mechanics, who complained that they were estopped from all recreations on Sunday. James needed no coaxing to utter pronouncements and the chance to encourage Sunday sports was not to be resisted. The upshot was the Book of Sports authorizing the people to enjoy themselves on Sunday afternoon. It was ordered to be read in all churches, an intended affront to the Puritans. Their ministers, like others, had to read it, although here and there a daring clergyman failed to do so.

Toward the theater the attitude of the Puritans was hardening. That the plays of the time of James I and Charles I had become licentious was no doubt one reason, but then the plays of Elizabeth's reign had not been stuff for green girls. The preachers had little to say about the subject, but zealous Puritans were more and more eschewing the theater. William Prynne, who represented the fanatic fringe of Puritanism, soon to exhibit itself, wrote with such abuse of plays and actors that he has been thought of ever since as the spokesman of puritan opinion. It is the fate of causes which become unpopular with posterity that they are judged by their extreme protagonists.

The Puritans were becoming more ascetic in outlook at just about the time when a few of them were embarking for Massachusetts Bay. One can hardly doubt that the stricter type of Puritanism was carried overseas. It is possible that the Puritans in New England, cut off from the main currents of English life, were more fanatical than their brethren in England.

It has become almost a convention to assume that the Puritans had bad manners and no sense of beauty. A more recent charge is that Puritanism was allied with capitalism. It is said too that the Puritans with all their godliness were not much interested in social questions and the problems of poverty. About these matters some comment is called for.

Those who dwell upon the absence of good manners among the Puritans can find much to support their judgment in the interference of the zealous with their neighbors. The aggressive type of Puritan was inquisitive, offered unwanted advice, and frowned upon the pleasures of others. The "do-gooders" in every generation are a trial to those who wish to live within their own castles. It has been observed that the Puritans were considerably recruited from the bourgeois classes. Neither Exeter merchants nor Norfolk clothiers nor Wiltshire wool buyers had the graciousness and poise of a Hampden or a Falkland. On the other hand, no better manners could have been found than among the gentle families of puritan tradition, quiet unassuming people with a courteous bearing toward all. In other words, manners were largely a matter of class rather than of religious outlook.

The Puritans have been censured for being unresponsive to the claims of beauty, and with justice. The charge deserves qualification. It is true that the beauty of holiness set forth by William Laud, the communion table set in orderly fashion with spotless linen, the stately ceremonies inherited from the old church, gave them no delight. They preferred sermons and exhortations. They had little time or interest to spare for the manifestations of the beautiful in any form because they were taken up with an active and continuous religious life. If they had imagination they did not allow it play in matters artistic. Few of the English of that generation did.[15] Yet there were some whose imagination was caught by form and color and rhythm, and among them Puritans. John Milton's father, a London scrivener, was devoted to music and skilled in the composition of it and gave his son every chance to develop his great talents.

[15] The sporting and hunting gentry cared as little for beauty in nature and art as they did for the puritan way of life.

There were puritan country families, as the Hutchinsons, who had a sense of beauty, whether expressed in line or shape.[16]

The idea of a connection between capitalism and Puritanism has been worked out by Max Weber as part of an interesting attempt to formulate a kind of philosophy of history, and has been taken up and modified by others. Weber began by thinking of capitalists as those devoted to making more and more money as an end in itself. This attitude, he found, flourished in communities that were Calvinistic. Later he restated his theory somewhat differently and in Germanic and sociological language not easily translated into simple English. He found that the Protestants and in particular the left-wing Protestants, that is, the Puritans, enforced a strict moral discipline upon their adherents which tended to develop certain traits of character, some of them ascetic. A man esteemed himself as he succeeded in meeting the norms set up for him, as he proved himself before God, attaining salvation, and as he held his own in his sect. It was to his interest as an individual to conform to the Puritan point of view and to propagate it. Hence individual motives and personal self-interest were directed toward maintaining and pushing the Puritan ethic. The men so imbued were admirably fitted to become capitalists.

It is easy to discover connections between Puritanism and capitalism. Were not the prosperous classes in London and the larger towns largely Puritans? The Puritans were hard-working, as they were taught to be; they were thrifty, they did not waste their substance on the vanities of this world, and were thus likely to save money and accumulate capital for investment. Some Puritans did indeed become capitalists, and moneyed men were often Puritans. There is also a connection between Puritanism and middle-class morality, but middle-class morality in England was older than Puritanism. Weber's theories are stimulating and provocative and cannot be

---

[16] The simplicity which Puritans affected in attire and in their homes, as opposed to the pretentiousness of the time, has some bearing on the question of Puritans and beauty.

ignored, but leave out many factors in both capitalism and Puritanism.[17]

The want of interest in social questions on the part of the Puritans, up to the middle of the Civil Wars, has at once to be recognized. Like their contemporaries they believed in an orderly hierarchy of society, in the degree and order set forth by Shakespeare. An occasional clergyman of puritan outlook inveighed against the gentry for pursuing their pleasures and for living idly, but neither he nor anyone else would have thought of doing away with that class. One of the straitest of the Puritans, in discussing the Sabbath, opposed feasts on that day, but made an exception of noblemen and great personages "because they represented in some measure the majesty of God on earth." [18]

The puritan preachers did insist, however, that men ought not to strive for great riches. Few, they implied, gained much wealth without the oppression of the poor. As for those who had too little, the Puritan had no social remedy to offer, but he might have gone into his own purse, or have collaborated with his fellow aldermen in voting money to the poor of the town.

Those who have described the Puritans have not said enough about their attitude toward women. It was of course much the same as that of others. Few there were, men or women, Puritans or non-Puritans, but would have accepted the duty of women to obey their lords and masters. It was written in all the old books; it was tradition and custom. Who had not heard the ballad of the Patient Griselda? For the subordination of women the Puritan could point out verses in St. Paul and abundant passages in the Old Testament, which reflected of course an eastern notion of the female; they could cite

[17] For example, the dynamic urge in Calvinism and among Puritans was directed less toward making money than toward bringing about the kingdom of God on earth. For a brief critique of Weber's earlier forms of his theory, see the introduction to Marshall Knappen, *Two Puritan Elizabethan Diaries* (Chicago, 1933). For more detailed criticism of Weber's entire theory by one not unsympathetic, see R. H. Tawney, *Religion and the Rise of Capitalism* (London), Preface to the 1937 edition, pp. xi–xix; also chap. IV and footnote 32 to that chapter, pp. 315–317.

[18] Nicholas Bownd, *A Treatise of the Sabbath* (London, 1595), p. 211.

William Gouge's *Domesticall Duties,* John Dod, and a host of commentators on Scripture. What is more, the wives never questioned their inferior status. Mrs. Hutchinson wrote of the just rule of her husband, "which it was her honor to obey." Lady Harley, who laid down the law to everyone in her castle and community, not only bowed to her husband's least word but stood in awe of him.

Yet the Puritans expected consideration for women. It was the duty of husbands to love their wives and to have due regard for them. It was even suggested that they should make financial allowances for them, as some puritan gentlemen did, and give them a certain control over the household. What is more significant, puritan writers had a great deal to say about the family and its unity. From diaries and biographies [19] one gains an impression that husbands and wives in their common effort [20] to bring about the kingdom of God on earth lived happily with one another. A common purpose was the best of all ties.

The Puritanism here discussed, most of it within the church, came to an end with the Civil Wars (1642–48). Those wars and their consequences brought to the front Presbyterianism, Independency, and other sects. We hear more of the Anabaptists; we read of Fifth Monarchy Men; Unitarians and Quakers appear on the scene. Not all these sects were puritan, but they were part of the indication that Puritanism was breaking into pieces. In itself it had been dissent from approved opinion, and now it was becoming dissent from dissent.

The variety of sects and opinion was a necessary outcome of puritan teaching. In going back to the Scriptures the Puritans had not been able to avoid the notion of the equality of all men before God. That was strong meat. Sooner or later it had to come to pass that Harry the tinker and Dick the tailor, who nowadays could read

[19] The Puritans in their biographical sketches did not leave out the godly women.

[20] Philip Stubbes of the *Anatomie of Abuses* tells of a woman who would be constantly "conferring, talking, and reasoning with her husband . . . asking him, what is the sense of this place, and what is the sense of that? how expound you this place?"

for themselves, would search their Bibles and find texts to suit them, and develop their own interpretations. In the agony and stress of the wars Harry and Dick decided that they were as able to preach as the learned men from the universities, and acted upon that belief. Puritanism came to cover many ideas and to have lunatic fringes.

With the Restoration (1660) Harry and Dick went back to their trades, and the lunatic fringes of Puritanism faded out. The Church of England came into its own, and good churchly gentry in Parliament put through the harsh Clarendon Code, which drove Nonconformity underground and made "conventicles" or meetings of any religious group except those of the Church of England illegal. Richard Baxter of *The Saints Everlasting Rest,* Edmund Calamy, Oliver Heywood, and all that devoted group had to hold their services secretly in private houses and were in and out of jail. Thanks to them and to others, who carried on in spite of persecution, Nonconformity, the lineal heir of the left wing of Puritanism, was spread widely among the artisans of the north and elsewhere. It took on more emotion and warmth than had been characteristic of Elizabethan Puritanism, but the Calvinism was still there, and the emphasis upon the daily walk with God.

With the Revolution of 1689 the Nonconformists received the blessings of toleration. The Presbyterians and the Congregationalists and other dissenting sects, such as the Baptists and Quakers, found wide support among the business classes in towns as well as among the small tradesmen and artisans. By mid-eighteenth century, Methodism appeared on the scene and was to gain a great following, especially among the working classes. It sprang from the Church of England, but had its pietistic roots in Moravia. It was an emotional faith far removed from that of the early Puritans, but not unlike that of the Nonconformists of the reign of Charles II. In some ways it resembled Puritanism, and it ranged itself eventually in the ranks of Nonconformity, as a collateral descendant of Puritanism.

The same may be said of a similar movement, but within the Church of England. The Evangelicals, who first appear at the close of the eighteenth century, became in the nineteenth century a powerful religious force. They captured the same type of religiously minded people among the merchant classes and even among the more serious gentry that Puritanism had won in the late sixteenth and early seventeenth century; they were indeed the spiritual heirs of that large body of Puritans who had remained within the church. They and the Nonconformists of all types, including the Methodists and the Quakers, became the bearers of the Nonconformist Conscience so powerful throughout the nineteenth century. The Nonconformist Conscience was behind the antislavery movement and social reforms of many kinds, behind Shaftesbury and Chadwick. It arrayed itself against the crasser forms of imperialism and opposed the Boer War. It was something the Continent could never understand and suspected as merely another form of English hypocrisy, like Puritanism. But above all it was something truly and characteristically English.[21]

From Wycliffe and his russet-gowned young evangelists to the Nonconformist Conscience is a long road and yet its course can be traced. It is like one of those upper New England roads where the old highway veers off now and then from the modern motor route and becomes a grassy path through the blackberry bushes that leads back eventually to the main thoroughfare. Puritanism had some magic out of the old church and something handed down from Reformers before the Reformation; it gathered zeal and drive from the returned exiles. By the later sixteenth and early seventeenth century it became a living force in English life and its influence lasted to the end of the nineteenth century and a little longer. Thus an English thing in its origins and evolution, it affected the character of the English. More than any other single factor it explains the differentiation of them from their continental cousins. It is a fashion in England nowadays to decry Puritanism; those who do so are

[21] That the Puritans hoped for the best of both worlds has been said so often with much illustration that it needs no elaboration here. We have all known Englishmen and Americans who were part saints and part men who missed no chances in this world. For an old-fashioned and whole-hearted denunciation of Puritanism, see Hippolyte A. Taine, *A History of English Literature* (New York, 1889), II, 202–221.

reviling that element in their inheritance which makes them most English.

Across the Atlantic Puritanism had its breathing center in New England, where divines made it even more formidable than in its old home and gave it something of a philosophic content. It was carried west by New Englanders to the Western Reserve, to the lands north of the Ohio, and at length to the new fields across the Mississippi and beyond the Missouri. It was reinforced by the Presbyterianism which the Scots and the Scots-Irish brought with them across the Appalachians and down to Virginia and through the Cumberland Gap to Tennessee. In the nineteenth century Puritanism with its many variants was a living force in the American scene. The Nonconformist Conscience had its equivalent here in the fierce, if intermittent, moral impulses of the public. Possibly the last great expression of American Puritanism was Prohibition, which the Elizabethan Puritans would have looked upon as passing strange.

Only within the last two generations has American Puritanism been losing its hold. The closing line of the song "Fair Harvard" runs: "Till the stock of the Puritans die." Today that stock is being outweighed by others and Puritanism is becoming a phenomenon for historians to examine and appraise.

CHAPTER 15

The Kingship and the Privy Council

TODAY the King of England is a symbol. He is the head of the government; laws, decrees, and appointments come forth in his name. He is also the head of the British Commonwealth of Nations and the one living tie between those independent nations. The new Queen, Elizabeth, is one of the greatest figures in the world and yet has no real part in making laws and would today hesitate to offer a suggestion about the appointment of a minister of state or of a bishop. That is the English of it. They delight in old forms but know how to give them new meanings. Their ruler is no longer a ruler but the embodiment of the state, one above parties and in general above criticism, to whom unreserved loyalty can be given.

In the early seventeenth century the sovereign was a great deal more, but then as now he was a symbol. He was the personification of the state, the anointed of God, a being of sanctity, and a legend. The ballads sold by Autolycus and sung in innyards and at fairs were full of the encounters of cobblers and tinkers and men from the greenwood with disguised royalty, and of their "amaze" when they learned with whom they had been talking.

As today the King was the focus of loyalty. He was an exalted and gracious figure to whom watermen and apprentices, merchants and squires, gave devotion. Even those intelligent enough to be critical wavered but rarely in their loyalty. The business classes suffered from the foolish policies of James I, but believed nevertheless in the good will of the Crown and laid the blame for their wrongs on evil advisers. The gentry and nobility found it hard to see Scots and favorites step in ahead of them at Court, but they were reared in the tradition, Fear God and Serve the King.

In the preceding reign the great Elizabeth had done nothing to lessen the loyalty to the Crown nor to impair its dignity. She would clap Hodge on the shoulder and talk familiarly with him and yet lose none of her queenliness and state. As for her progresses through the country, they were carried out with pomp and circumstance and punctuated with words brief and fitting. Her successor lacked her common touch and her air of majesty. He was afraid of Hodge lest he carry a knife. He lacked her feeling for her people en masse. "Your Queen did talk of her subjects' love and good affections," wrote an observant courtier in 1611 to Sir John Harington, "Our King talketh of his subjects' fear and subjection." His mind seldom strayed from the most interesting subject, his own importance. Even his pictures betray his self-satisfaction. His gait, a kind of strut, was like his talk.

He had no need to insist upon his greatness. Did not earls kneel before him and carve his meat? His progresses from place to place were attended by a large following. His Court was made up of lords and ladies-in-waiting, of members of the Privy Council, of such nobles as happened to be in London, and of favorites and their friends.

He was the fountain of honor. He dubbed men knights and thus "ladified" their wives; he created peers of the realm. In awarding titles Elizabeth had been sparing, but James delighted to give them to those near him and to those who would pay a round sum. He was further the giver of offices. He had at his disposal many posts of dignity and influence. The highly born and the courtiers looked to the beneficent bestower.

It was a role pleasing to James and he took an unpleasant advantage of it. "He hath found," wrote John Chamberlain, "the art of frustrating men's expectations and holding them in suspense."

When an important vacancy was about to be filled and everyone in Court was awaiting the outcome, he would send for someone known to be a candidate and before all the beholders make so much of him that the happy man thought himself as good as appointed and accepted the felicitations of his friends. At that point the King would drop him and take up someone else. There was in his character not only a Scottish taste for the dramatic but an element of subtle cruelty.

The power of making grants of money value to friends and favorites enhanced royal authority. That power James exercised constantly. All kings, said Francis Osborne, cast away money the day of their enthronement but James all his life. The story of the patents he conferred will be told in another chapter. He was equally lavish with the Crown lands, especially to his Scottish followers. The English wished also to be served and courtiers whispered, Give, give. Even great nobles with wide acres felt aggrieved if James did not bestow more manors upon them. He had no Scottish thrift in his make-up but a Scottish weakness for pleasing.

Eventually he got himself so far in debt that he could not raise the money to pay his long-suffering ambassadors or his other officials. When men who supplied him with goods found themselves arrested for debts incurred in his behalf and asked the King to pay them the thousands he owed, so that they could get out of prison, he would not reimburse them but give them instead letters of protection against their creditors, for six months at a time.

The King was the fountain of justice. To him belonged the naming of judges, though for those nominations he depended much upon the advice of the Lord Chancellor. The judges were his, and ought, as he saw it, to defer decisions in critical matters until they heard from him. He did not understand the common law nor the significance of old decisions as a guide to new ones. He was familiar with the civil law, or the Roman law as used in Scotland. When the judges hesitated to obey him, he showed royal anger and most of them agreed to comply with his requests. Sir Edward Coke, a man not unlike James in his self-importance, attempted to preserve the freedom of the courts and was severely handled and at length disgraced. James went a long way toward subordinating the courts to his will, and his successor went still further.

He was the supreme governor of the church. Archbishops and bishops, deans and lesser men with fat livings, owed their appointments to him and many of them looked for better posts. It was the part of wisdom to support him in ecclesiastical policy and in other matters.

The King was in charge of foreign policy, and was sometimes willing to listen to advice from councilors, but sought none from Parliament. His projects might, however, involve war and thus require many subsidies, and Parliament was reluctant to vote them unless allowed to discuss the reasons for them. James had precedents to support his view of his control over such matters and he believed that he understood diplomacy better than others. Had he not always been familiar with the European world? The peace with Spain in 1604 had been to his liking and he had come to fancy himself as a peacemaker. By the magic of his "kingcraft" he would save the Palatinate for his son-in-law, Frederick the Elector Palatine, and marry his son into one of the great royal families, that of Spain. It was a naïve idea and the outcome did not redound to his glory. The Elector Palatine was left in the lurch and the ill-considered jaunt of Prince Charles and the favorite Buckingham to Madrid to win the Spanish Infanta came to nothing. The young chevaliers came back with bedraggled plumes, crying out for war with Spain, while the bonfires blazed forth the exultation of the public at the failure. Even more inept was the diplomacy of Charles, who involved himself in war with both France and Spain.

The relations of James to Parliament will be dealt with in the next chapter and can only be touched upon here. James was accustomed to the Scottish Parliament, a very different body, and one of no great significance. In talking to the two Houses at Westminster he never grew weary of likening them to a body of which he was the head and informing spirit. In that simile he was not wholly wrong. He had indeed historically certain controls over Parliament. It was his right to call it together and to dissolve it when he pleased. He or his servants chose the Speaker. All the laws passed by the two Houses had to be approved by him and could be rejected. Furthermore his councilors had by old usage a considerable right of initiating legislation.

From the beginning he never had Parliament in hand and the decline of his influence over it was progressive. He patronized the members, speaking to them in a fatherly kind of way as if to inexperienced boys. He promised reforms "on the word of a king," and meant what he said only at the moment. He could talk oncomingly of freedom of speech in Parliament and then at the end of a session pack plain-speaking members off to prison. When things went ill with his plans he would whine and bluster and threaten. There was no least touch of that benignity and disinterestedness which good men crave to recognize in those to whom they would offer loyalty.

He could not, in any case, have ordered back the mounting waves that were breaking against the sea walls of prerogative. Too many able and informed gentlemen were willing to speak up in the Commons in good Norfolk or Sussex terms. They knew to a hair how to preserve the forms of deference, and yet to sidetrack legislation upon which the King had set his heart, and how to delay voting subsidies.

One could almost be sorry for the man. He was a spender, of course, but he did need money, much more than the two Houses ever gave him, and they could have afforded to give him twice or three times as much as they did. He had a good record in Scotland behind him; he had been more than a competent sovereign there, and had reduced a turbulent people to some order. Shrewd and unscrupulous, he had strengthened the position of the Crown, to the advantage of all. But when he came to the English throne he had an entirely new situation with which to deal. England had been long unified and needed no strong hand. He did not understand the English and their way of talking things over and of finding some common-sense solution in the middle. He had much uncommon knowledge but no common sense. Moreover, he was too old and tired to adjust himself to new men with ideas of their own, and to new ways.

He was fortunate during his first years in his chief minister, Robert Cecil, who had been brought up in Elizabethan statecraft by the elder Cecil. James could leave much to his "little beagle," as he called him. Once, when Cecil was ill, James had written him with unwonted graciousness that if anything happened to his Lord Treasurer there would be no good hunting for the King of England. But when in December 1610 the proposed Great Contract between King and Parliament failed to come off, James put the blame on the faithful Cecil and retained him in office with only the appearance of power. In May 1612 that great minister died to the relief and joy of the jealous little men around the King.

For a short time James tried to be his own secretary and dictated letters, but the hunting field called and would not be denied. The Privy Council would relay matters under consideration to Sir Thomas Lake, who was with the King in the country, and solicit the royal judgment. James would come in from a long day in the field and offer suggestions which would be at once sent on to Whitehall. Occasionally there would be two or three councilors with the King; at such times there were in effect two Councils, the one at Whitehall and the other in the country.

Before Cecil's death James had taken on as a favorite Robert Carr, a handsome young Scot on his way, and presently created him Earl of Somerset. In the words of Archbishop Abbott, looking back much later, the Kingdom groaned under the triumvirate, Northampton, Suffolk, and Somerset. Northampton was Henry Howard and Suffolk was his nephew, Thomas Howard. The new favorite cast his eyes upon Frances Howard, the daughter of Suffolk and grandniece of Northampton. She was the wife of the Earl of Essex and divorce was no easy matter. But the Howards were powerful. A commission was appointed and the titillating details that were given it entertained the prurient King and the Court. The lady secured her divorce and married Somerset in a ceremony that was the event of the year. The new Countess of Somerset could not forgive Sir Thomas Overbury, who, as a friend of Carr, had advised him against the marriage. When, through the influence of her great-uncle, she was able to have Overbury shut up in the Tower, she succeeded in making away with him. Eventually she was found out and, with her husband, tried and convicted. That blow to the power of the Howards was followed by the imprisonment of Suffolk for appropriating as Lord Treasurer large sums of public money.

Meanwhile James had had another good-looking man called to his attention, George Villiers, who became eventually Duke of Buckingham. James was still interested in foreign policy, but not in much else except his hunting. As he grew feebler he was inclined to give Villiers a free hand, and that agreeable young man was not unwilling to take control and, with the help of his mother, to look out for relatives and friends and to feather his own nest. The King retired slowly into the background, and we hear of him sitting at the door of his hunting lodge and watching deer driven before him. Near the end he grew suspicious of Buckingham, but he no longer had the will to interfere.

By the early twenties reflective men were becoming saddened and looked back wistfully to the reign of Elizabeth. A new sovereign, however, offered a chance for subjects to hope for better days. It was not long before wise men realized that things were not to be better under Charles, who leaned heavily on Buckingham. The new King was more attractive than his father and had much better manners. Although only five feet two in height he carried himself well and with dignity; in the Van Dyck portraits he looks a noble figure. His interests and his tastes were worthy of a king. Even his devotion to the high Anglican faith was becoming, had he not been determined to impose all its ritual upon all his subjects.

His mind had no edge. In his portraits one seems to read the sadness of a confused and worried being who did not know his way. The eyes are those of a dull-witted man. In his youth there had been concern about his backwardness. He had no imagination to enable him to see other points of view or to put himself in the place of others. He had no sense of men and situations, no antennae to catch from the air the waves of opinion. He was a weak character, emotionally unstable and dependent upon others, upon Buckingham and then upon Laud.

From his father's experience with Parliament he had learned nothing. He believed in an absolute monarchy and had no patience with the Commons. He had no capacity for concession and no magnanimity. He was opinionated and so unwilling to listen to plain speech that none of his advisers dared tell him that he was turning his subjects against him.

In March, 1629, he dismissed Parliament and set out to rule on his own with the help of Laud and of an able man, Thomas Wentworth, who became Earl of Strafford. For eleven years he managed to carry on, almost unaware of the tension in the country. When he tried to extend the Laudian high-Anglican ceremonies to Presbyterian Scotland, he roused rebellion, as he might have anticipated. To find money to resist the invasion by the Scots he had to summon Parliament (1640), and then the devil was loose.

Even after that he might have retained his throne had he shown consistency and firmness of policy. Instead he vacillated between a strong line and sheer weakness. He became angry; he had spells of weeping; he behaved like an unhappy child. His opponents learned that by enough pressure they could frighten him into yielding; he was terrified by the shouting apprentices outside the House of Lords, who had no doubt been sent there to frighten him. He sacrificed his best servant and gave away constitutional rights that belonged to the sovereign. Some compromise might have been arrived at between him and his subjects could they have trusted him, but at the beginning of his reign men had discovered that there was no truth in him and that promises meant nothing at all. He did not set out to deceive; he was too simple to understand the meaning of truth and of promises. His policies did have one effect that concerned the New World; they made some men ready to take ship for Massachusetts.

The Privy Council was the administrative organ of the Crown, a body associated with the sovereign and with him exercising wide powers. During the reign of Elizabeth it had been made up of from twelve to twenty or so members, but in the two following reigns it was expanded until there were over forty members. Many members did not attend regularly and most of the work was done by about fifteen or twenty men. The Council developed a system of appointing committees for this and that business. It was provided with a lord president and a clerk. The clerk recorded letters, orders, and some proceedings in the Register. He gave no account of the discussions, and all we know of them is from a few notes by members and from occasional letters in which one member of the Council describes to another what happened at a recent meeting.

In consultation with the King, who had the final word, the Privy Council dealt constantly with foreign affairs. The ambassadors were sent elaborate instructions and wrote in return detailed statements of what they had said to the rulers of foreign nations and of what had been said in reply. The French were detaining English ships; the Dutch were at odds with the English about the East Indies; the Italian cities were in negotiation about the Mediterranean trade. Not all such matters came before the Council. The King might make decisions himself and send instructions without consulting them.

Many other kinds of business came before the councilors. They were concerned about the great companies; they were worried about gold leaving the country; they were alarmed when they were told that Dutch ships were better built for carrying freight cheaply, and that English ships, of which there were never enough, were being sold abroad; they were distressed that timber which might be used for making ships was spent in smelting iron. English shipping was fundamental to the realm.

The oversight of the clothing industry came constantly within their purview. From 1616 on the declining market for cloth caused anxiety. The sudden unemployment of hardy and skilled workmen affected the country from Devon to Norfolk, and in the North as well. Something had to be done and the Council tried a Canute tactic. It sent letters to the justices of the peace to compel the clothiers to set the poor to work. Loyal clothiers did the best they could, for a time, but could not keep on making goods for which there was no sale.

In the long depression that followed the Privy Council dealt also with employers in difficulties. Samuel Salmon in Suffolk employed over two hundred people in the clothing business and was pressed by his creditors. Helen Manning, widow, of Culmstock in Devon used three or four hundred people and was unable to pay her debts. The Privy Council asked justices of the peace to deal effectually with their creditors and to make equitable agreements to put such useful citizens on their feet again.

The Privy Council moved to protect the Flemish and French émigrés who had settled in the east counties and were developing the new draperies there, bays and sayes, but were encountering the jealousy of native clothiers. It had to deal with the great controversy between Shrewsbury and Oswestry as to the Welsh woolen trade, which centred on Oswestry and which Shrewsbury was trying to take away from its neighbor town.[1] It kept a watchful eye on the middlemen of the clothing industry to see that they did not make undue profits.

The Council interested itself in the mining industry: in the new alum mines, in the lead mines of the Peak country in Derbyshire, in the copper mines of what is now called the Lake District. The coal mines of Durham and Yorkshire were a constant source of quarrels, and many petitions relative to those quarrels were sent on to the Council. Near Carlisle there was a strike of two hundred men who had combined not to dig peat or turf unless they might have their wages raised by a quarter. Such combinations were punishable by law, and the Commissioners on Mines Royal and the Bishop of Carlisle were ordered to examine the disorder, discover the ringleaders, and punish them with severity. Complaint was brought by the mayor and burgesses of Newcastle that the diggers and traders

[1] See T. C. Mendenhall, *The Shrewsbury Drapers and the Welsh Wool Trade* (Oxford, 1953).

of coal under a certain patent were mingling black earth with coal, and three important men were named to investigate the charge.

Harbors and rivers concerned them. Yarmouth badly needed new harbor works and the cost was more than the borough could sustain. The Council ordered "effectual" letters written to gentlemen and others in Norfolk and Suffolk and in the city of Norwich asking them to contribute to the project and arranged for a general collection throughout the kingdom. It never occurred to councilors that the government itself should help with such undertakings. Let the burden be put upon the rich. The River Foss in Lincolnshire needed opening up and scouring, "to the enlarging of trade," and certain great lords and knights and gentlemen in the county were solicited to give.

The Privy Council kept an eye open for new resources and new methods. In September, 1623, the Board renewed and extended an earlier order authorizing leases to anyone discovering new mines. Earlier in the same year it had listened to a proposal by Levine Van Hack, who promised that he would melt more lead and extract a greater quantity of silver from the same amount of ore than the workmen of Sir Hugh Middleton ever did. Two knights with experience in mineral matters and two others in the neighborhood of the mines were appointed to make a report. The Council was interested also in Vermuyden's plan to drain the fens and, in spite of the opposition, which it had anticipated, supported the project.

The Privy Council watched over food and drink. The existence of too many alehouses in any one town was bad and too strong ale was to be discouraged. Too much drinking raised the price of malt and thus the price of grain for the poor. The Council would hear of bad meat sold in London and would at once send peremptory letters to the butchers. It heard of a patent granted surreptitiously by which eating houses could sell ale without selling food and declared the patent invalid.

The activities of the Privy Council were so various that one could fill a book with them. On the whole the members were performing useful services, looking after matters that needed immediate attention. The councilors had the welfare of business in mind, they listened to the wrongs of the poor, and they were above all concerned to maintain order. As a body the Council had a tradition to maintain. We may suspect that the men who had grown old in the Civil Service kept other members to their work and pointed out customary procedures. What they failed to do was to look ahead.

The Privy Council watched Parliament.[2] The members were the King's servants, whose duty it was to forward such legislation as he desired. A great deal of time was spent in discussing whether a Parliament should be called at such a time, or not, and how many subsidies should be asked for. When Parliament refused to vote the money needed, or was dismissed by the King before the subsidies had been passed, the Council would send out seals and attempt to press the well-to-do into giving to the King in an extraparliamentary way. What is more important, it was interested in how public opinion expressed itself in debates in the House of Commons. As members exposed abuses the Council was likely to do something about them.[3]

One notices that the Council made more and more use of commissions. Three or four or five men would be named to make an investigation and to report. Such men as Bacon and Sir Edward Coke were constantly placed on commissions to investigate difficult matters. When the Council was puzzled as to what action was best and hesitated, the members found it easy to put the matter off by naming a commission. Some matters were ticklish. The King had possibly been induced by a favorite to grant a patent which was against the law and was doing harm to an important trade. The Council could not very well overthrow the patent without careful examination, and even then might find it hard. Not all commissions brought in reports and some of the reports offered temporary solutions. It would seem characteristic of the Council that it tried to alleviate the pains in the commonwealth rather than to develop long-term remedies.

[2] See D. H. Willson, *The Privy Councillors in the House of Commons, 1604–1629* (Minneapolis, 1940).

[3] See Chapter 16.

The nervousness of the councilors about riots over enclosure and over unemployment is interesting. There was no real danger in the reign of James I of any rebellion in the country, but there had been considerable danger in the time of Elizabeth, and old civil servants were easily alarmed. They had the recent Gunpowder Plot in the back of their minds.

The Privy Council was supported by two subordinate bodies, the Council of the North, which had its seat at York, and the Council of Wales and the four border counties, which had its seat at Ludlow. Each council had a lord president, a great nobleman in that part of the country. Various nobles and country gentlemen were members of the Councils and each Council had a body of underofficials. Each performed functions much like those carried out by the Privy Council, watched out for disturbances and riots, kept an eye on recusants and disaffected people, inquired into economic troubles, exhorted sheriffs and justices of the peace, gave orders about musters, and kept tab on all that was going on in its part of England.

It is hard to define the relation of the two subordinate Councils to the Privy Council. There was no sharp line of demarcation between the work done by the superior body and by the inferior. The London group did not hesitate to interfere in very small matters and might fail even to tell the subordinate Council what it had done. Occasionally the Privy Council sent an order to the lord president of the subordinate body, apparently to him alone, commanding him to do a certain thing. He was informed of its decision in a matter and told to investigate further, and to carry out its decision, unless he found reasons for not doing so, in which case he was to report back to London.

More important than the subordinate bodies was the inside group within the Privy Council. That group began to be evident about 1618 and centered round the committee on foreign affairs. The members of the committee were not yet called a Cabinet, but they were said to deal with "cabinet counsels," that is, with secret matters Not until the reign of Charles II did such an inside group become a fairly fixed body that was to develop into the Cabinet.

CHAPTER 16

Parliament

"WE BE the gentry:—an abstract of all the . . ." said a member in Parliament in 1610, and the last word is missing, but I suspect that he meant, "of all the commonwealth." That country gentlemen should speak for the nation seemed right to him, and would have seemed right to almost everyone in that time. The gentry were, as we have seen, the accepted leaders of their communities. In the county elections the shire chose gentlemen from prominent families who were in touch with London, and who were likely to be more than usually intelligent. The boroughs, often small-townish in their attitudes when they elected men to represent them in the House of Commons, thought it natural and even wise in most cases to go outside their limits and to pick country gentlemen in the vicinity,[1] or with some connection with the borough. The men the boroughs chose were among the better men of the gentry, usually reading men; men of that type were more interested in coming to Parliament. By the end of Elizabeth's reign many members were university men and not a few of them had continued beyond the

[1] The election of neighboring country gentlemen by boroughs was not a new practice, but was becoming more common in the Tudor period and very common in late Tudor days. The boroughs could save paying expense accounts to their representatives and they could secure members who might have influence and be able to put through such private bills as were desired. As the House of Commons became an assembly largely made up of such men, it was inevitable that it should show more spirit and more resistance to royal wishes. The gentlemen were accustomed to influence at home and were certain sooner or later to expect it at Westminster.

university at one of the Inns of Court. Thus England had in her legislative body a somewhat elite group. The colonists who came to the New World found it natural to choose their representatives from the same type.

A certain number of businessmen were elected to the House of Commons, generally merchants from London, Exeter, Barnstaple, Hull, York, and other towns of importance. These men, possibly a bit overawed by the mass of gentility around them, spoke little; but when bills affecting their interest came up they said their say. Probably they had a good deal to whisper to leaders when matters that concerned the export trade were in debate. Lawyers were more in evidence than merchants, barristers from London and the country (often younger sons of gentlemen). Their usefulness had long been recognized, especially on committees for framing bills. Sometimes a committee included "all the lawyers of the house."

Country gentlemen, merchants, lawyers, and a few others added up to something less than 440 members at the beginning of the reign of James I. Seldom was the actual attendance over 330, and that number was unusual. Toward the close of a session the numbers present fell off to less than a hundred.

The membership included two knights of the shire from each English county except Durham and one from each Welsh county. The burgess members were over three hundred, four from London, two from nearly every English borough that had the right of representation (five boroughs sent only one), and one each from the twelve Welsh shire towns.[2] There were also fourteen "barons" from the seven Cinque Ports and, a new thing, two representatives of each of the universities.

The representation by boroughs was very unequal. Many "decayed" boroughs with but a few inhabitants still elected two burgesses,[3] while some fairly important towns were without repre-

---

[2] The shire towns in Wales were associated in the election with certain contributory towns.

[3] James himself referred to the representation of Old Sarum in Parliament, with its few inhabitants, as an abuse, thus anticipating late eighteenth-century parliamentary reformers.

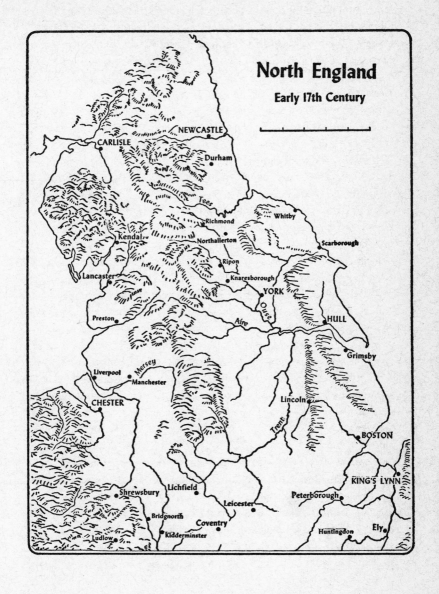

North England

Early 17th Century

sentation. Furthermore the number of parliamentary boroughs was unequally distributed as to counties. Such counties as Cornwall, Devon, Dorset, Wiltshire, Hampshire, and Sussex had a disproportionately large number of boroughs with the right to elect members, while other counties close to London and populous, such as Hertfordshire and Kent, had few boroughs with representation.

The knights of the shire were elected at a meeting of all men holding at least forty-shilling freeholds, called together by the sheriff. In boroughs the electors were in many cases a limited number of townsmen, a group of interrelated business families who managed the affairs of the town and constituted a kind of self-perpetuating oligarchy. One can read between the lines that the committee of privileges of the House of Commons was quietly throwing its influence, wherever possible, in favor of a wider franchise in towns.

Serious efforts are being made at present, under the auspices of Parliament, to analyze the character of the membership of the Commons throughout its history. The nearer those studies come to recent times, the more useful they will prove, and a comparison of the membership at different periods will afford some opportunities for generalization. It will be interesting to know about the membership of the Lower House in the reign of James I, what was the age, the wealth, of each man, how many had been to the Inns of Courts, and how many to the universities. But not all the answers can be given with enough assurance to make averages dependable, and the answers, if they could be given exactly, are hardly as important as they might seem. Some sixty or eighty men, no more, may be said to have done all the work of the House of Commons. It is in these men that we need to be interested, the little groups among them and what went on in those groups. Now and then we catch hints as to such inside circles, and that is all; it is just those social data that people did not put down on paper. We shall learn only enough to whet our curiosity and allow us pleasant speculation.

Alas that we have only one picture of the House of Commons in the early seventeenth century. The rare print we can look at in the Manuscripts Room of the British Museum shows Vandyked men sitting close together in a narrow chamber, St. Stephen's Chapel. When those sober-looking worthies came together their first duty was to elect a Speaker; they always chose someone suggested to them by a spokesman for the government, and not necessarily a well-known person or even one familiar with the ways of the Commons. The Speaker was an essential and important figure. It was he who by manipulation could push bills forward or find ways of delaying their progress. It was he who decided which man rising to address the House should be recognized; it was he who could rule that a man was not talking to the point, or was indulging in unseemly language. On the whole he was tolerant; he understood the tradition of the House—still a living one—that members behaved with informality.[4] If a member who was speaking became tedious, or wandered from the subject in hand, or uttered words not agreeable to the mood of the House, he would be "hawed and hemmed" and even shouted at. The Speaker seldom intervened to quiet the House or to discipline the man addressing it.

Next to the Speaker the Clerk was the most important official of the House of Commons. Appointed for life by the Crown, he took charge of bills, marked on the back of each bill, after its second reading, the names of the committee for the bill, and the time and place of the meeting of the committee. The whole business of writing out bills, of inserting amendments between the lines, and of engrossing bills when they reached the proper stage was in his hands. Furthermore he kept a journal of proceedings in which he set down the several readings of bills, and the messages to and from the King, etc. In the early Stuart period he was including in his record summaries of some of the speeches of members, but gave that practice up in 1628. It is fortunate for historians that some members were keeping notes, a few of them in shorthand, and others with prodigious memories writing up at night the speeches of the day. From such diaries we learn vivid details as to what was being said in the Commons. We can catch some notion of the ways in which

---

[4] The easy manners of our House of Representatives may be an inheritance from the English House of Commons.

men were thinking on political matters, of their methods of talking back and forth; occasionally we can light on the inception of ideas that were later to assume importance.

From these diaries we can easily discover that about twenty men took the leading roles in the Commons and that four or five might be called bellwethers of the flock.

There had not been much leadership in the old House of Commons. In the dim days, about which records are few and uninforming, the government seems to have indicated to the Commons what subsidies were needed and what laws should be passed. Now and then the Commons "grudged sore" the subsidies asked from them, and occasionally voted less money than demanded. A few of the measures put forward were rejected, and such rejection implies some leadership of men outside the government.

We begin to be more sure of leadership when opposition comes to be definite and continued. In Elizabeth's reign, from the early days, when the succession question was up (1566), to the last years, when the Commons pushed the Queen about patents (1601), it is evident that the opposition was more or less continuous and must have been well led.

From the volumes J. E. Neale [5] is writing about Elizabethan Parliaments we shall learn more about that opposition. Meanwhile we cannot but notice that it synchronized with an increasing interest by members in all the affairs of government. That increasing interest is easily understood. It was a new kind of House of Commons and these country gentlemen had recently been given greater powers in local government. As never before they were aware of what was needed in the way of laws to stop up loopholes and to strengthen the hands of justices. They could not be expected to be ciphers, as their predecessors seem largely to have been. They had suggestions to make, and were becoming less reticent about making them.

The new religion and the desire to promote it were pushing them further. The majority of the Commons in Elizabeth's reign and in

[5] See *The Elizabethan House of Commons* (London, 1949); *Elizabeth I and Her Parliaments, 1559–1581* (London, 1953). Another volume is being written.

the reign following were puritan in sympathy. They were fearful of the return of the Roman Catholic Church and thus constantly worried about the succession. They could not perceive as well as we can, looking back, that Elizabeth had to keep the middle of the road religiously. When in the last two decades of Elizabeth's reign Archbishop Whitgift became assiduous in disciplining puritan clergymen, the Commons were not happy about his policy. When James I after the Hampton Court Conference [6] turned sharply against the puritan clergy and threatened to harry them out of the land, there was anxiety among members of the Lower House. When Laud with the zealous support of Charles I began to enforce high Anglicanism, members of Parliament were mistakenly fearful that he was leading the country back to Rome.

But while the Puritans, many of them moderate men devoted to the Church of England, feared for the future and tended to be critical of the government, they furnished in the early years of the reign of James no solid front of opposition. Nevertheless an opposition was slowly forming. Over the projected union with Scotland, where national feeling was easily roused, Sir Edwin Sandys was able to muster a large group and manipulated matters smoothly and shrewdly to frustrate the King. By 1610 an opposition now centered on purveyance, wardship, and impositions [7] was exceedingly vocal. An attempt at a compromise, by which the King gave up some of his old feudal rights in return for a large sum of money, came to nothing. Meanwhile (1604–10) the opponents of the King were coming to be known as "mutineers," "commonwealth's men," and "the popular party," but they were far from being a well-organized group.

They were strong enough, however, to make the King and his councilors stop and think. Should a Parliament be called in 1614? Money was sorely needed. The councilors wavered as to what should

[6] See p. 156.
[7] Purveyance was the exaction from the subjects of provisions and cartage for the royal household, or its equivalent in money. Wardship was the right of the King to administer the estates of minors during their minority. Impositions were special import and export duties set by the King without consent of Parliament.

South England

Early 17th Century

be done. Bacon was optimistic. The opposite party was, he believed, now dissolved and broken. The members should be severed from one another by rewards, or intimidated, or held in hopes; the lawyers in particular should be made afraid to oppose the King.

The news from the country was not reassuring to those in Whitehall. Some of the royal servants who had labored for places in the Commons had been told by gentlemen of good quality that "all the shires are disposed to take care that none of his Majesty's servants be chosen." An anonymous correspondent wrote that people had not forgotten the last Parliament and were taking exception to all that had in any way a dependence upon his Majesty. It is hard for us fully to accept those statements. The country was not wholly happy about the King's policies and friends, but most of the voters were only slightly conscious of problems at Westminster.

By 1621 the leaders of the Commons were arrayed in opposition, and had little trouble in gaining and keeping the support of members. In the first three Parliaments of Charles I the opposition, now sometimes called "the country," was clearly a stronger body than those called "the courtiers," and there is evidence that the politically minded public was with them.

While the opposition was growing more definite and more outspoken, the issues were shifting. The abuses of purveyance and wardship had nòt been abolished after the meetings of 1610 and 1614; but while they were mentioned in 1621 and 1624, they were no longer pressed. On that issue the King had worn out the Commons. The attack on impositions led by Whitelocke and Hakewill in 1610 was taken up again in 1614, and had echoes in 1621 and 1624, but the Commons failed to win concessions. They had indeed been reviving the old effort to prevent the King from levying money without consent of Parliament. That effort took new forms in 1624, and in the first years of Charles I. But Charles took tonnage and poundage without grant by Parliament and continued the impositions. Over free speech the battle lasted longer. James and Charles would wait until the end of the session of Parliament, as we have already seen, and then shut up those who had been too outspoken.

By the time another Parliament met, the prisoners had long been released, and it was an old story. On that question, as on taxation without consent of Parliament, the King seemed to have the best of it.

It was not so. Whatever might happen to them at the end of sessions, members of Parliament were expressing themselves more openly and frankly. They were winning the battle of free speech simply because they were speaking more freely, and about everything connected with government. They were even forcing the King's councilors to discuss in Parliament the very things the King wished them to avoid discussing. They were making the House of Commons into a platform where public opinion could find its vent. They were widening the functions of the House.

So eagerly were they inquiring into abuses that officeholders dreaded an approaching Parliament. Those who believed themselves wronged were now bringing their cases to the attention of the Commons. In London organized groups, such as the apothecaries, the skinners, the grocers, were printing statements of their cases and circulating them to the members of committees. In Elizabeth's time they would have sought out a friendly Privy Councilor and laid their troubles before him. To councilors they still went, but they were pinning their hopes upon Parliament.

That the eyes of the country were turning toward the meetings at Westminster is increasingly evident in the letters of the time. The lady in the Herefordshire castle, the parson in Cambridge, and the gentleman in the Yorkshire dales craved news of it, and were supplied by friends in London. By 1626 the speeches of prominent members were being slipped to stationers, copied by them, and sold. By 1629 stationers were selling a weekly news report, in manuscript, of the course of proceedings day by day with excerpts from speeches; these little bulletins were often included by men in town in their letters to friends in the country, and sometimes inserted cleverly in the text, as if part of the letter.

Members of the Commons House were becoming more aware of their constituents, and of the desirability of pleasing them. Sir

Herbert Crofts tried his best to stand by his sovereign, but explained to a royal official that by so doing he was offending his constituents. The opposition in the Commons was not without support in the country.

Members were becoming more aware of one another. They were naturally, every one of them, devoted to their own counties. But experience in Parliament, now much more varied and significant than in the old days, was serving to break down much of that shire outlook.

When Sir Faithful went up from Devonshire to Westminster he learned that members from other shires, with local loyalties as intense as his, were after all men of his own kind. Some of them were cousins of his, or cousins of cousins. Sir James, whom he had met on a committee, was a Somerset man, but knew his brother-in-law. Sir John, with whom he happened to sup at the Seven Stars off Fleet Street, and who was on the same committee, was a Gloucestershire man, but kin to Devonshire friends. Both Sir James and Sir John thought the King was going too far. They talked sensibly, and mentioned to Sir Faithful abuses in their counties which he had seen in his. The more he thought and talked about it, the more he was inclined to go along with the committee in the statement being framed in answer to the King. Gradually, in committee service he was finding himself a working unit of an assembly that was dealing with the affairs of the Kingdom and he discovered, almost with surprise, that such affairs were as compelling as those of Devonshire. No loyalty is so binding as that of common service. Sir Faithful was becoming a House of Commons man.[8]

The committees on which Sir Faithful and his friends served were more important than in former generations. Step by step the House of Commons was developing committee machinery that was to prove useful. In the early years of the reign of James I the Speaker of the House had constituted himself a kind of royal agent and had used every means he knew to block opposition and to further the aims of

[8] That Parliament was meeting for a much longer session than in earlier days meant that men would become more interested in its workings.

the King. The Commons were not unaware of his maneuvers and hit upon a device to sidestep him. Since the last decade of Elizabeth's reign they had been using larger and larger committees. The committee on the subsidy had been made up of most of the members of the House, and had met in the afternoon. Usually it was provided that anyone who wished could come. The committee was nearly the same body as the House. What was more natural and easy than to formalize a large committee and make it into a committee of the whole house? Such a committee was developed in 1607, when the Speaker, in order to embarrass the Commons, had absented himself for a few days. The Commons resolved themselves into a committee of the whole house and chose a chairman for that committee. Then they could debate as they pleased, without interference from the Speaker. The new arrangement had a further unforeseen advantage. In committee unpracticed members who feared to make public speeches could from their seats throw in a sentence or two which they would have hesitated to utter formally.

It was little time before the committee of the whole house became a regular part of procedure. Even earlier there had been a committee of grievances, and by 1614 that committee had become a standing committee of the whole house. By 1621 three standing committees had developed and by 1624 there were four. The result of these committees was that more and more important matters were first aired in committee, before coming to the House. The House of Commons was likely to ratify readily what had been done in committee.

Those committees of the whole house went through much business. Some of it they apportioned among subcommittees where men behind the scenes did spadework of the greatest consequence. To understand what they were doing we have to go back to the committee of the whole house for grievances. Its function was to gather the abuses of the realm from what members knew and had been told, and above all from petitions presented to Parliament. In the British Museum may be seen two thick manuscript volumes of the grievances presented to the Commons in 1621 and 1624. On the margins of pages are the penciled notes of the unobtrusive but searching Edward Alford of Essex. Out of such notes as he made grievances were put into form and made the basis for preparing impeachments and attacks upon officials of the Crown. Out of such notes the Commons formulated a list of grievances to be laid before the King. They used an old tactic. They made ready the bill of subsidies but delayed a final vote upon it. When the King was ready to remedy their grievances, they prepared to vote him subsidies. It was bargaining with the sovereign; it was "merchant-like," as James remarked. But what else could be done with a sovereign who was showering gifts upon favorites, bankrupting the government, and undermining trade?

The promise of the King might be vague, or made only to be broken, and the Commons began to find it expedient to frame bills to remedy abuses. Those bills were brought in usually by individual members who had served on committees and knew what needed to be done. Later on they were brought in by subcommittees on grievances or by subcommittees of other standing committees.

The Commons could frame legislation. It was another thing to get it on the statute books. The King could stop bills through the influence of councilors and friends in the Upper House, and he was able to reject others. Moreover, in 1614 he had dismissed Parliament before the end of the session, and in 1621 he had dissolved it in anger; thus there were no laws enacted between the end of 1610 and 1624. The result was an accumulation of measures that needed to be passed. The Commons developed a useful practice of ordering the Clerk to keep copies of measures introduced and not passed, for the use of the next meeting of Parliament. The accumulation must have been considerable, for there were measures which had been introduced again and again in the course of the reign. Usually such a bill had been improved as a result of debate in one session after another; but however much improved, the bill was still not the law of the realm. Finally the flood gates were broken. The accumulated body of legislation passed in 1621, but not on the books, was brought up again in 1624, when King and Parliament were on friendly terms, and enrolled in the statutes at the end of that meeting. The year 1624 was a year to be remembered, the fulfillment of hopes long cherished.

The House of Commons did more than try to pass laws. In 1621 they were able to serve their country in a significant way. It will be recalled that Elizabeth had been impressed by the outcry in the Commons in 1601 against patents. Patents in that time meant licenses by the Crown to sell or deal in an article or commodity to the exclusion of other persons, and were practically never connected with inventions.[9] Of the outcry by the Commons in 1601 James probably knew little. He was surrounded by courtiers who asked favors every day; a few of them gained patents worth thousands of pounds which they deserved by no right of a new idea. Others received patents worth much less but burdensome nevertheless to the people. In every Parliament there had been complaints about them. In 1621 alert committeemen made such an examination of the abuses connected with patents that James and the Privy Councilors were frightened into canceling a large number of them. That cancellation marked an accomplishment by the Commons. Even if Parliament went back to the country with no laws passed, it had rendered a service constituents would not forget. In such ways the Commons were finding perhaps their greatest usefulness.[10] The legislative body was forcing the hand of the executive. Even before Parliament met, councilors, in anticipation of criticism there, would be shortening sail, would be remedying abuses.

We must look for a moment beyond the reign of James I if we are to appraise the importance of that period. The first three Parliaments of Charles I (1625, 1626, 1628–29) witnessed a continuing effort by the leaders of the Commons to hold royal ministers accountable for bad administration, to win freedom of speech, and to protect the rights of the subject. From March, 1629, to April, 1640, the King governed on his own. When the Long Parliament (Novem-

[9] See *New English Dictionary* (Oxford) under *patent*.
[10] Even the Archbishop of Canterbury might make a concession about two silenced ministers when waited upon by three M.P.'s, a concession which reveals the new influence of the House of Commons.

ber 3, 1640) came together Pym, Hampden, and their fellows were prepared with a program.[11] They moved quickly against the King's great minister and then proceeded to pass measure after measure; they were set to make the King supreme only when acting through Parliament, to render him dependent upon them. Charles wobbled and wept and gave way. The Civil Wars followed (August, 1642), a result of many causes, too many to be set forth here.[12]

It was the Revolution of 1688–89 that finally settled the supremacy of Parliament as well as the toleration of various types of Christian faith. Then it was that the manipulations of Sandys, the committee work of Hakewill and Alford, the management of Phelips, the racy speeches of Coke, and the smooth leadership of Pym and Hampden had their ultimate consequences. The supremacy of Parliament was embodied in the unwritten constitution.[13]

[11] A. P. Newton in *The Colonising Activities of the English Puritans* (New Haven, 1914) has shown how the men who guided the Long Parliament had been thrown together earlier in colonizing projects, and particularly in that one connected with the Providence Isle off Central America.

[12] Those who have read Chapter 5 on the country gentleman and who will read Chapter 18 on the justices of the peace will realize that those rulers of the countryside could not long be denied their say at Westminster. Those who have read Chapters 13 and 14 on Puritanism will gain some inkling of the causes of the Civil Wars. Archbishop Laud was determined not only to put down Puritanism wherever it reared its head but to enforce high Anglicanism and a great deal of ceremony. He had an ideal, the beauty of holiness, but it was one for which hunting squires and affluent townsmen were not ready. Moreover they resented the intruding powers of church officials who swarmed over the parishes exacting fees and censoring personal conduct.

To be more general about the Civil Wars, we must say, what the reader knows, that England was in a period of transition. New men were making new demands, and the stubborn and unseeing Charles and the men around him were resisting more than the demand for parliamentary sovereignty. Even before the end of the reign of James I, there were farseeing men who feared the outcome of the conflict between the sovereign and Parliament in alliance with the Puritans. What they could hardly have guessed was that the Civil Wars would release ideas more revolutionary than those of Pym, ideas that would have their influence both on modern English history and on American history.

[13] The American Congress in one respect took a somewhat different course from that taken by Parliament. The legislation by Congress is subject to review by our Supreme Court; laws passed by it can be declared unconstitutional. In England Parliament is the final authority and its legislation cannot be reviewed. In medieval days Parliament had been more than anything else a High Court

As the Lower House gained power and prestige, the House of Lords became gradually less important in public estimation. In the first years of James I there were just under eighty peers. At the beginning of the Long Parliament there were nearly one hundred and fifty peers. The twenty-five bishops and the two archbishops also voted in that body, usually as the King wished. The debates in the Upper House were not uninteresting; there were some able men who understood the law and could offer good suggestions. Unfortunately the *Journals* of the House of Lords do not record the debates and we have to depend upon a few notes kept by a few members in a few sessions. We know that among the peers were leaders of opposition to the sovereign. As the King created new peers, that opposition became less significant.

However little the Lords were able to do, Parliament in the twenties—long before the Long Parliament and the Civil Wars and two generations before the Revolution—was making itself felt in the country. A manuscript volume of the debates in the Commons in 1628, to be found in the Massachusetts Historical Society, is possibly an evidence of the interest of the Massachusetts colony in what had been happening in England. We do know that colonial legislatures soon adopted procedures developed in the English House of Commons in the reign of James I. The House of Commons in those years was pushing forward, as we have seen. It was preparing the ground for what was some distance off, for parliamentary-cabinet government, the most flexible and smooth-working political machinery yet developed. The members of Parliament hardly understood the changes they were making or even the direction in which they were moving; certainly they had no conception of what Parliament was to become. They could not have foreseen that they were fashioning a model which men overseas, in America and elsewhere, would find useful.

---

of Parliament (See C. H. McIlwain's classic, *The High Court of Parliament*, New Haven, 1910), and the distinction between judicial acts and legislative was only slowly developed. In the sixteenth and early seventeenth centuries judges still explained and in some degree interpreted legislative acts of Parliament, but their right to do so was coming in question and was slowly lost.

CHAPTER 17

The Sheriffs

THE OFFICE of sheriff had more history behind it than that of any other official in England except the King. It is, however, the fate of great offices to decline in power and keep only the prestige, and that was true of the sheriff. But he deserves consideration, for in the new world he continued to be a power in the county.

The election of the sheriffs took place on a day set apart in the government calendar. On the morrow [1] of All Soul's Day, the Privy Councilors and great judges gathered in the Star Chamber and made out a list of three gentlemen for each county, from which the King was to choose one as sheriff for the coming year. The judges were to be consulted; they were, said Bacon, well read in gentry of the Kingdom. Who knew so well what gentlemen in each county were wealthy and wise, what gentlemen had been to the Inns of Court and knew some law, and what gentlemen had experience as justices of the peace? [2] In the list of three men for a county which Privy Councilors made out after consultation, they usually put first the man who had been placed second the year before and in the second place the man who had been third. One new name they added and put in third place. When the list was prepared the King

[1] November 3. In the reigns of James I and Charles I the meeting was often postponed to a later date.
[2] Occasionally a lord lieutenant or another great nobleman in the county might offer suggestions as to possible sheriffs in his county.

was supposed to "prick" the first name, although he might prick one of the other two.[3]

Men were not eager to be pricked. From the last decade of Elizabeth to the Long Parliament (1640) the state papers are full of letters from country gentlemen importuning their friends at Court to help them avoid service as sheriff. Illness, want of means, arduous duties, service to the sovereign in other capacities, all were reasons alleged why they should be excused. It might be supposed that an important gentleman in the county would have admitted to himself that he had to serve once in his life and might as well take his term at once. The duty was only for a year. Not so. One year seemed too much.

For the office involved heavy expense. The fees the sheriff had to pay to various London officials when he assumed it, and when he left it, amounted possibly to something over a hundred pounds. Furthermore he never could collect all the money due from various debtors to the King; for four or five years after his tenure of the office he might find himself still pressed to pay himself what he could not wring out of others. His greatest expense was, however, the keeping up of the dignity and state of the office. When itinerant justices came riding into the county to hold the assizes, the sheriff was to meet them and to conduct them with pomp and ceremony into the town. Pomp and ceremony meant that he should be accompanied by at least thirty or forty men clad in his livery. In town the sheriff had to see that the judges were properly housed and dined, and usually, for at least four days of their stay, at his cost. A thrifty Lancashire sheriff who, with the approval of his fellow gentry, attempted to economize on the entertainment afforded the judges was heavily fined by them, ostensibly for other reasons. But that was not all. If the King or Queen happened to be passing through the shire, it was the part of a loyal sheriff to meet him or her at the boundary and accompany the royal progress until it left the county. He might even find himself compelled to entertain the King

[3] If a man's name had been on the list for four years and had not been pricked, it was usually withdrawn.

and the Court, at prodigious expense. Moreover, ambassadors proceeding through the county on their way to or from a port were to be accompanied in state by the high sheriff. It has been estimated that the Midland sheriffs spent during their year of office four or five hundred pounds a year over and above the fees they received,[4] and that may be an underestimate. The office was undesirable for another reason. The holder could not during his year leave the county except by special permission, a hardship for gentlemen accustomed to ride up to London frequently. One aged and ailing sheriff was shortly before his death refused permission to go to Bristol to see if the waters there might help him.

The Stuart kings took advantage of the unwillingness of gentlemen to serve as sheriffs. Now and then Elizabeth had turned aside from the list presented to her. James I and Charles I often pricked men not on the list. Favorites discovered that there was money to be made by getting men off the list. When a man learned that he was on the list, it was suggested to him that a good sum of money offered to a friend of a favorite might enable him to escape. Even if he had been pricked, it was possible, by paying money, to have a *vacat.* put opposite his pricked name, and another name substituted. Bacon wrote Buckingham that men who were never thought of, "nor yet of that worth to be sheriff," were nominated, because others had bought themselves off.

The Stuarts went further. They discovered that they could punish men by making them sheriffs. John Chamberlain wrote (1622) that men were pricked "for a kind of gentle correction, such as were too forward in the Parliament or too backward in the benevolence," and Rudyard said the same thing in another way. It will be remembered that Charles I in 1626 named six active members of the Lower House as sheriffs so that they could not sit in the Commons. He went on afterward to name men sheriffs who had refused to contribute to benevolences and forced loans, or who had opposed him in Parliament or in other ways. So nearly did this become a

---

[4] The estimate of T. Hallinan, who has kindly sent me his long article on the sheriffs in the Midlands.

fixed policy that men appointed to be sheriffs pled with the King that such an appointment meant to the public but one thing, that they were out of favor with Majesty.[5]

What a falling off was there! In the days of good King Alfred, in the days of the two great Henrys, of Edward I and of Henry V and Henry VII, the sheriff had been the great man of the shire. Then Tudor Parliaments began by this law and that to impose more duties upon the justice of the peace and, probably without realizing it, slowly whittled down the functions of the sheriff. In the Stuart period the registers of the Privy Council and the state papers indicate the progressive decline, almost year by year, of the importance of the sheriff. The King and his Council were turning naturally to the new rulers of the shires, the country gentlemen on the commission of the peace. The sheriff still had much work to do, but he had little part in making administrative decisions or in formulating policy.

The sheriff continued nevertheless to have many jobs of many kinds, most of them involving drudgery. To help him out he had an undersheriff, whom he chose, and various bailiffs.

He was still, as he had been in Anglo-Saxon days, the King's manorial steward, the shire-reeve. He looked after the Crown lands and revenues in the county, as any country gentleman's steward might do for his master. He gathered the rents, the annuities, the estrays,[6] the deodands,[7] the fees due to the King, the goods of felons and traitors. The Council might send him orders to stop the felling of trees in a royal forest; those trees were to be used for the Royal Navy.

He was still a means of communication between the Privy Coun-

---

[5] An examination has been made by Mr. Hallinan of the sheriffs appointed by James I and Charles I in the Midland counties, and it appears that some of them were neither important nor wealthy men in their counties; such appointees were probably those who could not afford to pay the bribes or who were unfamiliar with the ways of courtiers. Furthermore, the men named were often such as were untrained in the law and inexperienced as justices of the peace. Much of the last two paragraphs is based upon Mr. Hallinan's paper.

[6] Stray animals not owned by any man.

[7] Personal chattels which had been the immediate cause of a person's death.

cil and the county. It was the business of the sheriff to announce the new statutes passed by Parliament, "by sound of the trumpet and beat of drums," at the next county court,[8] and in "open market" in the shire town. The proclamations framed and set forth by the King and his councilors were also announced to the public by the sheriff. The carrying out of the policies of the Council was entrusted to the sheriff. If his county were on the coast he was asked to prevent the export of iron ordnance which might be turned later against the English by their enemies, and of fuller's earth, a kind of clay of which the English had almost a monopoly,[9] and which was essential in the cleansing of wool. The councilors ordered the sheriff to stop the planting of tobacco and to sequester that already planted, thereby helping out Virginia. When the great depression of the early twenties caused unemployment and poverty in the clothing counties, the sheriff was ordered to keep the poor within the parishes. The sheriff of Hampshire was to proceed against a riotous gathering of the poor, who in desperation were taking corn from the wagons going to market, to use a *posse comitatus* to disperse the gathering, and to apprehend such as he thought meet, thus exercising some discretion.

The Privy Council gave orders to the sheriff in more personal cases. He was to bring a man confined in jail before the Council; he was to reprieve one condemned to death by the assizes for purse-snatching and send him to Virginia, where he might prove useful. It had come to the ears of the Council that the Earl of Shrewsbury, who had great holdings in several Midland counties, was dying, and that his heir was prepared to seize all his properties at once. The sheriffs of those counties were warned that the heir was not to be allowed to seize those lands until the right of the daughters of the late earl had been determined.

In many instances the orders of the Council were directed to the sheriff *and* to the justices of the peace of the county. When the

---

[8] The county court, which had long ceased to be an important body, was the sheriff's court.

[9] There was fuller's earth in Silesia but that was a long way off.

councilors were anxious about the spread of the plague, when they wished to bring down the price of corn or to reduce the number of alehouses, they were likely to send a letter to both the sheriff and the justices of the peace jointly. But more letters were addressed solely to the justices. When the sheriff was included in the missive, it might be supposed that he and the justices would have consulted together, but the evidence for such consultation is not forthcoming.

Occasionally the councilors relied upon the sheriffs to get them some special piece of information. When the Privy Council in 1623 wished to find out the situation about grain in the county and how much was in storage, it asked the sheriff to get the data from the justices as individuals or in small groups. In matters of loans and benevolences for the King, extraparliamentary subsidies which the country resented, the Privy Councilors directed many letters to the sheriffs, and sometimes to the justices as well. Those letters would sometimes lay down the amount expected from the county, and would contain a few of those threatening phrases which the higher servants of Charles I were given to use.

The sheriff was the functionary of the assize court. He had to bring the men accused before the court; he had to see that those who were condemned to death were hanged and that the lesser penalties were carried out. He had to put in execution the instructions of the judges. The impaneling of juries was possibly his most important job. He had to find enough men of the various classes for the several juries and make sure that they were on hand. Packing juries in order to gain a certain verdict was one of the practices of the time and sheriffs were often suspected of being skillful at it. The judges had the right, whenever they wished, to "reform" the panels submitted by the sheriff, but little evidence that they did so has thus far appeared.

The sheriff issued the writs by which the quarter sessions was called together, but he left attendance upon that body largely to his subordinates. His greatest responsibility, as at the assizes, was to see that juries were impaneled. He had many actions to carry out, writs to deliver, etc. Some cases he arranged to have brought to his own county court. Those suspected of felony he was likely to put in prison to await the assizes.[10]

The sheriff had to deal with many officials. By his oath he was under obligation to help ecclesiastical courts. If he were a sheriff of one of the four western counties, he had to assist the Council of Wales. He had to serve the coroners and the commissioners for sewers, and those for bankrupts and the subsidy. He was responsible for the county jail and for the appointment and conduct of its keeper. He had to pay the grand jurors their fees and the justices of peace their wages for service at quarter sessions. He might be asked to help out the lord lieutenant of the county about musters or to support the constables in pressing men for military service abroad. Occasionally he was asked to examine by himself, or in association with certain selected justices of the peace, into a disputed matter, and if possible to find a solution.

The sheriff was at his worst in carrying out elections for knights of the shire. From the chancery the writs would be sent out to him; upon receiving them he would proclaim the time and place of the meeting of Parliament. He announced as well the place and day and exact hours of the county election. This interested everyone of importance in the county. For months there had been talk of a probable election, country gentlemen had been writing letters to one another canvassing names, and several well-known figures had indicated their willingness to stand, if their friends insisted. In counties here and there were two families which had long been at cross-purposes, perhaps since a quarrel over a bridge in the time of Henry VI. If a member of one of those families sought election, the other family was likely to throw its support to a rival candidate, possibly to one of its own connection. In any case there emerged usually two sets of candidates with their arrayed supporters. Those supporters

---

[10] That the undersheriffs and bailiffs used their offices for profit was generally believed in the time. For some reason they failed many times to find and bring in to the sessions those whom they summoned. When they distrained property for the recovery of fines and penalties, they had chances to do well by themselves. The undersheriff had usually paid the sheriff well for the right to serve under him, and probably because he had the chance to make more than his fees.

would gather in for the great day and might be given hospitality. They would include many forty-shilling freeholders, who had the right to vote. But one of the candidates might bring in a lot of substantial-looking yeomen. Who was to say offhand that they were not forty-shilling freeholders? The crowds gathered round their candidates shouting "a-Phelips" or "a-Paulet." The sheriff, at what he deemed the right moment, called for a vote and listened to determine by the shouting which was the majority party. If there were doubt he called for a show of hands and proceeded to a count. Too often the sheriff was not a wholly disinterested party; he might use tactics to help his friends. He might suddenly move the election from one side of the castle to the other; he might resort to a show of hands before one of the groups had drawn all its men away from the alehouse to the designated place; he might delay the show of hands until his friends could muster more voters. Such maneuvering was rather common and resulted often in an appeal to the House of Commons and in the summons of the sheriff and others before the committee of privileges. There the chicanery of the sheriff might be proved, and he might find himself in jail until he would admit his fault publicly on his knees before the Speaker of the Commons.

In the years just before the Long Parliament, the situation of that already-driven official became impossible. Charles was carrying on without a Parliament and finding money in what ways he could. He imposed ship-money,[11] and the sheriffs found again and again that they could not collect it. The government had an answer. It apportioned so much to the sheriff to gather, and, if he could not gather it, he was to be himself responsible for the whole sum. The sheriffs were at their wits' end.

The sheriff comes into his own again and figures largely in the late seventeenth century and in the years following. Slowly he has become more and more an honorary official, one of great dignity, still carrying out the more formal duties of his office, but leaving

[11] An ancient tax levied in time of war on the ports and maritime towns, cities, and counties to provide ships for the King's service, revived by Charles I (with an extended application to inland counties).

much to subordinates. He performed a function so necessary that his office was transported to the colonies in America and incorporated in their community organizations. With us he has remained in some degree what he was in Elizabethan England and earlier. We think of him in Bret Harte's stories and in the "westerns" as one who deals with bad plainsmen and cowboys gone wrong. But he has a real existence outside of fiction as an executive official in the county and is still concerned with criminals.

CHAPTER 18

The Justices of the Peace

It is sessions with me every day all the day long here, and I have no time for my own occasions, hardly to put meat in my mouth. . . . There was yesterday fourteen brought before me and presented that are so fit for no place as the house of correction, all of one parish . . . 4 or 5 of them idle whores, that had had 1, 2, 3, and 6 bastards.

So wrote William Capel of Somerset to another justice of his daily activities. In addition to his constant occupation with the poor and with petty criminals, he had to attend the quarter sessions and intermediate sessions. Such men were kingpins in their own communities, powers in the county, and useful to the kingdom, as they and others knew. "There was never in any commonwealth devised," wrote Sir Thomas Smith, "a more wise, a more dulce and gentle, nor a more certain way to rule the people." Sir Edward Coke was even more enthusiastic and thought no other Christian country had as good an office, if duly executed. How it was executed is what has to be set forth here.

The justices of the peace were chosen by the Crown, usually by the Lord Chancellor, who was likely to consult Privy Councilors, judges of assize, and sometimes lords lieutenants of the countries. They were of two kinds, ordinary justices, and those of the "quorum," men who had some special knowledge of the law and had perhaps attended one of the Inns of Court.

The justices, except those in towns,[1] were drawn almost exclusively from the ranks of country gentlemen.[2] It was the ideal of the government to choose gentlemen whose families were well known and looked up to in the county, and so well did it succeed in that purpose that the roll of justices of a county was regarded as one of honor.[3] The justices savored the dignity and consequence of their position, and delighted to recall their experiences on the bench, not failing to mention Privy Councilors, great judges, and famous noblemen who had at one time or another sat with them.

The justices did not all measure to the ideal. It was the delight of playwrights to picture them as pompous and ignorant, and sometimes as downright dishonest. Men who used the office to advantage themselves and their friends could have been found in most counties. The phrase "basket justices," to describe those who received baskets of fruit and fowl from such as hoped for favors, was heard in villages and at Westminster.

But the assumption of political thinkers and observers that the justices constituted one of the bulwarks of the commonwealth found wide support. Members of Parliament thought equally well of them—many of them had been justices—and grew indignant at colleagues who were critical of them. The man on the land respected the justices, who seemed to him to know as much about statutes as about soils; occasionally he had a suspicion that Sir John might now and then favor his own class,[4] but in general he set him down as

---

[1] In all corporate towns the mayor, bailiff, and recorder, if there were one, and a varying number of the senior aldermen were *ex officio* justices of the peace. But only boroughs in which there was a recorder had the privilege of holding their own quarter sessions.

[2] The qualifications for a justice were residence in the county, suitability of moral character, religious uniformity, and the possession of lands or tenements worth £20 a year.

[3] Many of them were men of affairs, judges, officials, and practitioners in the central courts; some had been sheriffs; a goodly proportion would be or had been members of Parliament.

[4] There was favoritism upon the part of justices to men of their own breed. It was natural for Sir John to believe that Sir Thomas, a neighbor and a good fellow, was speaking the truth, and that Tom the poacher and Ellen the old hag suspected of witchcraft were lying. Yet not uncommonly the justices decided

one who sought to do right and was not far off in his judgment. Many justices searched matters out thoroughly and knew the uses of reason and fairness.

The justice had men brought before him on many kinds of charges, upon his own summons, or upon the initiative of the petty constable. He could punish men for drunkenness, for playing cards on the Sabbath, for refusing to work in the harvest; he could order a "sturdy rogue" or vagrant to be whipped. Those accused of more serious crimes, of felony, he could bind over to the quarter sessions or to the assizes,[5] or hold them in jail.

When a man was brought before him the justice did his best to draw him into confession. "Speak him fair to the end that you may get him to confess," wrote one justice to another about a man suspected of thievery. In theory such an effort was contrary to legal procedure; in practice a justice commonly cross-examined a man in such a way as to draw him into an admission of guilt and to learn also what accomplices he might have. In the report which the justice would prepare for the quarter sessions, he would often say of one he had questioned: "Will confess no more."

His main duty was to keep the peace whenever it was threatened. As a Lord Chancellor had declared, the justice was to withstand all beginnings. The beginnings were usually quarrels. Hodson was a fire-eater in the community; he had not only had high words with Winwick but had threatened to do him harm. Winwick feared that Hodson might assault him or burn his barn, and went to the justice. Two actions the justice had at his hand. He could compel Hodson to give surety of the peace, that is, a bond that he would keep the peace. He could take a more inclusive action. If four substantial neighbors complained of Hodson, the justice, associating with himself another justice,[6] could compel Hodson to give bond of good-a-bearing (*de bono gestu*), pledging himself in a sum of money (two friends pledging themselves with him) that he would present him-

against Sir Thomas and refused to yield to the pressure of Earl High-and-Mighty.

[5] In most instances he bound felons over to the assizes.

[6] In an emergency he might act by himself.

self at the next quarter sessions, and that in the meanwhile he would keep the peace as against Winwick and everyone else. This action the justice found convenient not only to hold in check troublesome and dangerous men, but to bind over to the quarter sessions small thieves, alehouse-haunters, drunkards, those suspected of begetting bastard children, and loose women.[7] If a man behaved himself up to the next quarter sessions, he might be released from his bond; if he were held for a crime, his bond was security for his appearance. Jails were few and room in them limited. It was easier to take bail. At the same time that the justice bound the accused over, he also bound the accuser to appear and prosecute.[8]

Anticipating trouble involved preventing riots and public disturbances. If the justice heard of a riot, or the likelihood of one, he with his servants was to go to the place mentioned, compel the individuals assembled to give bonds of good-a-bearing, and perhaps cause a proclamation to be made in the King's name charging them to disperse. If they refused, he might commit them to ward or take their arms from them. He could not himself punish the rioters.

Two justices, or better three, could do more. They could move "with the power of the county" to arrest the rioters and to "record" the riot and send on word of it to the assizes and to the Privy Council. If the riot had taken place before their arrival, they could make an inquiry by a jury within a month and certify to the King and his Council what had happened.

A justice alone, two justices together, three justices together, had more capacities and functions than can be enumerated here.[9] More-

[7] The intentions of the justices were often thwarted. By a writ of supersedeas a man bound to surety or good-a-bearing might carry his case to the King's Bench or to Chancery in London, and there get "knights of the post," "base and beggarly men," who had managed to get themselves assessed at high rates in the subsidy book, to be accepted as sureties. The surety was worth nothing and the accused would fail to appear. This dodge was stopped by legislation in 1624.

[8] The justice might on the basis of his own knowledge bind over a man suspected, in which case the clerk of the peace prosecuted.

[9] As individuals and as members of small groups the justices varied in their ways of doing business from county to county, and even within counties. They were not always as learned in their duties as they should have been, but there

over, when a special case came up two justices or more might call upon the sheriff to impanel a jury which would deal with it at once. There was also what may be called "divisional" sessions,[10] where the justices of an artificial "division" or "limit" [11] met together [12] and performed much the same functions as quarter sessions. In many cases they devoted attention to the giving and sometimes to the taking away of licenses to alehouses.[13] Now and then they named high constables and less often petty constables.

The quarter sessions was the field day of the justices and the omnium-gatherum of the shire. The more active of the country gentlemen who were on the bench were to be seen. One of them might be an earl, accompanied by his lawyer, who was also one of the justices and would sit beside him to help him. A bishop might serve as a justice, and possibly another ecclesiastical dignitary. The *Custos Rotulorum* was supposed to be in attendance and of course the Clerk of the Peace was always there. But many not on the bench would be waiting their turn to take their parts: the high sheriff and his undersheriff and bailiffs; the coroners; the stewards of the leets [14] and all the high constables; and, in theory at least, all the petty constables; the jailer, and the masters of the houses of correction. In addition all the jurors returned by the sheriff for the grand jury and for the hundred juries of presentment and for the petty (trial) juries were required to be ready for their duties. Furthermore all

---

was excuse for them. They had to administer an increasing body of statutes, many recently passed. Those statutes imposed new duties, and were often vaguely stated. Only slowly could justices learn what they could do and what they could not, and some were cautious and others inclined to take matters into their own hands.

[10] These were sometimes called "petty sessions," but must be distinguished from the petty sessions of the high constables.

[11] In Warwickshire the unit was the hundred.

[12] As business increased these divisional sessions met oftener, in some shires once a month, and did much of the routine legal and administrative work. There was a tendency for the quarter sessions to confine itself to the more important matters, referring the smaller to the divisional sessions, or to a few justices.

[13] If they dealt with alehouses alone, their meetings were called "brewster sessions," usually a special meeting held just before the Easter quarter sessions.

[14] A court held by the lord of the manor. See references to it in Chapters 19 and 20. The steward of the lord usually presided.

the persons bound over to the peace or to good behavior and all those who had to prosecute or give evidence were required to be available.

By the reign of James I the Commission of the Peace [15] in a county included from about forty to seventy members,[16] a multiple of the numbers in early Tudor days. Country gentlemen aspired to be on the Commission and brought pressure to bear toward that end. In 1608 the Lord Chancellor complained of the many knights that came in their bravery and stood there to be gazed upon and did nothing. Such men came once or twice, but found it pleasanter to remain in London three-quarters of the year and to take their country duties lightly. In few meetings of the quarter sessions were more than twenty justices present; from ten to fifteen was a more usual number. In most counties eight or ten justices showed by their regular attendance their interest in the work.

The leading officials of quarter sessions were the *Custos Rotulorum* and the Clerk of the Peace. The *Custos* was, as his name implies, the keeper of the records, but by the Stuart period his office had become an honorary one, sought after by great nobles or by men of wide acres. The man who kept the records for the *Custos* and looked after all the details at sessions, and before and after, was the Clerk of the Peace. He continued in office usually as long as the *Custos;* was often one who had been a steward or legal assistant to the *Custos,* and of the small gentry or the country-lawyer class. He saw to it that the order of business was followed, that all documents were in order and at hand, that all recognizances had been turned in and all writs delivered, and that all the many orders of the sessions were carried out.

The quarter sessions met four times a year, as the name implies. By statute it was expected to meet for three days, but often finished its business in two. In rare instances it lasted four days.

In their judicial capacity the justices assembled in sessions dealt

[15] The Commission of the Peace was the authority given under the Great Seal empowering certain persons to act as justices of the peace in a specified district.

[16] Rutland had less and Kent more.

usually only with minor crimes, with petty larceny, assaults, forcible entries upon land, sheepstealing, housebreaking, trespass,[17] etc. As for felonies, murder, rape, highway robbery, and witchcraft, they had the right to deal with them, but usually left those offences to the assizes.

In many cases they used a kind of short cut to justice. When a jury brought in an indictment [18] against a man he might "put himself on the country," in which event his case was postponed for trial by a petty jury at the next sessions,[19] or he submitted to a fine, without further trial. The case did not then come up before a petty jury but was settled by an appropriate fine, and the man went away without having been convicted of a crime.[20]

When the justices were uncertain about the proper procedure in a case, they would refer it to the itinerant judges at the assizes. Cases could not be appealed, but they could be removed by a writ of certiorari. The justices looked to the assizes for direction. They were expected to attend the assizes—where they were given seats of honor —to watch the great judges in action, and to learn what laws were at the time most in need of enforcement.[21]

The justices were drawn almost necessarily into dealing with matters that amounted to civil actions. Two men quarreled and were bound over to keep the peace and presently released, but went

[17] The weakness of the quarter sessions was that in a large number of cases the sheriff or the undersheriffs reported that the man sought for could not be found. Unless the man pleaded to the indictment he could not be convicted. Writ after writ, venire facias, distringas, capias, etc., in increasing order of importunity, would be sent out against him, and, if he never appeared, he would be finally outlawed, no severe punishment for the ordinary man. Some of those who never appeared must have been lying hidden in remote alehouses or in the homes of friends. But so many men were reported as unfound that one suspects that the undersheriffs and bailiffs were skillful in failing to find men.

[18] Petty offences were often determined on the same day the indictment was found.

[19] If a man put himself on the country, that is, asked for a jury, he was bound to appear at the next sessions, but his case might be dragged out over several sessions.

[20] But thieves, receivers of stolen goods, alehouse keepers, etc., might be given a fine at this session, and another two years later, and perhaps again pay their fines and continue in their nefarious ways.

[21] They were often sent instructions on the matter.

on bickering until something had to be done. Two yeomen had a difference about the ownership of a lamb. Seventeen harvesters declared that they had not been paid for reaping, shearing, and inning the corn grown on a baronet's land. What the justices did in many cases was to name one, two, or three of their number to look into the matter and arbitrate it. Sometimes they appointed neighbors of the disputants as arbitrators, occasionally a clergyman.

The petty quarrels of the village were brought in to quarter sessions. The assembled justices were told what the parson said in his anger about a parishioner and what parishioners said of the parson. They were given the most frivolous stories: a woman had spoken ill of her mother-in-law; another woman by her great show of overmuch familiarity toward men in the parish had bred disquiet between them and their wives; a man had delighted more to sing ungodly songs in the alehouse than to hear the word of God in church. The justices sitting together stuck pretty close to administering the law, unless a fellow justice were slandered, and then they came down on the offender and made him beg pardon on his knees. Village squabbles could be ignored until one of the troublemakers went too far, as he was likely to do, and put himself within easy reach of the law.

More exacting and significant than the judicial duties of the justices were their administrative labors. They received orders from the Privy Council [22] and they were expected to inform that august body of any serious trouble in the shire. They had to deal with an infinity of local matters. The business of musters and of the full attendance at them of those of the proper ages belonged to the lord lieutenant and his subordinates, but the justices might help him by

[22] They expected instructions from the Privy Council, but resented deeply interference by the subsidiary councils, those of Wales and of the North. It was natural that men who had to deal with the Privy Council regarded themselves sometimes as spokesmen for the county. When James was trying in 1614 to get a benevolence, or grant of money, without consent of Parliament, the Devonshire justices refused to pay it from "the fear of the just blame of after ages." In the same county they made representations earlier to the government about purveyance; in the reign of Charles I the Essex justices resisted the extension of the forest laws. The Somerset justices were acting for the shire but in a different way when, in 1632, they importuned the King's judges for the suppression of disorderly wakes and revels.

bringing pressure to bear upon local officials. They had to see to it that the constables pressed men for military service. They had to cooperate with high constables in making certain that masters paid and servants accepted the specified wages, no more, no less. They had to keep tab on the apprenticing of the children of the poor and to deal with those who mistreated such apprentices. They had to check on those who had taken up trades and "mysteries" without undergoing an apprenticeship in the particular skill. They had to exercise control over markets and supervise the keepers of weights and measures. They had to arrange that money was collected for the prisoners in the Marshalsea and King's Bench prisons in London and in the jail in their own county. It devolved upon them to vote suitable pensions or lump sums to maimed soldiers returned from wars, and to vote money to those who had suffered heavily from fires or inundations, a kind of county insurance. Sometimes they gave "briefs" to those who had suffered, allowing them to beg for money. They checked the accounts of overseers of the poor and compelled parish officials, if necessary, to levy rates for this and that purpose. Other administrative functions they had, more than can be enumerated here. Most of them consisted in the oversight and prodding of smaller officials.

The cries of the poor went up from parish officials to the quarter sessions. The husbandman could not feed his family wrote the dramatist Dekker, and his wife wrung her hands and his children pined. In some shires the farm laborer was hard put to it to keep his family fed and warm, and even in the better farming regions did not live abundantly. When in trouble he looked to the churchwardens and the overseers of the poor; they were often slack, as we shall see, and begrudged the use of parish funds, or failed to bestow the sums they had voted, or were slow about it. Housing the poor was almost as much a problem as feeding them, and officials were now and then at their wits' end to find them roofs. They would make room in houses already tenanted; widow Ashton would be paid something to take on a homeless woman. But a man with family required more space. The churchwardens could have asked the lord of the manor for four acres from the waste land upon which to throw together a cottage; [23] they were inclined to turn over the making of that request to the justices, who found lords nearly always amenable. The justices would then order the overseers to erect a cottage, and the lord of the manor might cooperate by allowing the overseers to procure timber for it from the manorial woods. If the parish were swamped by crowds of the poor who had lost work or who had moved in, hoping for work or help, the justices might order the inhabitants of two or more adjacent hundreds to assist with money.

If the justices did much to supplement the duty of churchwardens and overseers to feed and house the poor, they did little to keep them warm. At Christmas the overseers might bestow a little wood and coal, but not enough to last through January and February. The poor were likely to shiver and, if desperate, to go into the woods and cut down branches or break hedges in the fields, thus creating new work for the justices.

The necessities of the aged and infirm were constantly being called to the attention of the justices. Hodge had labored long as a lead miner in the Mendips, moving here and there to find work, and shoring up sometimes the end of a cave as a habitation. Never had he been an idle man or a vagrant; he had been one to pay his parish rates. Now his arms had gone back on him and he could not work. The churchwardens in the last parish in which he had resided had sent him on to the place of his birth, at the other end of the Mendips, and he was promptly sent back by the local authorities there, who professed to know nothing of him. Again the churchwardens pushed him off, this time on a parish where he had labored years ago, and that parish refused to support him. The worn-out miner found himself shunted by constables from parish to parish, [24] and no help in sight. The parishes were so intent on getting rid of those who

[23] A cottage of clay and branches of trees could be set up for three or four pounds, a ramshackle affair, no doubt, but proof for the time being against wind and rain.

[24] Stubbes in his *Anatomie of Abuses* (1584) wrote of the poor: "They drive them from city to city; from parish to parish. . . . Here they dare not tarry for this justice, nor there for that . . . whereas a man would think their old age, their hoar hairs, their blindness, lameness . . . should be passports good enough for them to go abroad."

might prove an expense to them that they would even anticipate the end of a man's working years and take steps to send him away. If he had a wife they were determined to be rid of him and of her. If he had offspring living, they would try to put off the burden of support upon them, but the sons and daughters had often gone far away. What were the quarter sessions to do about the old and weak whom the parishes were pushing off on one another? The parishes had the right to send vagabonds, "sturdy rogues," and beggars back to their places of birth or to the places where they had resided a year; but they were in many cases doing the same thing to those no longer able to work, even when they had been long in residence, and the justices were not exerting themselves to protect those unfortunate creatures. There had been Elizabethan laws, and custom that one year's "settlement" in a place constituted residence there, and the justices in Somerset and in the West Riding of Yorkshire had attempted to establish a three-year or one-year settlement as giving a man a right in a village or town. Such a good principle had, however, its disadvantages. It made it hard for working people to move and better themselves in a new situation. If they lost their jobs in their new location, they were likely to be sent away. It placed them more than ever under the thumb of parish and county officials.

In times of distress, as when the clothing industry came to a standstill in the 1620's, the justices showed up well. They were quick to inform the Privy Council of conditions and to plead for action. If the grain crops failed and the price of bread soared, the justices would go as individuals into the market and buy grain at as low a price as possible and then sell it for less to the poor, to their own personal loss. They kept watch to prevent monopolists from forcing up prices. It was their business to license "badgers," who bought and sold commodities, and when they detected them buying up large quantities of corn, butter, or cheese to hold for higher prices, they would fine them heavily.

We do not know how much the justices did for the poor who lived away from the village, on the heath, on the low-lying lands near the river, or along the inlets of the sea. Such people were often squatters, outlanders, who moved from one place to another and were not easily amenable to discipline. They slipped into the village and helped themselves in barns and fields and chicken pens, partly because they sorely needed covering or food. They were not popular in the village and were naturally afraid to ask for help or to appeal to the constable or to the justice of the peace. The justices could not do much unless cases were brought to their attention.[25]

The matter of alehouses was not unrelated to that of the poor, and received attention from the justices. The laws, the old laws as well as the new, gave the justices a great deal of authority over the sellers of ale. To keep an alehouse a man was supposed to be licensed by two justices,[26] one of whom was of the quorum, or by divisional sessions. The justices demanded that the licensee should be a respectable character, vouched for by the parson, the church-wardens, and some of the worthies of the village.

They expected him to close his house rather early in the evening, say by nine o'clock; to allow no one to tipple more than an hour; to sell wholesome beer at prices that were fixed and named; to prevent games such as dicing, and all gambling; to put a quietus on quarrels; and to keep out all vagrants and sturdy rogues.

The keepers of alehouses did not always live up to such expectations. The hostess in Henry IV, Part II, had been warned the day before by the constable, and was for the moment on her good behavior: "Shut the door—there comes no swaggerers here." Widow Johnson was more wary about doubtful characters, but she was a good fellow with the boys and allowed them to stay late and throw dice. Hopkins had fizzed out as a blacksmith and as a butcher; everyone in the village was sorry for him and anxious lest he prove a burden to them. The justices listened to community opinion and

---

[25] J. Willis-Bund has pointed out in his introduction to the *Worcestershire Quarter Session Records* (Worc. Co. Council, 1899), I, xxxix–xl, that there were few recognizances in Worcestershire exacted from those who lived away from main roads. That proves little, but does suggest that those in remote districts may have been many times overlooked by the justices.

[26] Single justices often gave licenses. It was said in villages that justices would help out indigent former retainers by giving them licenses.

gave him a license. He set up two rooms in his house and sold a poor grade of ale and stale bread. A gang of woodmen working nearby happened to seek their meals at his house and he prospered. But the woodmen were noisy and even violent; villagers complained and the constable went to the justices, who canceled Hopkins' license. Poor Hopkins! The village knew that he was easygoing and careless, but a wave of sympathy for one dispossessed of his living swept the cottages. Moreover Hopkins promised amendment. His license was renewed. Not always was it easy for the justices to follow the twists and turns of village opinion.

The justices were on the whole doing a fairly good job with the alehouses when they suddenly found their control threatened. In 1616 Sir Francis Mompesson devised a scheme by which all inns were to pay a license of five pounds. Inns were houses that provided food and lodging for travelers and were usually of a somewhat higher character than alehouses, but if they sold ale, as they usually did, had to be licensed as any alehouse. Mompesson had the King's favorite, Buckingham, behind him, and the patent he secured for administering the licenses gave him control over the licensing of every inn and every least alehouse that might lodge a stray traveler for the night. That control meant that Mompesson and his friends, to whom he farmed out the rights of licensing in various counties, could exact large sums as bribes for giving licenses. At the same time a brother of Buckingham, and his associates, gained a patent for alehouse forfeitures which meant that they could collect other sums from alehouses. It looked as if the justices of the peace were to lose much of their control over alehouses when the Parliament of 1621 began an investigation. Mompesson fled the country, and the plans of unscrupulous patentees went by the board. The defeat of the "projectors" revealed the power of the justices in the country and did not lessen their prestige.

Unlicensed alehouses were another story and a continuous problem for justices. Many of them were small places where the wife of an artisan or a worn-out laborer made a little ale and presently gained a clientele. Some of the houses were in the midst of the village; many of them were on the other side of the common or beyond the woods or near the ferry. They had no good name and were often suspected of harboring vagrants and rogues, and sometimes of receiving stolen goods. But if they had gained the rights that belonged to old custom, the constable might ignore their want of a license, though he would visit them, and the justices of the peace might let well enough alone unless the houses became too disorderly. Now and again the Privy Council would show concern about the number of such places, and then the justices would become zealous in closing them up. A year or two later they would be operating again at the same old stand.

From the legal treatises about the duties of justices one would scarcely learn what stands out in quarter sessions records, that they gave much of their time to roads, and not a little to footpaths, causeways, ferries, and bridges.

They needed to look after roads. Not a traveler but made his moan about them. Coaches were overturned, packhorses with heavy loads were mired, the man on horseback had to go a long way round, and the parson could not visit the sick. The bad roads of winter men endured as a necessary evil but hoped for better in summer. James I, who loved to hunt between London and Royston, found the royal progress slow, and there was royal indignation. Privy Councilors hastened to write importunate letters to the justices of the counties north of London. The justices blamed the ill state of the roads on the carriers from Norwich and Ipswich to London, who drove heavy four-wheeled wagons and teams of eight or ten horses,[27] and did the roads no good. In many places heavy loads of timber, of coal and iron ore, were making those sloughs which Bunyan was to remember.

It was to look after the roads in every parish that surveyors of the highways (called "waymen" or "waywardens" in some counties) had been established. They were elected usually by the parish or

---

[27] In 1632 the justices of Hertfordshire ordered a census made of wagons which passed to and fro from Cambridge, Norwich, and Bury St. Edmunds to London, and asked that the names of the owners be reported to the Privy Council.

vestry [28] in the early spring at the same time as the churchwardens. It was then the duty of the churchwardens to set aside six days in which the men of the parish were to work upon the roads, the better-off to bring plows or carts and two workmen, the cottagers and smaller fry to be present themselves or by substitutes.

In theory the workmen gave six days to repairing the roads. It was said that many regarded the job as a formality to be got through with and would drift off early in the afternoon to the nearest house of refreshment. They could not but notice that important land-owners would now and then ignore the summons to the roads, and that the poor were often let off, so that the burden fell on those who needed to be sowing their fields. Did the road menders have any boss to take charge and keep them working toward a plan? I find one instance where "orderers of the works" are mentioned. Did the surveyors of the highways choose such men, or did they supervise the work themselves? I do not know. Occasionally they did order a certain man to bring cartloads of gravel or broken stone for the use of the workmen. If there were a boss a great deal would depend upon him, as to how much he knew about making roads. Few principles had as yet been developed upon the subject, although such principles were just beginning to be enunciated. Too often the workers scoured the ditches at the side of the road, filled up holes, and covered the middle of the road with loose dirt and some stones and gravel, if those commodities were available near at hand. In many instances they left the roads worse than they were before.

The surveyors of the highways had little to encourage them to take pains. They received no salary and none of the fees accruing to other small officials; their post brought them neither much con-sideration nor honor. They had little money to spend upon the repair of roads; they had the fines levied upon those who failed in their duty, the money given them by those who commuted their services by cash payments; occasionally they had the income of a

[28] In some places they were named by the leet court. We find instances where they were chosen by the constables, possibly because the parish had failed to do its duty.

small endowment left for the parish roads, and rarely the money raised by a parish "ale."

The surveyors were often so lax that the justices were forced to interfere. Presentments about the ill condition of roads would come in from single justices, from churchwardens, and most often from constables, who ventured to take a hand. The justices in sessions would amerce (fine), not the surveyors or the churchwardens, but the parish or the inhabitants of the parish for their failure to keep up such a piece of road, and sometimes in sizable sums. If the parish did at length repair the road, by using other funds for the purpose, or by levying a special rate, the amercement might be remitted.

The justices dealt also with landlords on both sides of a road, who were bound to keep the ditches scoured and the culverts in good order on that portion of the road bisecting their property.[29] Moreover if a great landed gentleman or his father had been accustomed to look after a certain length of road, the justices were only too glad to take advantage of custom and to order him to continue the work.

The justices had to deal with many cases where the main trackway had been blurred or the road lost. In the North—and elsewhere —travelers across rough and boggy moors were wont to alter their route to the right or left, in order to find solid and smooth ground, until it became doubtful where the main line of the road was. Furthermore a road generally disused, perhaps because it had become so nearly impassable, would disappear entirely. Then sharp North Country landlords would see their chance and put up walls and enclose most of the road or all of it. North Riding justices were often appointing inquests to determine where a road had been, and then ordering its restoration.

The justices were also interested in footpaths, causeways, and bridges. Many of the footpaths had been long used and were thus

[29] This duty fell often upon the manorial court. The problem of water running across a road was always coming up. Men diverted watercourses in order to keep water out of a field, or to make a pond, or to furnish more power to a waterwheel, and such diversions might flood the road.

almost as sacred as roads, but were always being fenced in.[30] Causeways across low and swampy ground had to be well kept up. About bridges justices and high constables cooperated. If a bridge were to join two counties, the justices attempted to divide the costs with the other county. As often as possible they pushed the expensive business of a new bridge off upon great landlords. In some parts of England the good monks had taken care of bridges and drawn the material for their repair from their own woods. If very old men could be brought in to testify that the monks had always looked after such a bridge, then the great lord who now owned what had been monastic lands might be informed that it was his obligation to make a new bridge or to repair the one standing. The great lord might go to court about the matter, but he had old custom against him.

It is a favorite saying that the justices of the peace were the Tudor maids of all work. Multifarious indeed their activities were, but maids of all work they were not. They were as a body the major-domos who ruled the underservants and kept them going. If the cooks or the scullery maids or the upstairs maids were slack, the major-domos brought them to time. It was they who made local government work.

[30] The problem of footpaths was complicated by the fact that men in going from their homes in the village to their various strips of land in unenclosed fields developed innumerable paths, most of which were no longer useful after enclosure had taken place.

CHAPTER 19

The Constables

I. THE PETTY CONSTABLE

THE PETTY constable was more than a policeman; he was the executive official of the village; he kept it going. In larger towns he was less important. He was elected for a year and sometimes served longer. He was chosen by the suitors to the leet court of the manor, and in theory was an official of the manor. Leet courts were not as many or as active as once, and the constable was occasionally chosen by the lord of the manor, sometimes named by the high constable of the hundred, and less often imposed on the village by the justices of the peace. In villages here and there the obligation of serving as a constable was passed round in rotation to the various farms and houses in the township.

He might be a husbandman or an artisan, a carpenter, a shoemaker, or many times a tradesman, a butcher or baker. It was the notion in London in governing circles that the constable ought to be a substantial citizen, one not in debt or in service to another, and preferably not one of the poor.[1] But the better-off did not welcome the office, whereas the poor man from his petty fees could probably

---

[1] Sir Thomas Smith in his *De Republica Anglorum* (written between 1562 and 1566) said that in villages the constable was commonly chosen from the artisan class, from tailors, shoemakers, carpenters, etc. He wrote that the office was "at first in greater reputation than now."

228

gather more sixpences than he had ever seen before,[2] and gain some little prestige as well. Not that the office carried much prestige. The constable was the butt of village jokes, and the dramatists missed few chances to present him as a little man, ignorant, and puffed up with authority.

He had no easy role. He needed to be one who was not afraid to speak up to a "cloak lined with velvet" and did not "tremble at the sound of a jingling spur." He had to overawe the quarrelsome man and lead the dangerous man away to jail. It was desirable that he should be a man of strength and of an impressive bearing. Yet he had finally to depend upon the law—he was the spokesman of the King—and upon the support the local inhabitants would give him when he called for their help in mastering the unruly.

He had to be readily available. His abode was at least in some cases marked out by the sign of the broad bill.[3] He was usually to be found near the center of the village, not far from the alehouse. In the alehouse he could see much and learn more. The youths on the street had been teasing queer old Joan and she had been heard to mutter threats against them; young Jenny, it was whispered, was in trouble, and the man suspected was missing; the common was overcrowded with cows and horses; the deer were breaking through the palings of the lord's park and nibbling in the gardens and corn-fields; the poor were breaking down the hedges for fuel and cutting branches in the woods at the top of the common; a road was flooded over at a point where goodman Foster had failed to clean his ditches, the unlicensed alehouse at the other end of the village was serving new ale and unwholesome bread, and, worse, was tolerating gambling. A laborer had become intoxicated and had to be fined or put in the stocks. All such matters came to the attention of the constable. He had to see that the streets were watched at night and

[2] In *Measure for Measure* (Act II, Scene I) Elbow is asked why he had been constable for seven years: "Are there not men in your ward sufficient to serve it?" and answers: "Few of any wit in such matters. . . . I do it for some piece of money."

[3] The staff or weapon he carried.

was bound to keep an eye on houses where there was noise and much coming and going after dark.

There was aften more than one man could do. In a large and populous parish there might be two or three townships and a constable for each township. In borough towns there might be several constables, and in small towns the constable might have watchmen to assist him who would take turns during the night. But in a village the constable had to be his own watchman and hope that nothing went wrong after he went to bed.

He expected the villagers to bring him word of petty thieving, of household and farm utensils that disappeared, of the clothes hung out to dry that were nipped off by those with not enough to wear, of a duck or hen that was gone and had perhaps supplied hungry squatters with a meal.

When a householder came home from the fields and found something missing, he was likely to go at once to the constable and report what had been stolen and whom he suspected. The constable had to act quickly while the stolen article or animal could be found. Seldom did he wait to get a warrant from the justice for search of a cottage. He could depend upon the stupidity of the pilferer who took few precautions to escape detection. He would hurry with the complainant to the dwelling of the man or woman suspected. When Thomas Lightbowne of Pendleton in Lancashire reported that he had lost two geese, the constable moved quickly with Lightbowne to the hut of Travis, searched it and found two geese wings of the color of the missing geese, and discovered in the paunch of a newly killed goose some French wheat. Lightbowne's geese had been roaming in a field of French wheat. With such evidence the constable would soon have Travis before the nearest justice. Not always was the collecting of evidence as simple as that. The constable might have to make many inquiries round the village before he was ready to bring a man before the justice.

If a horse had been stolen, the thief would be someone who lived at a distance and who would make a quick getaway with the animal. In that case the constable raised hue and cry; that is, he sent word to all neighboring constables that a horse of such a description was missing and that a man of such a description was suspected of having stolen it. If word were sent quickly enough, the thief might be caught and the animal recovered.

Any violence or possible violence called for the attention of the constable. If he learned from B that A was threatening him with injury to his person or buildings, the constable would bring B before the justice to tell his story. Rumors of quarrels, many of them at the alehouse, were carried quickly to the constable. If two men were about to use bludgeons or knives upon one another, the constable would warn them in the King's name to desist, and, if they ignored him, he had the right to call upon all bystanders to help him "force a quiet." If the affray resulted in serious bodily injury, the constable would at once hold one or both men and bring him or them as quickly as possible before the justice.

Trespasses and forcible entry into fields in order to take possession were matters for two or more justices to deal with. But if the constable heard of a plot to seize a piece of land, he informed the nearest justice. If the justice were away the constable could warn the intruders, and, if he could not prevent the trespass, he would gather the evidence about it.

Vagrants and "sturdy rogues" were a worry to the constable. In many instances they pretended to be looking for work, perhaps in the harvest field, but they were usually looking for something to take with them. They sought refuge in unlicensed and remote alehouses, and in the cottages of such as would hide them.[4] It was the duty of the constable to be forehanded and to make surprise visits at intervals to the places where they might be found. Occasionally they assembled in numbers in a barn and were too many for the constable and a menace to the community and to property. If vagrants had no pass showing who they were and why they were traveling, the constable was to arrest them and whip them—women as well

---

[4] That the rogues were protected and hidden shows that there was some sympathy for them. Indeed the constable himself would occasionally affect not to see them, or might even find lodging for them and give them a few pence, a kindness for which he was liable to be presented to the quarter sessions.

as men—on the bare back until they were bloody, and then to give them a certificate that they had been whipped and should be sent from constable to constable back to the place of their birth. For the whipping the constable was supposed to get the consent of the clergyman, but the punishment of such people and the sending of them on rested largely in his hands.

In his efforts to maintain the peace and catch evildoers the constable was sometimes roughly handled and occasionally maimed or injured for life. Now and then he was so terrorized that he lost his usefulness as a constable. Those who had attacked him were often fined and occasionally imprisoned, but were not as severely punished as those who resist the police today.

The problem of illegitimate children haunted the constable because the village was likely to find itself compelled, if the supposed father had disappeared, to support mother and child. Hence as soon as the constable heard of an unmarried pregnant girl, he was likely to make inquiries as to the paternity of the coming child, so that the father could be found and made responsible for the upkeep of the girl and her offspring. If the girl refused to make charges, or if there were suspicion that she was blaming the wrong man—she was sometimes persuaded or bribed to do so by the real father—the constable, perhaps with the agreement of the justice, arranged that certain women in the village should attend the young woman at the birth of the child, and cross-examine her during her pains as to the father. It was believed that at such a time, with the fear of death before her, she would reveal the truth.

The constable might resort to extreme measures to save the village charges. In December, 1605, a woman carrying a peddler's pack came with two female friends to Ardleigh in Essex and was harbored in an alehouse. The woman proved to be in travail, and when turned out of the alehouse tried desperately to rent a room. The constable, fearing that the child would be born in the village and become a future charge upon it, went out in the cold rain and carted all three women a mile out of Ardleigh, just beyond the bounds of the parish, depositing them at a farmer's barn door. The farmer demanded by what right he had brought the women to him and wished them taken back again, but the constable left the women in the barn, where the child was born that night. Seven or eight days later the mother decamped, leaving the newborn child to the mercy of the parish of Langham. The justices decided that the village of Ardleigh was to pay for the upkeep of the child.

The constable had to keep an eye on the apprenticing of children. The parish apprenticed the children of the poor to artisans and farmers and had thus responsibility to see that they were properly fed, lodged, and taught the skills of a trade or occupation. Not infrequently the masters proved negligent or cruel, and sometimes the apprentices themselves and sometimes their parents complained. It was often the constable who knew about the matter and who brought it to the attention of the justice. When the apprentices had finished their time of service and required testimonials of their training in order to find posts, they had to get them from the justice, but it was the constable who was likely to look out for them and bring them to the justice.

The duties of constables in harvest time were precise. Though hundreds of men took a holiday from their town jobs to take part in harvesting, many communities lacked enough helpers in the fields. It was the obligation of the constable "upon request" "to cause all men artificers and persons as are meet for labor . . . to serve for the moving, getting, or inning of corn." Those who refused were to be put in the stocks by the constable or to forfeit a sizable sum, forty shillings.

The constable had many functions as a subordinate to the high constable, as errand boy to the justice of the peace, and also in connection with the deputy lieutenants and undersheriffs and sheriffs. Writs, precepts, mittimuses he had to carry and deliver by the dozen. He had to keep an eye on A until he appeared at the next quarter sessions; he had to distrain B for unpaid taxes by driving off a cow; he had to escort C to the house of correction; he had to go through D's barn carefully to make certain that in a time of scarcity he was not holding back corn for a higher price. It was his business on behalf of the deputy lieutenants to see that all men between eighteen and sixty attended musters, to press men—sometimes quickly—for military service in Ireland or the Low Countries. He had to lead women and carry babies and cripples from his village to the next constable. He had to jog overseers of the poor and the surveyors of the highways about the neglect of their duties, and perhaps present them to the high constables or to the quarter sessions for their failures. Even churchwardens who failed to mention recusants, or churchwardens who were themselves recusants, might be presented by him. In other words he was often the final authority as to the conduct and efficiency of other officials of as high rank as himself and often of higher.

His most onerous task was possibly that of gathering taxes. The subsidies voted by Parliament were to be collected by treasurers for the county, but those officials relied upon the high constables and they upon the petty constables. The money for purveyance, that is, for supplying the King's household, the money for maimed soldiers and for various kinds of prisoners, which the parish had to pay, fell upon him to collect. He had to gather money for the expenses of the parish. Parish officials were often slow to levy assessments and meanwhile debts owed by the parish accumulated, and the poor were not paid the sums allotted them. The constable might have to bring pressure to bear upon the parishes and their churchwardens to levy the sums necessary. Better than anyone else he knew how much had to be levied; sometimes he suggested the amount. If he failed to get the money he was likely to find himself in trouble with higher officials. In some places the various sums to be collected were lumped together so that the constable could gather them at one time; in other places it would appear that the constables had to collect this tax and then that. There might be a special tax for the repair of this bridge or for building a new house of correction, and the constable would find himself with an extra and burdensome task. Now and again he met with resistance, perhaps from the strong and well-to-do, but in general the English were good about paying their taxes.

There were many kinds of constables. A few proved something like leaders in the village, but most of them were little more than servants of the justice. The position of the constable depended somewhat on his personality. It depended also upon custom and practice, and there were almost infinite variations of methods in shires and hundreds and parishes. The role of the constable was not as simple as it sounds in this brief chapter. Two large volumes would be scarcely enough to set forth aright the duties and limitations of his office. The variations of practice were not only in place but in time. Ways of doing things were always changing. New laws were being made, and sometimes those laws seem to follow practices that had developed in certain shires.

In any case it is safe to say that the constable was often the spokesman of village opinion. Again and again ten or twelve substantial men of a parish, including the constable, would send a statement to the quarter sessions saying that there were too many alehouses in their village, or that the method of assessment for taxes needed overhauling, or that something else was wrong. In some instances the constable was perhaps the man behind the statement. More often the actions of the constable followed village opinion. The presentments sent up to higher officials were sometimes merely the formal phrasing of conclusions arrived at by influential members of the community.[5]

II. THE HIGH CONSTABLE AND THE HUNDRED

The "hundred" as a political unit had been brought to England from northern Europe at least two centuries before the Norman Conquest. It was probably an old unit in Teutonic territories. In thinking of it the reader had better divorce from his mind any possible connection with the numeral 100. In England the hundred became a division intermediate between the shire and the township or parish, a much smaller unit in the eastern and southern counties

[5] In some places we can detect the beginnings of discontent among the lesser fry that they were allowed so little part in affairs. There was often an oligarchy in the village and the parson was likely to cooperate with it; the constable, if he were a good one, was likely during his term to be accepted by it.

than in the northern and western. In a few Midland and northern counties the hundred was called by the Scandinavian word "wapentake." It was an administrative and judicial unit; there was a hundred court and here and there a "sheriff's tourn," by that time almost a relic. Hundred courts still were to be found in the seventeenth century, and manuscript records of them can be looked at in the British Museum. But the hundred court was becoming an unusual thing; what was left was the high constable's post and an old loyalty to the hundred. Those who have read Smyth of Nibley's *History of the Hundred of Berkeley* will remember the note of pride as he wrote, "we hundredors."

The high constables, two of them, were officials of the hundred, though not chosen by the hundredors. They continued to be important even where the hundred became no more than a geographical expression. They were chosen by the justices of peace of the county at quarter sessions, and sometimes by the justices of a "division" or "limit" of the county. They were usually of the small gentry, though often well-to-do yeomen served in the post. Their terms of office were unspecified, but they were generally expected to carry on for three years, and did sometimes carry on longer. It was a yeoman high constable in Ben Jonson's *A Tale of a Tub* whom the tinker addressed as the very bellwether of the hundred. At another point in the play the headborough remarks:

> The High Constable is the Thumbe, as one
>   would say,
> The hold-fast of the rest.

It was the duty of the high constables to relay instructions from the justices of the peace to the petty constables. At times the listing of all recusants might be stressed; at times the needs of the poor, or the menace from sturdy rogues. He had constantly to be an intermediary to gather information from the petty constables for the justices, who in their turn might have had orders from the Privy Council. He would make inquiries about the alehouses and about tillage (plowed land) that had been turned into pasture.

He had to see to it that the sums levied from parishes and townships for the hundred and the shire and for all purposes outside parish and township were gathered and turned over to the proper treasurers. It had long been his function to maintain the King's peace within the hundred, and that might involve much cooperation with other officials. It was his particular duty to take pains that watches were kept by local authorities and that all beacons in the hundred were in repair, and, if necessary, to make certain that a rate was levied for the purpose. Moreover, he had to cooperate with the lord lieutenant and his deputies concerning the militia.

The presentments made by the petty constables, in some cases with the assistance of the churchwardens, were brought before the high constables gathered together in "petty sessions," just before the quarter sessions. In other counties there were no petty sessions, but the high constables came to the divisional sessions of the justices, or to the quarter sessions, and delivered in the presentments they had collected from the petty constables. Too often the petty constables and the churchwardens would report, *Omnia bene,* all well. The high constables might know better; they might have heard of disorderly alehouses not reported, or of crimes not mentioned. For such failures to report they could impose fines upon the petty constables and they might also fine them for not appearing before them at petty sessions. Now and then the high constables would realize that a petty constable had too much to do and would compel him to take on a watchman as an assistant.

The high constables exercised one of their most important functions in connection with wages. Once a year the justices of the peace were obligated to formulate a scale of wages to be paid for various types of service, and especially for farm labor. It was the high constables who enforced the scale determined upon. In the autumn after harvest the two high constables of a hundred sent word to each of the petty constables to attend them at a certain place on a certain day for a "statute sessions" about laborers and masters. If the hundred was large, the two constables might divide it up and arrange that one of them should hold statute sessions at one place and the other at another. When the petty constables were summoned to the statute sessions, they proceeded to send out instructions to all masters and servants to appear at the time stated. By no means all of those summoned did appear, but it is probable that laborers seeking work and masters looking for laborers would turn up.[6]

The meeting of the "statute sessions" was an occasion in the hundred. Just how it was related, if at all, to the old annual fairs where servants and masters met and made contracts we do not know. This was an official business. We can imagine the high constables taking their place at the market or in front of the inn. They would call the petty constables in order before them and scan their lists of masters and servants. As their names were read aloud, the men were expected to make their appearance. The master would be asked if he released Tom, and if so, the high constable would then issue a testimonial for which Tom had to pay $1d.$ to $2d.$ When Tom received his testimonial he would then go to the rendezvous appointed and enter into a bargain with another employer for a year, accepting in token a God's penny, usually $2s.$ or $2s.$ $6d.$ If the master wished, however, to keep his servant for another year, no testimonial was required. Once a bargain had been struck between master and servant, the high constable made a record of it, which he was supposed to keep in a book. If later there was any infraction of the wage set down, either by master or servant, the high constable presented the offending party to the quarter sessions.

The high constables cooperated, as we have seen, with the justices in the matter of bridges. In the hilly counties of England, especially in the North and West Ridings of Yorkshire, in Westmorland, Cumberland, Lancashire, Derbyshire, and Shropshire, the bridges were likely to be washed out by sudden floods or at least seriously damaged. The building or repairing of such a bridge might cost from £100 to £500, sums beyond the financial resources of a single or of two hundreds. It became the duty of the justices of the peace

---

[6] In this paragraph and the next I owe much to George Dodds' unpublished thesis, "The Rural Constable in Seventeenth Century England" (1939), now in the Yale Library.

and of the high constables in association to determine the probable cost of a bridge. Once that was settled they had to hire workmen and allocate costs. The same cooperation was required for raising a new house of correction or for a new jail.

If the high constables were a little lower than the justices of the peace, it is to be said that at least once they were asked to check upon the justices. In 1605 the Privy Council sent out a letter addressed to the justices and to the clerks of the peace, the executive officials of the quarter session, asking the clerk and the constables of the several hundreds to certify the judges of assize upon their oath as to what justices of peace were absent from divisional sessions, and as to what services had been done by every justice in apprehending murderers, robbers, and thieves, in the punishment of rogues and vagabonds, and in the suppressing of unlicensed alehouses. The information the high constables gathered in answer to this request was to be relayed by the judges to the Lord Chancellor. In other words, while justices kept an eye on high constables, those officials were in this instance to report on the faithfulness of the justices. So far as I know, this scheme was not tried a second time. It may have aroused opposition from the justices, who were jealous of their authority and of any encroachment upon it. Ben Jonson makes Turfe, the high constable, gloat over a justice:

> Well, I have carried it, and will triumph
> Over this justice, as becomes a Constable;
> And a high Constable.

Actually there was seldom a chance for such gloating.

CHAPTER 20

The Churchwardens and the Parish

O NLY rarely are we fortunate enough to catch a glimpse of the churchwardens together. In a play we see them coming into the alehouse for breakfast, ordering ale, nutmeg, and toast.[1] The host foresaw that they would spend little and expect much. Perhaps they were paying their own "shots" that morning. More often they met at the alehouse at the expense of the parish. Another time a traveler meets them in the church; they have bought a new organ and are tuning it and trying it out, while with the parson and his guest they sip a cup of good liquor.[2]

At the breakfast in the alehouse there were four churchwardens, and in large boroughs there were sometimes that many, but two was the common number; in very small villages there was occasionally only one. By the reign of James I, and indeed shortly before, we hear of "sidesmen," who were to assist the wardens, and who often graduated into churchwardens.

The churchwardens were at the top of the village organization. Now and then the gentleman in the manor house consented to election to the office. Those who filled it were in general drawn from the more important families in the town or village, the well-to-do householders. In villages it was sometimes hard to find enough good men

[1] *The London Chanticleers,* Scene 5, in J. P. Collier (ed.), R. Dodsley, *A Select Collection of Old Plays* (London, 1874–76), XII, 336.
[2] L. G. Wickham Legg (ed.), *A Short Survey of the Western Counties,* Camden Misc. XVI, 60. The traveler was William Hamond.

to take on the necessary offices, but that of churchwarden had so much tradition behind it, good ecclesiastical tradition, and such respectability that few men asked to be excused. It was an office where the holders were in close relation to the parson, who often kept the accounts for them and was at times their moving spirit.

They were elected at the annual meeting at Easter. In some parishes a churchwarden already in office was reelected for a second year and a new churchwarden elected, so that there would always be one old hand and one new hand. In earlier days they had been chosen in many cases by all the parishioners who attended the parish meeting. By the Stuart period the right of choosing churchwardens had fallen in many parishes into the hands of an inside or more or less exclusive group. In some places there had long existed "the four," "the twelve," "the sixteen," or "the four and twenty," who had gained complete control of parish affairs. In other parishes those who attended the meetings regularly, possibly at first a rather unfixed group of the more important and well-to-do, or sometimes "the neighbors," came slowly to be regarded as "the vestry," and eventually assumed all powers. Such a narrow and responsible body was likely to be more efficient, and had been often favored by various ecclesiastical authorities, and possibly by the lord of the manor. No doubt the householders and the better-off villagers who had to pay the taxes felt themselves more competent to vote money and to choose those who had to administer the funds, that is, the churchwardens. It was a time when oligarchies grew and flourished.

In some places the parishioners or the vestry made many of the decisions about parish affairs. In other places the decisions fell largely upon the churchwardens, who probably consulted others of the parish. They constituted a legally corporate body, which could sue and be sued for movable goods.

The parish which they served was the base unit of the English political structure. Originally an ecclesiastical unit, it had become as a result of Tudor legislation not less political than ecclesiastical. There were more than eight thousand parishes in England, in most of which there was a clergyman and his rectory or vicarage. The boundaries of that parish were "perambulated" ceremoniously every year at Rogation tide [3] by the parish officials accompaned by old men who could recall the boundaries and by boys who were expected to remember those boundaries when they became old men. Those boundaries were in many instances approximately those of the land held by the lord of the manor and corresponded often to the township, though in places a large parish might contain two or three townships.

Up to the break with Rome the life of the village had revolved around the church, its fabric or structure, its appurtenances, and its ceremonies. The activities of the church in some parishes, and particularly in the southwest of England, had been highly organized, with different groups performing different functions. The matrons looked after a certain altar, the maidens raised money for a chapel or saw to the gilding of the images; the older men collected money for reparations or for some other object in the church; the younger men organized the church ales and the church plays. In addition the various guilds in the town had this and that chapel for which they cared, and where they had perhaps arranged windows with painted glass. The several groups were friendly rivals as to how much they could do for the church and as to the amount of money gathered. Out of such rivalry grew loyalty to the church and pleasant social relations in which men and women, youths and maidens, had a part.

With the Reformation much of the cooperation in church activities ceased and the good will was lost. The altars and images disappeared, the paintings on the walls were covered with white or erased, and Scripture texts put in their place; Bibles were bought and the *Paraphrases* of Erasmus and Foxe's *Book of Martyrs* and the works of Bishop Jewel. Were not their minds now on higher things, on matters of the spirit, on men's chief duty?

Meanwhile, as medieval local government was breaking down, the state was reaching out to find new means of putting communities to the task of managing their affairs. What better unit could be used than the parish? Almost without intention the makers of law

[3] The three days before Ascension Day.

were putting duties upon the churchwardens and upon other parish and township officials. The whole course of mid- and late-Tudor legislation was directed to using the officials already on the scene. In their own communities the churchwardens found themselves administering the new laws about the poor and about apprentices. They had now much money to distribute and much money to take in: all the property that had accumulated in church hands.

For the parish tended to gather to itself possessions. From the late Middle Ages many parishes had secured to themselves church houses, rooms which they sometimes rented out for money, or turned over to the poor, or used to brew ale or bake bread for the church ales, and part of which they often retained as a kind of social center. They were always profiting from wills. Sir Roger at the manor house might leave the parish certain houses or certain strips in the open fields, the rents of which would give the parish an annual sum. The old parson, who had possibly some property in another village, would leave the rents to be used by the churchwardens for the poor. Goodman John in his will—the parson had perhaps helped him draw it—bestowed upon the church a cow or a few sheep. The cow or sheep could be leased out to villagers. The tradesmen in the town or village were likely to leave sums of money to the church for this and that purpose. Even a farm laborer might leave a pig or a hive of bees or a few shillings.

From such gifts the churchwardens ought to have found themselves eventually able to meet all the expenses of the church without levying any rates. That is precisely what happened in some important parishes in the towns, where the churchwardens not only kept the capital but added to it. Not so in most villages. The churchwardens often lost the property bequeathed to the parish. They would lease out sheep and cows to villagers who would avoid payment by pleas of poverty. They would rent houses and fields, and the tenants would fail to pay and by and by claim a prescriptive right to them. The churchwardens would loan money and get neither interest nor the money back. They were sometimes too sympathetic with their neighbors and allowed themselves to forgive debts

due to the parish which they would not have forgiven if due to
themselves. Moreover a certain number of churchwardens were
dishonest, keeping for themselves the funds they handled. They were
supposed to submit their accounts to the justices and in some places
to the vestry, and were sometimes exposed and occasionally forced
to repay. Too often they profited from the slackness of the justices
and of their colleagues in the parish.

The churchwardens had other sources of income. Since the
Reformation, and probably before, pews had been rented, and the
price for a pew was steadily going up.[4] Burial fees brought in
revenue. Those who wished to be buried within the church left
usually 6s. 8d., a sizable sum, to pay for the preferred position.
The fines and amerciaments for violations of the laws about highways accrued to the churchwardens to be used for the highways.
The fines for swearing, for drunkenness, for keeping an unlicensed
alehouse, or for keeping an alehouse open during church time on
Sunday belonged to the churchwardens and were earmarked for the
poor.

In earlier times the church ales had been a source of income to
the parish and were still in a few places profitable. The churchwardens or their assistants or a group of young men in the parish
would be furnished malt by the maltsters and would arrange to have
the beer brewed and the bread baked in the church house or elsewhere. The parishioners would contribute eggs, butter, cheese, and
fruits. To encourage the sale of the ale the alehouses would remain
closed during the celebration. The village gave itself up to the festivity. He who ate and drank most proved himself a helper in a good
cause, bringing in the most money. Many who could not afford it
and more who liked a good excuse to imbibe took part and sometimes showed unnecessary zeal in the good cause. In the early sixteenth century as much as £10 or £15 or even £20 might accrue to

---

[4] There was much bickering about pews, since their position in the church
was not unrelated to the social position of the family. The churchwardens were
given pews at the front and near them were the leading parishioners. Men tried
to keep the pews their ancestors had held and the newly prosperous wished
recognition in better pews. Hence arose bitter quarrels and even lawsuits.

the coffers of the churchwardens from these ales. In early Stuart days the profits seldom came to more than £4 or £5.

With the rents, the fees, and the profits accruing to the parish, the churchwardens had less than enough to meet the calls upon the parish. Like the churchwardens of pre-Reformation times, they had still the continuous problem of keeping the church in repair and were pushed by the ecclesiastical authorities as their predecessors had been. On the tower some stones had fallen off and others were loose, the west and south walls needed refacing. Stone and lime had to be bought and masons called upon. It might become necessary to repair the roof and to bring lead from the Mendips or the Peak. Two new windows on the north side would improve the lighting in the church. The bells were constantly getting out of order and had either to be mended or replaced, always a ticklish job. Bells were expensive and had to be carried in from a distance and the men who could repair them were scarce. New floors had to be laid, new pews and benches for the servants crowded in, and possibly a new gallery to meet the needs of a village that was growing. That meant the hauling of timber from the woods and the employment of carpenters and possibly of woodcarvers.

The floors were "strawed" over, or covered once a year with rushes, and here and there the churchwardens put down rugs and even a carpet. Occasionally the churchwardens bought enough coal to take the chill off the church in winter and charcoal and incense to sweeten the air. For festival occasions they arranged that the interior should be decorated with greenery, ivy gathered by the children, or with bays and rosemary.

They were accountable for the good appearance of the churchyard. It was often required of them that they should wall or fence it about so that the village pigs should not root among the graves, nor the children make it a playground, nor the alehouse at the corner use it as an out-of-door extension.

The churchwardens found themselves compelled to spend several times as much on the poor as they had spent in mid-sixteenth century. The "old Church," that is, the Catholic, had set aside occasional sums *pro caritate* (for charity) and the monks had kept something like open house for the wandering poor. But the monks were gone, and, owing to economic changes, there were more poor than ever before.

We have seen that the Elizabethan Parliaments put upon the parishes the obligation of caring for them. When it was found that the collectors for the poor at the church services, whatever importunity they used in passing the plate, could not raise enough, the justices of the peace were empowered (1572) to assess the inhabitants. By the Poor Laws of 1597 and 1601 overseers of the poor were set up; they and the churchwardens could levy a poor rate on the parish. Moreover the overseers of the poor, with the churchwardens, who were always to act with them,[5] were to establish stocks of raw materials upon which the poor could work,[6] and furnish weekly sums of money for the aged and those unable to work. They had also to find rooms for the poor or build cottages for them on the waste, and to apprentice their children. It was a task that involved consideration and wisdom. Thomas was too old to work and had a bedridden wife. Henry had eight children, and had been crippled by a fall from a ladder. A stonemason was no longer able to carry on, and he and his wife had been sleeping out of doors in November. A farm laborer needed to be sent to Bath for the recovery of his leg, and the churchwardens gave him 10s. toward his expenses. They allowed 20s. for a child who needed an operation.

The churchwardens and overseers of the poor had many times to be pushed by justices of the peace into doing their duty by the indigent. Even when they voted the small sums necessary, they did not always see to it that the money was dispensed regularly. Poor Agnes was old and worn out, and had been allowed 6d. a week, but lingered on for months without seeing any money, and perhaps survived only by the kindness of other poor. Alice in a similar situation

[5] In some places the churchwardens seem to have been responsible for casual relief and the overseers of the poor for regular relief.

[6] They were required by law to establish such stocks. I have found fewer cases than I expected in which they did so. But see E. M. Leonard, *The Early History of English Poor Relief* (Cambridge, 1900), pp. 325-329.

did not survive, but her shroud and funeral expenses were paid for by the churchwardens.

The quality of mercy was not always lacking. Churchwardens in towns were more generous and on the job than in villages. Even in villages they would contribute 2d. or 3d. to bona fide travelers with passes,[7] to soldiers home from the wars with visible wounds or loss, to those who had suffered from the Barbary pirates or been wrecked at sea. Men from afar with vivid stories for the alehouse no doubt fared best. The churchwardens gave money to the plantation of Virginia and to those who had returned from there and could tell of Indians and massacres; they voted sums to towns in England which had suffered from fire or plague; they were known to have appropriated shillings to "our poor Protestant brothers in the Palatinate."

The problem of bastardy was closely related to that of poverty, and involved expense. If the constable and the churchwardens could discover the father of the expected child, they would order him to pay 8d. a week for the upkeep of mother and child. But if not, or if the suspected father disappeared, they might be able to push off the burden upon the relatives of the mother or father, even upon the grandfather.[8] Otherwise they might be compelled to draw upon parish funds for the support of mother and child until the child reached the age to be apprenticed.

The churchwardens had to pay the expenses of minor officials in the church. The parish clerk they did not choose, but they usually paid his quarterly wages. He was supposed to be a man of good conversation [9] and of some skill in singing; he was sometimes also sex-

7 That is, certificates that the bearer was a person of good conduct, no vagrant or sturdy rogue.

8 With the moral questions involved the ecclesiastical authorities were most concerned, and, as a result of their pressure, the churchwardens might order the girl whipped or command that she and sometimes the erring man should stand in a white sheet at the door of the church and then later in church should publicly confess their sin and promise amendment.

9 In Devonshire and other parts of southwest England the parish clerk was sometimes called a deacon and was in minor orders and wore a gown. He might conduct part of the service and carry on when the parson was absent.

ton and bellman and town crier. He might even be the organist. Now and again the churchwardens hired a schoolmaster to teach the A B C's, in rare cases using the parish clerk in that capacity. They might add a few pounds or shillings to the income of the parson or curate in token of appreciation. In some well-endowed puritan parishes the churchwardens hired a "lecturer." [10]

In places where the leet court had disappeared the churchwardens paid for sundry local helpers, the shepherd who cared for the sheep on the common, the swineherd who looked after the pigs in the woods, the poundkeeper who shut up stray animals,[11] and the dog-rapper who whipped dogs out of church. Now and again they gave bounties for killing foxes, wildcats, polecats, badgers, and sparrows.

The churchwardens might even consider the general needs of the village and spend a considerable sum to restore the village cross or, like a modern chamber of commerce, seek the right to establish a market in the village.

The churchwardens had expenses in connection with appearances at court. The summoner was always turning up and calling them to come to the archdeacon's court or to the bishop's court. There were fees for being summoned and fees right and left when they presented themselves. A swarm of church officials went round spying upon conduct in order to draw people into their courts and gain more money. Nothing irritated the churchwardens and parishioners more than the overbearing ways of these busy officials,[12] and the abolition of church courts by the Long Parliament was popular even with many of those who loved the church. The expenses borne by churchwardens in their relation to high constables and quarter sessions were chiefly those of travel. Now and then one of the churchwardens had to go to London about a suit, or the parish had to

[10] See Chapter 13.

[11] A lost beast could not be shut up by the poundkeeper until it had been proclaimed in the church as an "estray."

[12] In the parish of Bishops Stortford in 1634 the churchwardens voted 5s. to the bellringers for not ringing the bells when the chancellor came, and 2s. 6d. for ringing on the day that he went away.

employ a lawyer in a county town or in London, and that cost money.

As a result of their many expenses a large proportion of parishes had to pay rates; a few of them indeed had been levying rates even earlier than the time of Elizabeth; by the early Stuart period it was becoming a common practice. This levying of rates by the parish has been hailed as a great democratic process. As a matter of fact the parish was forced to pay money; if it neglected to do so, the churchwardens, under pressure from higher officials, would have had to find the money anyway. I cannot discover majority and minority votes. I do come upon cases where the parish would fail to come together or fail to make a vote. It had to pay in any case.

It will be seen that the churchwardens were above all businessmen concerned with the collection and expenditure of money and thus deeply involved in the activities of their communities. They were as well administrative officials with almost inquisitorial powers. When they dealt with the poor and with bastardy, they had to pass judgments upon their inferiors in the village. They had sometimes to pass judgments upon those at least nominally their superiors. If the parson was failing to wear a surplice, or omitting a required part of the service, or leading an unbecoming life, it was their duty to present him to the church officials. The churchwardens were, together with the constable, the purveyors of community opinion. Many things they knew only by common report, and they had to act on such report. It was whispered in the village that the squire was at heart a Catholic; it was even believed that he entertained priests in a priest's hole in his house.

To report him to the church courts or to the quarter sessions was not lightly done by churchwardens; they owed him a kind of feudal loyalty; usually they paid him rents and were thus somewhat in his power. But the justices, urged on by the government in London, wished to know of all recusants. It became the duty of churchwardens, however much they might try to evade it, to report such men, even when they had only community opinion as to the facts in the case.

CHAPTER 21

The Companies and Colonization

THE COMPANIES which sent out colonists to Virginia and Massachusetts Bay were the outgrowth of a long development. The stories of those companies, of their dealings with King and Council and Parliament, of their explorations, of their negotiations with strange despots in Russia, in Persia, and India, are hidden away, many of them, in archives or in the proceedings of learned societies. Those narratives tell us not a little about the merchant classes, who were not only imaginative and enterprising but patient and long-suffering. Here we are more concerned with their forms of organizing their foreign ventures, forms which were originally derived in part from the medieval guilds but were adapted with skill to the needs of traders in distant ports. The forms slowly became rather fixed.

The companies were of two kinds, regulated and joint stock. The oldest of the regulated companies and the "great prototype," [1] was that of the Merchant Adventurers. It was recognized by the government as early as 1407, although already long in operation, and it was given a charter in 1564. The governing body was to consist of a governor and twenty-four assistants, as had been the custom. These officials were elected in the early seventeenth century by members of the company at the continental port of trading. At that

---

[1] Astrid Friis, *Alderman Cockayne's Project and the Cloth Trade* (Oxford, 1927), pp. 26, 57. I have made much use of this work.

time the governor was usually a Londoner and was represented at the trading port by a deputy.

The London group was central, and of great influence, but there were also Merchant Adventurers at Newcastle, Hull, and York, and lesser groups at Norwich, Ipswich, and Exeter. Each of these local bodies had its own rules and special modes of government at home, but was subject to the deputy governor and the twenty-four assistants at the continental port or ports where sales were made. Taken together, the company at the beginning of the seventeenth century included probably between three and four thousand members. It was, said the governor, "the most famous company of merchants in Christendom." [2]

Such a company with its several branches could hardly have been managed except as a regulated company, which allowed freedom to its members. Each merchant could ship on his own a certain number of cloths [3] each year (the number depending upon the length of his membership in the company) and sell them himself or by his factor at the place where the company had privileges of a market. But strict rules governed the conduct of each member. He was to make sales only on specified days and at certain hours of that day. All disagreements were to be settled by the governor, or his deputy in residence, and those officials dealt with such disputes as arose between members of the company and continental officials and buyers. It is probable that a large proportion of the business was done by a rather small number of the merchants.

In joint-stock companies each member took a certain number of shares and all the selling of the goods of each merchant was carried on by the officials of the company. In general, joint-stock companies were necessary in far-flung enterprises and in those where the company had to make special arrangements with the foreign countries. The device of joint stock might take the form of a fully incorporated body or of a somewhat informal and unincorporated syndicate. The

[2] Friis, *Alderman Cockayne's Project,* p. 69.
[3] A "cloth" consisted of a long piece of cloth of a fixed size. A common size was twenty-four yards in length and a yard and a half in width. But every kind of cloth had its own sizes, and the sizes were slightly different at different times.

Muscovy Company, which had constantly to make new arrangements with the Czar of Russia, had been established in 1553 as a joint-stock company with a subscription by each member of £25 and a total capital of £6,000. The several privateering expeditions of Drake against the silver fleets were joint-stock enterprises organized, however, not as incorporated companies but as joint-stock syndicates. The Levant Company, which developed trade with Turkey, seems to have been a joint-stock company, although it became eventually a regulated company. The greatest of all joint-stock companies was the East India Company, established at the end of 1599 and under the management of Sir Thomas Smith and twenty-four assistants.[4] It included 218 members all named in the charter.[5]

The companies proved useful to England in critical times. In her first years as Queen, Elizabeth wanted money to help the Scottish Protestants, to repel French invaders, and to pay her debts. That she was "on the high road to lose her throne" was the judgment of the Spanish ambassador. It was Sir Thomas Gresham, who had been the agent of Henry VIII and of Mary, who forced the Merchant Adventurers to loan the Queen the money coming in from foreign sales. By the most intricate financial operations, described by W. R. Scott,[6] Gresham managed to keep Elizabeth's government solvent.[7]

Hardly less helpful to the Queen were the joint-stock syndicates

[4] The Lord Treasurer put pressure upon the company to choose as head of the expedition a friend of Essex, but the company asked that it be allowed "to sort their business with men of their own quality . . . lest the suspicion of the employment of gentlemen . . . drive a great number of the adventurers to withdraw their contributions."

[5] It was provided that the sons of members, at the age of twenty-four, the factors of the company and their apprentices, and those subsequently admitted to the freedom of the company could become members. The factors and employed were given a share of the profits.

[6] The Constitution and Finance of English, Scottish, and Irish Joint Stock Companies to 1720 (Cambridge, 1910), I, 27–28, 51–54.

[7] The company had its reward. In 1564 it was given a license to export 30,000 undressed cloths a year. Its great rival, the Hanseatic League, was prohibited from exporting any white or undressed cloths, and was at length frozen out of the English market.

for privateering organized by Drake. In that sailor's voyage around the world the Queen was a heavy investor and made such a profit that she was able to assist in the financing of the Levant Company, in the putting down of the Irish rebellion, and in helping the Dutch against Spain.

The companies justified themselves by their support of exploration. The City men who founded them and financed them were surprisingly willing to take a far view and to send out expeditions to cold seas and across dangerous deserts. They studied maps and picked up information about voyages already taken, believing that sooner or later they could find a northwest or northeast passage to the Far East. They found instead new lands and occasional openings for trade. They lost a great deal of money, but sometimes the next generation did well. The Muscovy Company hoped to find a northeast passage to China and, after many ups and downs, developed a trade with Russia. That country was to it only a stepping-stone. Hoping to discover "how men may pass from Russia either by land or sea to Cathaia," Anthony Jenkinson persuaded the Czar to allow him and his company to seek an overland trade route to Persia and China. Six times the Muscovy Company sent travelers toward those lands, with great peril to the men, and gained a little silk and a few precious stones, but failed to establish a trading route.

The English had to acquire Oriental commodities in other ways. They procured them from the Venetians, who had tapped in the Near East the overland trade routes from India and China. When the Venetians had their commerce halted by the Turkish control of the eastern Mediterranean, the English looked to Portugal as the intermediary from which they could buy the spices and silks of the East. But when Portugal was overcome by Spain, the English had to find new means of gaining the goods they required from Asia. The establishment of the Levant Company in Constantinople, the result of carefully laid plans and of elaborate negotiations, which the French did their best to defeat, proved in the long run one of the most profitable of adventures.

Other ways were to be found to tap the East. Out of the Levant

Company grew the East India Company. The English had observed that the Dutch were getting a footing in the East Indies and they organized the East India Company in the hope of competing with them. The earlier expeditions of that company were mostly to the East India Islands, where the Dutch proved too much for them. It was not until the seventh expedition that the company secured a foothold on the mainland of India at Masulipatan, nearly two hundred miles north of Madras, on the east coast. In 1612 the English landed at Surat on the west coast, and from there were able to set going trade with Persia. Slowly they penetrated inward from Masulipatan and Surat and developed a great commerce with India.

The new companies affected English life. The hope of making money quickly, as Drake had done, possibly several hundred per cent in a year or two, induced merchants to buy shares in every new company organized and drew in as investors many of the nobility and gentry. They forgot the enormous losses undergone and remembered the few successes. One result was that the investing classes and the whole English public gained a wider outlook upon the world. The news of this ship's arrival, of that one lost, of rich cargoes just landed at Plymouth, and of new privileges conferred on the English at Constantinople or at Surat was relayed over London as fast as the disgrace of a courtier. The merchants took on a new importance in the minds of members of Parliament and Privy Councilors and the King. To the public they were becoming almost heroes.

The explorations east and west and the success of some of the companies led men to look westward. Had not the Spaniards found treasure in the New World? Had not English privateers profited thereby? Even after peace with Spain was declared in 1604, those privateers were able to carry on underhand trade with Spanish possessions in the West. In their many trips along the trade routes the English had learned not a little about the long American coast north of Florida; had come to realize how thinly populated it was and what a chance it offered. The Spanish claims to that coast might well be ignored. Were not the Spanish the traditional enemies

of England and the offending front of Catholic power? The idea
of colonizing North American lands could not long remain merely
an idea. As early as the 1570's Sir Humphrey Gilbert had schemes
for setting up plantations in America and in 1583 almost established
a settlement far north at St. John's. The first man who planted a
colony was Sir Walter Ralegh. After an exploratory trip which
touched what is now North Carolina, he sent out two expeditions,
the second putting ashore more than a hundred people at Roanoke
on the Carolina coast. When two years later relief was sent them,
no trace of the colony could be found.

While Ralegh was starting off his first expedition and before it
returned, Richard Hakluyt, a Bristol clergyman who had from youth
studied geography, was asked by Secretary Walsingham to make
"diligent inquiry of such things as may yield any light unto our
western discoveries," and to suggest measures for the furtherance of
settlement.

Hakluyt was known to Ralegh and may have assisted in drawing
up a memorial about colonization. It is possible that Hakluyt
decided to expand that statement. In any case he wrote *A Particular
Discourse concerning Western Discoveries,* of which a manuscript
copy was sent to the Queen. It was destined to become the classic
statement of the case for English colonization.

Hakluyt had read Spanish, Italian, and French travelers, and had
accumulated more information of the American shore north of
Florida, of its appearance, soil, and inhabitants, than any two or
three navigators. It was a country which the English ought to settle
quickly, he believed, before the Spanish who were already in
Florida, or the French who had explored the St. Lawrence, gained
a foothold. Was it not by reason of Cabot's discovery in the reign of
Henry VII properly an English possession? Hakluyt held out hope
that the English would find timber for masts, dearly needed at that
time, as well as pitch, tar, and ashes for soap. About silver and gold,
which men always hoped to find, he had little to say. Nor did he
expatiate upon those spices of the East which might be brought by
a northwest passage to India. He talked like a man with his feet on

the ground, unless when he suggested that the savages of New England would be eager to buy English cloth. In fact they did buy a little.

He was one of the first Englishmen, but not the last, to make the best of both worlds, trade and religion. Colonizing would be a means of converting the natives to the Christian faith. It would also be a means of setting up merchants who had gone bankrupt and were in debtors' prisons. Hakluyt held out the hope that the large vagrant population of England might be shunted to the New World and learn new ways there.

It would not do, however, to rely upon broken merchants and vagrants. Colonies, he pointed out, required many kinds of artisans: ironworkers, carpenters, sawmill-makers, gunpowder-makers, shipwrights, basket-makers, etc. An impressive list he drew up of types of workers needed, a list that might well have been examined by the founders of the Virginia Company.

Hakluyt's manuscript, passed no doubt from hand to hand, affected a considerable circle in his time. It presented ideas that were in the air, but was supported by a more exact knowledge than was common. More people than Ralegh became interested in colonization. In 1605 the Earl of Southampton (Shakespeare's patron) sent out Sir George Weymouth, who touched Nantucket and the coast of Maine and fetched back five Indians. Sir Ferdinando Gorges, a naval and military man who carried weight in that west country where sailors lived and men were ready to plan expeditions, took charge of the five Indians. They proved an excellent advertisement of the New World. Meanwhile all sorts of people were sending out ships to engage in fishing. By the early years of James I so many kinds of men were interested in the lands across the North Atlantic and were so experienced in developing companies that the formation of the Virginia Company became almost inevitable.

The story of the Virginia Company belongs in another volume of this series and can only be touched upon here. In 1606 a patent was granted for two Virginia companies: "the first colony," commonly called the London Company, was to plant a settlement in southern

Virginia; "the Second Colony," called usually the Plymouth Company, was to make a settlement in northern Virginia. Over both settlements was instituted a Council of thirteen members appointed by the Crown. The project was not well considered. The English were more experienced in establishing trade facilities than in founding colonies. Neither the merchants of the London Company nor those of the Plymouth Company had a clear notion of what they intended to do and of what they could do. They sought immediate returns from their investments, although in earlier projects they had seldom made a profit quickly. In Virginia income at once was not likely unless valuable minerals could be discovered. But they also wished to establish colonies, forgetting in their hope for quick returns that new settlers needed all their energies and capital to put themselves on their feet.

In 1607 a small body of colonists was sent out and in 1609 six hundred more. In that year the company for the southern of the two colonies envisaged in the plan became a joint-stock company, somewhat on the model of companies already mentioned. The stockholders put pressure upon the settlers to ship home salable commodities, but aside from small amounts of timber, soap ashes, pitch tar, and dyes nothing profitable was exported until eight or nine years after the first settlement, when tobacco began to offer a prospect of profit.

Things were not going well. Too many unruly gallants and men and women undesired at home had been shipped out. The settlers suffered from disease, from want of food and from poor food, from bad water in the low grounds, and from attacks by the Indians.

One device after another was used in England to keep the colony going. Reorganizations were instituted and auxiliary companies established. The main company sent shipload after shipload of new settlers, but bettered the situation little; it sent out a stern governor as a kind of dictator, and recalled him. It advanced money until the stockholders refused to go further into their pockets. A national lottery brought in some income and saved the colony, and by that time the grants to auxiliary and subordinate companies and to those who would establish plantations of their own within the territories assigned were alleviating the situation.

At home a furious conflict was developing between Sir Edwin Sandys, a great figure in Parliament, and Sir Thomas Smith, perhaps the leading financier of London. At last in 1624 the King, who cherished a grudge against Sandys and was weary of the quarrels, dissolved the company. By that time, however, new settlements were being opened up and the colony was about ready to stand on its own feet.

The Virginia Company was a natural extension of company enterprise. The Plymouth and Massachusetts Bay colonies used traditional forms of organization, but were more purely colonial enterprises. Their establishment was related to the immediate situations in the reigns of James I and Charles I. The hardships imposed on religious extremists by James I led to the project of the Plymouth colony.

The story of that colony, of the "Pilgrims" who settled at Plymouth, is central in the American tradition. On the borders of Yorkshire, Nottinghamshire, and Lincolnshire, in a level and dull countryside crossed by the Great North Road, in the villages of Scrooby, Bawtry, Gainsborough, and others, were two groups of Separatists,[8] one of which met at the home of William Brewster in the little manor house where he conducted the post office. Simple folk they were, most of them engaged in the skills connected with clothmaking.

Their life was uneasy, as their historian Bradford tells us, "for some were taken and clapt up in prison, others had their houses beset and watcht night and day." They had been told that in the Netherlands they could gain freedom of worship, and thither they fled, settling finally in the lovely city of Leyden. There they set up their own meetinghouse where their beloved pastor, John Robinson, ministered to them. Other Separatists from England joined them and their congregation grew steadily.

[8] See Chapter 13.

They found occupation at Leyden, but with heavy labor and hard fare. The bodies of their children were bowed under the weight of the labor and became decrepit in youth. Some of the young people were drawn away by the temptations of the place. Meanwhile the Separatists at Leyden were hearing stories from England about the progress of Virginia. It was said the company was offering special opportunities to those who would go out and establish their own plantations, and that those who did so could live subject to slight control from the government of Virginia. It is possible that they heard also of John Smith, who had been going up and down the New England coast drawing maps and writing of the possibilities of the country. Meanwhile they were being solicited by some of the Dutch to make a settlement on the Hudson, or to find a home in another part of Holland.

After much weighing of pros and cons they determined to go to Virginia. William Brewster, Jr., and their pastor were acquainted with Sir Edwin Sandys of the Virginia Company. That company was induced to look with favor on their scheme, to accept them as settlers, and to loan them £300.

They were not yet out of the woods. They had trouble with the Royal Council for Virginia and had finally to content themselves at the last moment with a patent to Pierce and his Associates for land in Virginia, subject to the Virginia Company, and not independent of control, as they had hoped. Moreover, with great honesty they had drawn up seven articles stating their religious opinions, and those articles did not please the Archbishop of Canterbury. Nor was the King gracious when their request for religious liberty was brought before him, but they persuaded themselves that he was not against them, and would perhaps not interfere with their liberty if they carried themselves peaceably.

The company they set up was not incorporated but was to be a voluntary joint-stock enterprise, or syndicate, with a business group in London and a group of settlers in the New World. Those who paid money (£10 a share) or gave supplies were to receive shares and the colonists themselves were allowed one share apiece, in land.

The profits and the stock were to belong to the joint stock for seven years.

Just before the Pilgrims embarked they heard that the voyage sent forth by Blackwell, one of their Leyden elders, had suffered the loss of 150 out of 180 persons on board. They may have heard too of the fearful death rate in Virginia. But they were not deterred. "Their condition was not ordinary, their ends were good and honorable; their calling lawful and urgent, and therefore they might expect the blessing of God."

Of those who sailed in the Mayflower in September, 1620, only thirty-five were from Leyden, and sixty-six were from London and Southampton, the latter, most of them, not of the religious outlook of the Leyden group.[9] With them they took household furniture and a good supply of provisions. In November they sighted Cape Cod and turned south, but met storms, and went ashore in mid-December at Plymouth on the north side of the Cape, which was far from the country allotted to the Virginia Company, and thus territory to which they had no claim.

The hardships of that first winter are part of the American saga. More than fifty colonists died and at one time only seven were fit to carry on. It was an English saga too. They were of the same stock as the men who had adventured into the White Sea and developed trade with Muscovy; their yeoman ancestors had known all about cold and rain and illness and heavy mortality. They kept going, but their progress was slow. In 1624 the population was only 124 and in 1630 less than 300. Those few hard-working men cleared the woods and planted fields. They made friends with the Indians, who found that they would keep their promises and would treat them fairly. On the whole they were not quarrelsome among themselves, as men in a far country shut off with one another are likely to be.

Their position as squatters on the land was ended in 1621 when they secured a patent to the merchants and planters together for a voluntary joint-stock company in New England. But the English

[9] I am following closely C. M. Andrews, *The Colonial Period of American History* (New Haven, 1934–38).

end of the company, the businessmen behind it in London, became dissatisfied, disapproving of the emphasis upon religion as likely to stir up the government against them, and ceased to ship out supplies. They were further embarrassed by the ill success of their fishing enterprises, which they had hoped would enable the company to pay its way.

In spite of such discouragements the colony was by 1626 doing well enough to enter into an agreement with the London branch to pay £1,800 to them at £200 a year for nine years, and to take over the £600 of the debt of the company. A hard bargain it seemed to the men on the ground, but they were determined to pay their way. They were extending their activities with the Indians. They were developing pasture and breeding cattle and growing wheat and corn.

The story of the emigration to Massachusetts Bay has to do, like that of the Plymouth colony, with the desire of the Puritans to escape persecution. Under Charles I and his ecclesiastical high command the Puritans could no longer hope that better days might be ahead. The great depression of the 1620's had no less to do with the emigration to Massachusetts Bay. That depression is connected with the grant made in 1613 by James I to William Cockayne and his associates to export dyed and dressed cloths. The Merchant Adventurers had sold "whites," or unfinished cloths, to the Dutch, who took over the finishing processes. Cockayne had gained the ear of those closest to the King and had persuaded His Majesty that Cockayne and his friends would be able to give employment to London dyers and other workmen, and so displace the Dutch in the finishing processes of clothmaking. The new project was not welcomed by the Privy Council, which foresaw its dangers but was unable to move the King. The new company offered to bring in the Merchant Adventurers, but that company, believing that the project was sure to fail, refused to meet them halfway. At length the King forced the Merchant Adventurers to yield up their patent and charter, and gave the new company, the King's Merchant Adventurers, advantages never enjoyed by their predecessors.

From the start the new company proved a fizzle. The Dutch refused to buy the finished cloth, and the new company was not able in any case to produce it in sufficient quantities. What it did do was to bring the cloth trade to a standstill. The clothiers in the western shires complained pitifully to the justices of the peace, who relayed their complaints to the Privy Council. It was not, however, until 1617 that the new company, unable to carry out its promises, had to give up its charter.

Meanwhile the old company had lost its market and the whole machinery of the cloth industry and its selling facilities on the Continent had been so disorganized that the business never wholly recovered. What was even worse, the Thirty Years' War broke out in 1618 and cut off many markets for English goods. The clothing counties were hard hit. Norfolk, Suffolk, and Essex were among the counties that suffered most and those counties were full of Puritans uneasy about their future in England. As the depression went on through the twenties, these men had a double incentive to take ship for new shores. Other motives in the twenties and throughout the century led men to think of going away. The craving for land of their own must have affected many who had not the capital to purchase land in England. Furthermore, among the yeoman and artisan classes all over the realm were young men of vigor and initiative who were willing to venture far if they could improve their status.

To many the possibilities across the Atlantic must have looked promising. It was a West Country man, one of moderate puritan principles, the Reverend John White of Dorchester in Dorset, who must be called the father of the movement to Massachusetts Bay. He lived in a town ruled by an oligarchy of alert businessmen who were in contact with the nearby gentry. The men of Dorchester had observed that the neighboring port of Weymouth was sending out fishing vessels to Maine. In 1623 Sir Walter Erle, an active Dorset gentleman who had been a member of the Virginia Company, secured for himself and his associates a patent from the Council for

New England [10] for a plantation, of which he was to be the governor. The company consisted of fifty gentlemen from Dorset and six from Devon; thirty merchants from Dorchester, Exeter, and Shrewsbury; twenty clergymen; and others. From shares of £25 apiece the company was able to raise a capital of about £3,000.

Behind their plans was a good idea. They hoped to make money from fishing, as others were doing. But the fishermen needed to get an early start in the season. It was proposed therefore to send out settlers who could hunt, trap, and raise food for themselves and for the fishermen, and thus save their time. The good Dorchester parson, as no doubt others, was greatly interested in Christianizing the natives.

In 1623 the company sent out a small ship which left fourteen men at Cape Anne north of what is now Boston. The two vessels which went out the following year caught a few fish and left on shore thirty-two men. As head of the settlement on shore the company named Roger Conant, a brother of one of its stockholders.

When the fishing at Cape Anne proved a disappointment and the company in 1626 withdrew its settlers, Conant conducted thirty who remained to Naumkeag (Salem), and wrote White that he hoped Naumkeag would prove a "receptacle for such as upon the account of religion would be willing to begin a foreign plantation." White urged him to stick to his plans and promised to secure a patent and to provide men and provisions.

He lived up to that promise. He conferred with others in his own part of the country, with London merchants, and with East Anglian Puritans, and the result was the organization of the New England Company of about ninety members, of whom six were of the original Dorchester group. In 1628 the New England Company sent John Endicott and forty others to Naumkeag. In March, 1629, the King granted a charter to the Massachusetts Bay Company, which now took the place of the New England Company. To secure that

[10] The Council for New England was incorporated by the Crown in 1620 as a successor to the so-called Plymouth Company created in 1606 by the same charter that established the London Company.

charter great pressure must have been exerted upon a government not friendly to puritan leaders; among those who had part in the negotiation of the charter were such influential Puritans as the Earl of Warwick, his relative Sir Nathaniel Rich, and Lord Saye and Sele, as well as several London merchants. The new company was to have a governor and eighteen assistants much in the old manner. But a curious arrangement was made, destined to have consequences. Taking advantage of a loophole in the charter, the company brought the charter and the organization to Massachusetts and thus distorted the joint-stock company structure into the political frame of a self-governing colony. This arrangement gave the colonists a certain independence of King and Parliament.

Political events favored the Massachusetts project. Just before the first ship sailed, the dissolution of Parliament had occurred in March, 1629. That was a great discouragement to all Puritans and especially to the zealous men in the east counties. Sempringham, the seat in Lincolnshire (near East Anglia) of the Earl of Lincoln,[11] became a kind of center where men gathered and discussed plans for furthering the emigration to Massachusetts. Among them were John Winthrop of Suffolk; his brother-in-law, Emmanuel Downing; Isaac Johnson, Lincoln's son-in-law; and others. Winthrop and Sir Richard Saltonstall resolved to take part themselves in the emigration.

The first fleet sailed in April, 1629, with five ships and arrived late in June at Cape Anne, from which the colonists were escorted by Endicott to Naumkeag. There they found ten thatched houses and a building for the governor. In 1630 eleven ships sailed, including a freight of horses, goats, and cows and provisions on a considerable scale. Earlier in the same spring a vessel from Bristol, with eighty passengers, and another from Plymouth, with 140 West Country people, had sailed. In all seventeen vessels bound for various ports around Boston Harbor went out in 1630 with over a thousand

[11] Lincoln was a son-in-law of Lord Saye and Sele and a brother-in-law of John Humfrey, who had been interested in John White's project.

lives on them. Those emigrants settled at Charleston, Watertown, Roxbury, Dorchester, and at other points.

The emigration to Massachusetts continued apace, and with no setbacks, from the American side. By 1634 it was estimated that there were four thousand people in the colony.[12] Its success was due in part to the body of knowledge that had been accumulated about what a colony needed. The immigrants brought with them not only horses, cows, and utensils, but a large number of those skilled men in which the east counties and the West Country abounded, men who could make fortifications, houses, ships, and fishing shallops. They were men who could put their hands to ax and plow; they expected hardships and were ready to take hold. Moreover the colonists had some talent for organization, which we think of as typically American, but which was characteristic of many English of that time.

Intangibles came with them over the seas: English law and precedents, safeguards against tyranny wrought out in courts and Parliament; experience in leet and parish and town government, and thus practice in working together, in finding the mean between extremes, in arriving at common-sense solutions; confidence in humane education and in learning; and, above all, faith in God.

Those intangibles they hoped to preserve and in the main were able to do so. But they were in a new country and had to face new obstacles and think of new methods.

> And those that came were resolved to be Englishmen,
> Gone to the world's end, but English every one,

---

[12] In 1634 Henry Dade, Commissary of Suffolk, reported that 240 persons were about to sail from Ipswich and that 360 more were expected to go. *Cal. St. P. Dom. 1633–1634* (London, 1863), p. 450. Emigrants went also from Essex and Norfolk in considerable numbers. The number of town names in Massachusetts from the three counties is impressive. It may be added that the people from those counties were among the most vigorous and active in the kingdom. The emigration to Massachusetts and elsewhere was not unnoticed. John Milton said the prelates by their policy had "unpeopled the kingdom of so many thousands." William Prynne spoke of ministers and people leaving from the diocese of Norwich, and said thousands more were ready to go. In the articles of impeachment against Bishop Wren of Norwich it was estimated that his persecution of the Puritans had sent 3,000 to Holland.

And they ate the white corn-kernels, parched in the sun
And they knew it not, but they'd not be English again.

They would try, they would swear they were, they would
        drink the toast,
They would loyally petition and humbly pray
And over them was another sort of day
And in their veins was another, a different ghost.

For the country is where the life is, not elsewhere.
The country is where the heart and blood are given.

Bibliography

This book is based considerably upon the *Calendars of State Papers Domestic* from 1603 to 1629 and, as far as social history is concerned, upon the original papers in the Public Record Office (P.R.O.). Some of the material derives, however, from that great mélange, the *Reports* of the Historical Manuscripts Commission (H.M.C.). That official Commission has been able over a period of some eighty years to investigate and publish materials from the muniment rooms of country houses and borough halls and from cathedrals and churches. The *Reports* were at first largely lists and calendars, but have become volumes of related documents published almost completely. They include great collections of family papers. The most important for the reign of James I are those of the Cecils, of which eighteen volumes have been published in chronological order down through 1606, the last four dealing with the first years of James I. The unpublished Cecil papers (1607–1612) are available in transcript in the P.R.O. and repay close examination. Among other collections are the letters of the Manners (Earls of Rutland), Coke (Sir John), Sidney, and Harley families.

No less useful are the periodicals of the many local societies, known as the Archaeological and Natural History or Record Society of this or that shire. Some of these societies started in mid-nineteenth century as field clubs where gentlemen came together, lunched well, listened to speeches, and then went off to look at a Roman villa recently uncovered. They would establish a quarterly and publish papers on the local birdlife, on rock formations, on odd bits of folklore, or about a famous battle fought in the county.[1] Slowly they became more historical. Their historical papers were often amateurish, but they became progressively more professional. Through the decades the improvement has continued and today some of the local societies are staffed with trained archivists who search the country houses, town halls, and lawyers' offices for manuscripts, and who show themselves old hands at editing them. Such men are going to make over English history.

These periodicals, even the less useful of them, and even those called

[1] Some of the periodicals were archaeological and historical from the start.

Notes and Queries for this and that county, the scrap bags of antiquarianism, have been worked through almost page by page, and they have given many clues to life in the early Stuart period. One finds documents from the P.R.O. and from the British Museum (B.M.) that concern the particular shire, but many more from the local repositories: country houses, town halls, law offices, and church chests.

The sources the historian of early seventeenth-century life is looking for are of many kinds: diaries, autobiographies, biographies by contemporaries, letters, tracts, books of advice, account books, household inventories, sermons, books of travel, plays, and poems.

Diaries above all other sources should carry us into the midst of an earlier generation. We have too few of them for the early Stuart period. A certain number are catalogued in Godfrey Davies' *Bibliography* (mentioned later) and more have since been found and are being published by local societies. What would we give for a long diary of a clergyman or yeoman such as that of Parson Woodforde for the late eighteenth century! The diary of a York-shire lady in late Elizabethan days (Margaret Hoby), of a Lancashire hunting and drinking gentleman (Nicholas Assheton), of a West Riding yeoman returned from the Civil Wars (Adam Eyre), such diaries give only brief entries. Yet if we examine closely the routines of those men and women, their comings and goings, and note what they did not do, we can learn not a little about them.

Autobiographies are less satisfactory because they depend upon fallible memories and because they were often written in that time for a purpose. Yet they do reveal attitudes and prejudices and sometimes details of life among the neighbors of the writer. One of the best of autobiographies is that of Richard Baxter, a little late for our purpose, but full of the rough village life of Shropshire and Worcestershire. Biographies by contemporaries are likely to be eulogies and to go little below the surface. Yet William Hinde's account of his friend, a Cheshire puritan gentleman (John Bruen), tells much that we are glad to know.

The letters, where there were many of them from the various members of a family or connection, are full of information. The correspondence of the Gawdy and Barrington families fills volumes in the B.M. (in film in the Yale Library), and gives details not only about the family and their kin but about their retainers, their tenants, and their lawyers, about the villages near which they lived, about the schoolmasters and the university tutors who taught their boys, and about connections of the family with the county town and with London. A single writer who wrote continuously over a long period is extremely useful. John Chamberlain wrote letters from 1597 to 1627 (Norman E. McClure, ed., *The Letters of John Chamberlain*, 2 vols., Phila-delphia, 1939) and told of the City and the Court and of the families he visited in the country. His letters are often vivid and sometimes amusing; his gossip is unusually trustworthy. From such letters more is to be learned than the casual reader realizes. One needs to read through the whole body of them and come to know the receivers as well as the writer, their circles, their and his likes and dislikes; and then one should reread the letters two or three times. Social historians are somewhat like boys who raise the slab on the ground and watch the scurrying life underneath.

The pamphlet literature is enormous. Two good collections of tracts republished are the *Harleian Miscellany* (10 vols., London, 1808), and the *Somers Tracts* (13 vols., London, 1809–15). Other collections exist, some of them in local societies. The pamphlet literature is of many kinds. The Wagner Collection at Yale has much about economic conditions. The little pamphlets about witches and witch trials, to be found in the British Museum and in the Harvard and Cornell libraries, sometimes throw light on the ways of poor people in small villages. The largest bodies of pamphlets are to be found in the British Museum and in the Bodleian, but the Harvard Library and the McAlpin Collection at the Union Theological Seminary are not far behind. The Yale Library has a good collection; that at the University of Minnesota must not be overlooked.

The letter or book of advice, ostensibly written by a father to his son, and circulated usually in manuscript, turns up often in family papers, sometimes the same letter in several collections. Such letters were evidently passed around. They are of importance as showing the ideals about family life and conduct, and about estate management. That by the Earl of Northumberland (Henry Percy, the 9th Earl), though wordy and involved, shows what nobles thought of themselves. The letters of advice by Sir John Oglander and Sir John Strode in C. F. Aspinwall-Oglander's *Nunwell Symphony* (London, 1945), pp. 47–49, 50–54, are revealing about the ideals of the gentry. One of the best of letters of advice is that recently turned up by John Cooper of Trinity College, Oxford, in the Wentworth-Woodhouse MSS. (now in the Sheffield Public Library) and presently to be published. It is a document that throws light not only upon the Wentworth family and the gentry but upon Yorkshire as well.

More and more account books are being published and countless others are to be found in manuscript in the British Museum and elsewhere. They give us not only prices but changes in prices, always upward; they offer clues as to the style in which a family lived, as to where it procured supplies, and what kinds of supplies.

The personal inventories made after a man's death are beginning to be published. F. G. Emmison brought out in 1938 (Bedfordshire Historical Record Society, XX, 1–143) *Jacobean Household Inventories,* with a useful introduction. Those Bedfordshire inventories afford information about the rooms, furniture, dishes, wall hangings, home industries, clothes, books, farm equipment, and livestock of yeomen, husbandmen, laborers, shepherds, carpenters, weavers, bakers, and occasionally of clergymen and gentlemen. When many such inventories have been published and analyzed, we shall know more about country life.

Of sermons a vast body exists, especially in the Bodleian, British Museum, Yale and Harvard libraries, and in the McAlpin Collection already mentioned. Perhaps 95 per cent of them have little for one interested in everyday life, but now and then a preacher would call attention to local abuses and perhaps offer advice to justices of the peace.

The literature of travel and of observation of places is not as much or as helpful as one would expect. Fynes Moryson went all over Europe and as far as Turkey, and made comparisons between other peoples and the English, seldom illuminating. William Camden, the historian, in his *Britannia* of many editions, described England by counties but was more aware of antiquities than of living people. A few highborn Germans left their impressions of London and the nearby country (W. B. Rye, ed., *England as Seen by Foreigners in the Days of Elizabeth and James I,* London, 1865). A military man, William Hamond, left *A Relation of a Short Survey of 26 Counties* (ed. L. G. Wickham Legg, London, 1904), and *A Relation of . . . Survey of the Western Counties* (Camden Misc., XVI. London, 1936). The most informative traveler was the water-poet, John Taylor. In early life a waterman, he developed a better method of making money. He would announce a proposed trip, book advance subscriptions for verse about it, and then on his return publish windy doggerel recounting his adventures. He told of inns and innkeepers and their wives, of men on the road and at the inn, and of mayors and gentlemen who gave him lodging and food and who hoped to be mentioned in his verse. A few men wrote descriptions of shires: Tristram Risdon and Thomas Westcote described Devon; Erdeswick, Staffordshire; Lambarde, Kent; William Burton, Leicestershire; Reyce, Suffolk; and John Norden, Essex, Middlesex, Hertfordshire, Cornwall, and probably Norfolk. Those contemporary topographers had too much to say about landed families and their monuments, but they did afford bits of useful information. John Smyth of Nibley, in his *The Berkeley Manuscripts, The Lives of the Berkeleys . . . from 1066 to 1618; With a Description of the Hundred of Berkeley* (3 vols., ed. Sir John McLean, Gloucester, 1883–85), tells us much about villagers in that hundred. William Harrison's *Description of England* is known to all.

The plays of Shakespeare, Ben Jonson, Marlowe, Dekker, Ford, Marston, Massinger, Beaumont and Fletcher, and scores of others, to be found in J. P. Collier (ed.), R. Dodsley, *A Select Collection of Old Plays* (13 vols., London, 1825), 3rd ed., and elsewhere, have been read attentively. Their value as social history has been less realized by historians than by scholars of literature, whose editorial notes on manners and customs, most of them published a good while ago, deserve to be better known. The plots and the main themes (borrowed often from the Italians) are unreal, the characters violent and often unlike Englishmen, and the motivations farfetched. Moreover, when the playwrights did describe the English they tended to exaggerate social differences. One reads many pages to find a few lines that are significant for the historian. Now and then the dramatist without realizing what he is doing allows a character to betray an attitude, a scruple, or a prejudice that has the very hallmark of the Jacobean age. Ben Jonson set out deliberately to show the manners of his time, too deliberately, and we read him with less sense of reality than Dekker or Heywood. Shakespeare, because he understood country life and the forms and pressures of his generation, is indispensable for the historian, almost as much so as for the scholar of literature.

In this book I have used a small fraction of the notes made from the dramatists; those notes add up to a body of comment upon the time by men of more than usual intelligence.

One reads much indifferent poetry to find bits that tell us what we would know. George Herbert, Robert Herrick, John Donne, Samuel Daniel, Michael Drayton, good poets every one, give us not a few clues as to the spirit of the age. Lesser poets are often helpful.

The bibliography of the chapters has to be brief and many useful titles must be left out.

Chapter 1, on England up to 1603, is an attempt in the fewest possible words to bring the reader up to the Stuart period. The discussion of early man is written from popular works of the anthropologists. The constitutional and economic paragraphs are summaries of what is in every textbook. The last part of the chapter, dealing with heroes and national feeling, is based upon the Elizabethan historians, poets, and dramatists.

Two chapters are devoted to the English character. Chapter 1 is in two parts. That about the Villages and the Country owes much to churchwardens' and leet court records, to quarter sessions orders, and to tidbits of evidence here and there. Part II of the chapter, Economic Factors, is based upon general reading and it is impossible to suggest sources unless one fills up pages. Chapter 3, on English character as revealed in intellectual and cultural life is grounded upon the writings of scholars and upon the literature of the time. The comments on the men and women of that generation as shown in their portraits and letters are put forward with some assurance, but not without the hope of starting a discussion.

The same may be said of Chapter 4, The Nobles. Those great personages figure in the literature of the time. A lively controversy has been provoked in England by Lawrence Stone's article, "The Anatomy of the Elizabethan Aristocracy," *Econ. Hist. Rev.*, XVIII (1948), 1–53. That paper was sharply attacked by H. R. Trevor-Roper in "The Elizabethan Aristocracy, An Anatomy Anatomized," *Econ. Hist. Rev.*, 2nd ser., III (1950–51), 279–298. Stone's rejoinder, the best he could make, will be found in the *Econ. Hist. Rev.*, 2nd series, IV (1951–52), 302–321, "The Elizabethan Aristocracy, A Restatement." Trevor-Roper has the best of it.

Chapter 5, The Country Gentleman, depends upon a wide variety of sources printed and otherwise. No one can talk about the country gentleman without reading Tawney. See *The Agrarian Problem in the Sixteenth Century* (London, 1912); the introduction to Thomas Wilson's *Discourse of Usury* (London, 1925); "The Rise of the Gentry, 1558–1640," *Econ. Hist. Rev.*, XI (1941), 1–38; and *Harrington's Interpretation of His Age* (London, 1941). H. R. Trevor-Roper will presently publish (*Econ. Hist. Rev.*) an attack upon some of Tawney's theses about the gentlemen. Tawney's writings are touched with genius; they show imagination and betray on every page wide reading. He is a pioneer in his field and hence closer research—so many more materials are becoming available—over a long period by many workers may modify and even alter some of his conclusions. His sympathies for the underdog cause him to view the land-owning class with a certain suspicion. When that dying species has become extinct, its services in its time will be favorably appraised. See also David Mathew, *The Social Structure of Caroline England* (Oxford, 1948). His *The Jacobean Age* (London, 1938) and *The Age of Charles I* (London, 1951) are suggestive about many subjects, including the gentry. The unpublished Yale thesis of Francis Squire, "The English Country Gentleman in the Early Seventeenth Century" (1935), is useful and deserves expansion.

The Clergyman (Chapter 6) is mentioned in diaries, letters, and biographies. After his death a funeral sermon printed or short biography might give details of his life. He appears in churchwardens' accounts, in borough records, and in quarter sessions orders. A few visitations by archdeacons have been published in local societies and more are to be found in manuscript, and will eventually give us much useful information. George Herbert's *A Priest to the Temple, or the Country Parson* is a sketch of the ideal clergyman; all Herbert's writings are important about his profession. *The Diary of Ralph Josselin* (*Camd. Society*, 1908, 3d ser., XV), a puritan parson, is good reading.

Among recent studies C. W. Foster's *The State of the Church in the Reign of Elizabeth and James I as Illustrated by Documents Relating to the Diocese of Lincoln* (*Linc. Rec. Soc.*, 1926, XXIII) deserves first mention. Mrs. Alice Kimball Smith's thesis, "The English Country Clergy in the Early Seventeenth Century" (Yale Library, 1936), contains much information from print and manuscript. Miss M. Barratt's Oxford thesis (in the Bodleian) deals with the clergy in Oxfordshire, Gloucestershire, and Worcestershire in the late sixteenth and early seventeenth century, and is a careful and intelligent study.

The materials about the Yeoman (Chapter 7) have been collected, analyzed, and put together in delightful fashion by Mildred Campbell in *The English Yeoman under Elizabeth and the early Stuarts* (New Haven, 1942). An intelligent review of that book by W. G. Hoskins (*Econ. Hist. Rev.*, XIV, 193–196) points out how much yeomen differed from one another in different parts of the country. Hoskins has written "The Leicestershire Farmer in the 16th Century," *Trans. Leic. Arch. Soc.*, XXII (1941–42), 33–94. See also L. A. Parker, "The Agrarian Revolution at Cotesbach, 1501–1612," in *Studies in Leicestershire Agrarian History* (Leicester, 1949). In W. G. Hoskins and H. P. R. Finberg, *Devonshire Studies* (London, 1952), will be found further information about yeomen. The reader may well consult *Robert Loder's Farm Accounts 1610–1620*, ed. G. E. Fussell (*Cam. Soc.*), 1936, 3d ser., LIII; Henry Best, *Rural Economy in Yorkshire in 1641*, edited by C. B. Robinson (*Surtees Soc.*, 1857), Vol. XXXIII; Gervase Markham, *The English Husbandman* (1613–15) and his *The Countryman's Recreation* (1640) and above all Adam Eyre's "Dyurnall" in *Yorkshire Diaries* (*Surtees Soc.*, 1875), Vol. LXV.

The Yeoman appears in many plays and sometimes is presented in action. He is portrayed sympathetically in some of the character books. He figures in churchwardens' accounts, in leet court records, and in quarter sessions proceedings.

Chapter 8, The Inns of Court and the Lawyers, depends much upon the published records of the four great Inns: *The Black Books* of Lincoln's Inn, ed. W. P. Baildon (4 vols., London, 1897–1902); *The Pension Book* of Gray's Inn, ed. R. J. Fletcher (2 vols., London, 1901–1910); the *Middle Temple Records*, ed. C. H. Hopwood (4 vols., London, 1904–1905); *A Calendar of the Inner Temple Records*, ed. F. A. Inderwick (3 vols., London, 1896–1901). Sir William Dugdale's *Origines Juridiciales* (1666) gives some light on legal education. See also W. B. Odgers (ed.), *Six Lectures on the Inns of Court and of Chancery* (London, 1912). The biographies of lawyers and judges and the many brief accounts of their lives afford information. The literature of the time, the tracts, the letters, and the plays, mention many lawyers and their work.

The Physician (Chapter 9) appears in autobiographies, diaries, and letters. He is made fun of in many plays and pamphlets. We have few records of physicians themselves. Of great value is *A Seventeenth Century Doctor and his Patients, Doctor Symcotts, 1592?–1662?* (*Beds. Hist. Rec. Soc.*, 1951), XXXI, with introduction by F. N. L. Poynter and W. J. Bishop of the Wellcome Medical Historical Library in London. Many of Dr. Mayerne's medical records are to be found in the Sloane MSS. in the B.M. Very useful is John Raach's Yale thesis (unpublished) "The English Country Doctor in the Province of Canterbury, 1603–43" (1941). See also the chapter on medicine by Alban H. G. Doran in C. T. Onions (ed.), *Shakespeare's England* (2 vols., London, 1917).

The Businessman (Chapter 10) appears most often in the many records of boroughs and towns and to a less degree in those of leet courts. Few diaries of businessmen exist, but that of William Whiteway of Dorchester, 1618–34 (B. M. MSS., Eg. 784 and in transcript in Thomas Murphy's edition, Yale thesis, 1939), furnishes a picture of the bourgeoisie in one country town. Edgar I. Fripp's *Shakespeare Man and Artist* (2 vols., London, 1938), and his several other books, although they repeat one another, do afford information about life in Stratford-on-Avon in Elizabethan times. Louis B. Wright's *Middle Class Culture in Elizabethan England* (Chapel Hill, 1935) is important not only about townspeople but about other subjects.

For Chapter 11, many histories of famous grammar schools embody documents dealing with the foundation and early course of such schools in the sixteenth and seventeenth centuries. Borough records are filled with the troubles of the town authorities with the schoolmaster. Autobiographies and contemporary biographies relate early experiences at school. About the classroom it is best to read the works of schoolmasters, of Roger Ascham, John Brinsley, Richard Mulcaster, E. Coote, and C. Hoole. *An Apologie for Schoolmasters* (1619) is a rare tract that bears reading. Among modern monographs, see A. F. Leach, *English Schools at the Reformation 1546–48* (Westminster, 1896); Norman Wood, *The Reformation and English Education* (London, 1931); A. R. M. Stowe, *English Grammar Schools in the Reign of Queen Elizabeth* (New York, 1908); Foster Watson, *The English Grammar Schools to 1660* (Cambridge, 1908); and especially J. Howard Brown's *Elizabethan Schooldays; An Account of the English Grammar Schools in the Second Half of the Sixteenth Century* (Oxford, 1933). See also Foster Watson, *Tudor School-Boy Life, the Dialogues of Jean Louis Vives* (London, 1908). The articles on schools in the various Victoria County histories are indispensable. About women's education see D. Gardiner, *English Girlhood at School* (London, 1929). For comparisons read what S. E. Morison says about New England grammar schools in *The Puritan Pronaos, Studies in the Intellectual Life of New England in the Seventeenth Century* (New York, 1936).

About Universities (Chapter 12) much is to be learned from reading in the two series about the colleges of Oxford and Cambridge known as College Histories Series. They are often based upon manuscript and out-of-the-way printed material. Much is also to be found in the memoirs of the time, since few men failed to describe their university careers. We know a good deal about tutors because many of them made enough mark to have their lives set down. About Oxford, Anthony Wood's *Athenae Oxonienses* (1691–92) and John Aubrey's *Brief Lives* contain fact and gossip. Thomas Fuller's *History of the University of Cambridge;* Charles H. Cooper's *Annals of Cambridge* (5 vols., Cambridge, 1842–1908), and J. A. Venn's *Alumni Cantabrigenses* (Cambridge, 1922) must be consulted. The standard histories of the two universities are J. B. Mullinger, *The University of Cambridge* (3 vols., Cambridge, 1873–1911), and Sir Charles Mallet, *A History of the University of Oxford* (3 vols., London, 1924–27). Mallet deals with more aspects of university life but Mullinger is more interested in the intellectual history.

The two chapters (Chapters 13 and 14) on Puritanism derive much from the biographies and diaries of puritan divines and laymen. Something can be gleaned from the sermons they preached. The records of boroughs contain not a little about Puritanism in practice. Notable among monographs on Puritanism are Marshall Knappen's *Two Elizabethan Puritan Diaries* (Chicago, 1933) and the Introduction; his *Tudor Puritanism* (Chicago, 1939); William Haller's *The Rise of Puritanism* (New York, 1938); Perry Miller's *The New England Mind, the Seventeenth Century* (New York, 1939), his *Orthodoxy in Massachusetts, 1630–1650* (Cambridge, Mass., 1933), his *The Puritans,* with T. H. Johnson (New York, 1938), and his article, "The Marrow of Puritan Divinity," in *Publications of the Col. Soc. of Mass.,* XXXII (1937). An important article is that by L. J. Trinterud, "The Origins of Puritanism," in *Church History,* XX (1951), 37–57. The reader should also consult the various writings of Kenneth Murdock and S. E. Morison. It is interesting that in the last generation the best work on Puritanism has been done on this side of the water.

The chapter on the Kingship and the Privy Council (Chapter 15) is written from the State Papers Domestic in the P.R.O., from the *Acts of the Privy Council,* and from many other sources including Chamberlain's letters. The Cecil correspondence, the Winwood letters, and the unpublished letters of the Earl of Northampton and of Sir Thomas Lake are relevant (P.R.O. and B.M.). Great quantities of letters in the B.M., in the Bodleian, and at the P.R.O. reinforce knowledge. We all await David H. Willson's life of James I.

The chapter on Parliament (Chapter 16) is based upon the *Commons Journals,* the *Lords Journals,* and upon private diaries of proceedings, published and unpublished. Bits of information can be gleaned from letters written to English ambassadors abroad and from letters of members to their friends.

The discussion of the Sheriff (Chapter 17) is based in the main on the

Calendars of State Papers Domestic, on the *Acts of the Privy Council,* and on bits of material in the county societies. The article by Jean S. Wilson, "The Sheriffs' Rolls of the Sixteenth and Seventeenth Century," *Eng. Hist. Rev.,* XLVII (1932), 31–45, and an unpublished paper by T. Hallinan of Balliol College, which he has sent me, about the sheriffs in the Midlands, have proved helpful.

The literature about the Justice of the Peace (Chapter 18) is large. Most important is William Lambarde's *Eirenarcha or of the Office of the Justice of Peace* (London, 1614). It was first published in 1581 and went through edition after edition. William Fleetwood, *The Office of a Justice of the Peace,* was first published in 1658 but was written in the 1580's. Michael Dalton's *The Countrey Justice* was published in 1618 and went through many editions. The MSS. Room of the British Museum has an almost unlimited amount of material dealing with the justice. The Quarter Sessions of Staffordshire for the years 1581–1606 in five volumes (*William Salt Soc.,* 1931–1940), with introductions by S. A. H. Burne, are valuable. So are the Worcestershire Quarter Sessions, with a long introduction by J. Willis Bund, in two parts (*Worc. Co. Council,* 1899–1900). The Northamptonshire Quarter Sessions have little for our period and the Kesteven Sessions have nothing (*Lincoln Rec. Soc.,* XXV–XXVI), but the two introductions by S. A. Peyton deserve reading. The Quarter Sessions Records for Somerset (*Som. Rec. Soc.,* XXIII, XXIV, XXVIII), are interesting, as are those for Hertfordshire. No less so are those for the North: the *Lancashire Quarter Sessions Records* (with introduction by James Tait, *Chetham Soc.,* new ser., LXXVII); the West Riding Quarter Sessions (*Yorks. Arch. Soc.,* rec. ser., III and LIV, 1888 and 1915); the first three volumes of the North Riding Quarter Sessions (ed. J. C. Atkinson, *N. R. Rec. Soc.,* 1883–84); the *Manchester Sessions,* Vol. 1 (by Ernest Axon, *Lancashire and Cheshire Rec. Soc.,* XLII, 1901). The introductions by H. C. Johnson to the Elizabethan Quarter Sessions of Wiltshire (1949) and to Quarter Sessions of Warwickshire, with S. C. Ratcliff (*Warwick Co. Recs.,* I, 1935) are excellent. The voluminous Middlesex quarter sessions records have been omitted as more about London than the country. A. H. A. Hamilton's *Quarter Sessions from Queen Elizabeth to Queen Anne,* chiefly from Devon (London, 1878), give sidelights on the justices in western England. I am told that all the quarter sessions for Devonshire are now to be found in film in the Harvard Library. The quarter sessions records for Essex have been used in the typed calendars to be seen in the Essex Record Society at Chelmsford.

C. A. Beard's *The Office of the Justice of the Peace in England* (New York, 1904) is not among the best works of that distinguished scholar, as he was wont to admit. The Webbs deal much with the justice of the peace, using sources printed and unprinted and, as always, with illumination. They were pioneers, and thorough ones, in local government. The various Law Reports touch upon the justices. The justices appear in the plays of Shakespeare and other dramatists as well as in Butler's *Hudibras*, in Breton, and in the pamphlets of the time.

The literature about the Constable (Chapter 19) is larger than might be expected. William Lambarde in his *Eirenarcha* (ed. 1614, already mentioned) has at the back a pamphlet called *The Duties of Constables, Borsholders, Tything Men and such other low ministers of the peace*. In 1655 William Sheppard published *The Office and Duties of Constable or Borsholders*, which dealt more with law than practice. A few accounts of constables exist. The Mauleverer diary of a constable, with the accounts of the parish of Arncliffe, is to be found in the Appendix to George Dodds' "The Rural Constable in Early Seventeenth Century England" (thesis, 1939, Yale library). Constables' accounts for Stathern (Leicestershire) are in the *Arch. Journal*, LXIX; those for Repton in the *Derbyshire Arch. and Nat. Hist. Journal*, I, 27–41. Unpublished accounts of Great Easton are in the Essex Record office at Chelmsford and those for Wymeswold (Leicestershire) are in the B.M. Add. MSS. 10457. The constables' accounts for the manor of Manchester in three volumes (Vol. I, 1612–33) have been published with an introduction by J. P. Earwaker (1891).

Most useful for the activities of the Constable are the quarter sessions records mentioned earlier, especially those for the North Riding, Worcestershire, Staffordshire, and Essex (MSS.). Many churchwardens' accounts carry allusions to the constables. The leet court records contain much about them. The constable appears in many plays, as in Middleton's *Blurt, Master Constable*, Ben Jonson's *Tale of a Tub*, Glapthorne's *Wit in a Constable*, and Marston's *The Insatiate Countesse*. He is mentioned in Law Reports.

The only monograph is by George Dodds, already cited. I have made use of it, notably about the hiring fair of the high constables, but especially as a guide to sources.

In connection with Chapter 20, many churchwardens' accounts for the early seventeenth century have been published, most of them in county society periodicals, but occasionally in other places. A list of churchwardens' accounts then in print was published in 1900 by Elspeth Philipps (*Eng. Hist. Rev.*, XV, 335–341). How many hundreds exist in manuscript would be hard to say. William Lambarde in *The Duties of Constables, Borsholders* . . . (in the back of his *Eirenarcha*, 1614) has given some pages to the churchwardens (69–82). Bishop Hobhouse published some churchwarden records for Somerset for an earlier period (*Som. Rec. Soc.*, IV) and discussed the functions of that official. The largest secondary work is that of Sedley Ware, *The Elizabethan Parish in its Ecclesiastical and Financial Aspects* (Baltimore, 1908). The churchwardens appear often in quarter sessions documents and are occasionally discussed in the introductions. They are mentioned again and again by Sidney and Beatrice Webb in *English Local Government from the Revolution to the Municipal Corporations Act: the Parish and the County* (London, 1906).

The most useful work on the Companies (Chapter 21) is of course W. R. Scott, *The Constitution and Finance of English Scottish and Irish Joint Stock Companies to 1720* (3 vols., Cambridge, 1910–1912). The first two volumes are relevant to this topic and have been much used. Almost equally helpful is Astrid Friis, *Alderman Cockayne's Project and the Cloth Trade* (Oxford, 1927). The writings of Sir William Foster about the East India Company and about commercial adventures in the East should be consulted. Occasional volumes of the Hakluyt Society deserve mention: E. D. Morgan and C. H. Coote (eds.), *Early Voyages and Travels to Russia and Persia* (2 vols., London, 1886), and James T. Bent (ed.), *Early Voyages and Travels in the Levant* (London, 1893). The reader should also read Inna I. Lubimenko, *Les relations commerciales et politiques de l'Angleterre avec la Russe avant Pierre le Grand* (Paris, 1933). A. C. Wood's *A History of the Levant Company* (Oxford, 1933) is relevant. About the Virginia Company and the settlement of Plymouth and Massachusetts Bay, Charles M. Andrews, *The Colonial Period of American History* (4 vols., New Haven, 1934–38), is the latest word.

Some general works deserve mention. Special bibliographies for the period covered are Conyers Read (ed.), *Bibliography of British History: Tudor Period, 1485–1603* (Oxford, 1933), and Godfrey Davies (ed.), *Bibliography of British History: Stuart Period, 1603–1714* (Oxford, 1928). Both are somewhat out of date, but may be supplemented by A. T. Milme (ed.), *Writings on British History* (London, 1934 ff). Stanley Pargellis and D. J. Medley (eds.), *Bibliography of British History: the Eighteenth Century, 1714–1789* (Oxford, 1951), contains a number of more recent titles that overlap into the early Stuart period. L. B. Frewer (ed.), *Bibliography of Historical Writings 1940–45* (Oxford, 1947), lists scholarly reviews as well as books and articles. Other bibliographical guides may be found in J. B. Black, *The Reign of Elizabeth* (Oxford, 1936), and in Godfrey Davies, *The Early Stuarts, 1603–60* (Oxford, 1937) which happen also to be good surveys of the late sixteenth and early seventeenth centuries.

For the beginnings of English colonization and overseas expansion, particularly into North America, the following books may be noted: J. H. Rose, A. P. Newton, and E. A. Benians (eds.), *Cambridge History of the British Empire* (8 vols., Cambridge, 1929 ff); W. F. Craven, *The Southern Colonies in the Seventeenth Century* (Baton Rouge, 1949); A. D. Innes, *The Maritime and Colonial Expansion of England under the Stuarts* (London, 1932); A. P. Newton, *The British Empire to 1783* (London, 1935), and *The*

Colonizing Activities of the English Puritans (New Haven, 1914); H. L. Osgood, *The American Colonies in the Seventeenth Century* (3 vols., New York, 1904–07); J. A. Williamson, *A Short History of British Expansion* (London, 1941–43); Louis B. Wright, *Religion and Empire: The Alliance between Piety and Commerce in English Expansion, 1558–1625* (Chapel Hill, 1943).

Index